NEGOTIATING TRANSCULTURAL RELATIONS IN THE EARLY MODERN MEDITERRANEAN

Transculturalisms, 1400–1700

Series Editors:
Mihoko Suzuki, University of Miami, USA,
Ann Rosalind Jones, Smith College, USA, and
Jyotsna Singh, Michigan State University, USA

This series presents studies of the early modern contacts and exchanges among the states, polities and entrepreneurial organizations of Europe; Asia, including the Levant and East India/Indies; Africa; and the Americas. Books will investigate travelers, merchants and cultural inventors, including explorers, mapmakers, artists and writers, as they operated in political, mercantile, sexual and linguistic economies. We encourage authors to reflect on their own methodologies in relation to issues and theories relevant to the study of transculturism/translation and transnationalism. We are particularly interested in work on and from the perspective of the Asians, Africans, and Americans involved in these interactions, and on such topics as:

*   Material exchanges, including textiles, paper and printing, and technologies of knowledge
*   Movements of bodies: embassies, voyagers, piracy, enslavement
*   Travel writing: its purposes, practices, forms and effects on writing in other genres
*   Belief systems: religions, philosophies, sciences
*   Translations: verbal, artistic, philosophical
*   Forms of transnational violence and its representations.

Also in this series:

Negotiating Transcultural Relations in the Early Modern Mediterranean

Ottoman-Venetian Encounters

STEPHEN ORTEGA
Simmons College, USA

ASHGATE

Published by
Ashgate Publishing Limited
Wey Court East
Union Road
Farnham
Surrey, GU9 7PT
England

Ashgate Publishing Company
110 Cherry Street
Suite 3-1
Burlington, VT 05401-3818
USA

www.ashgate.com

British Library Cataloguing in Publication Data
A catalogue record for this book is available from the British Library

The Library of Congress has cataloged the printed edition as follows:
Ortega, Stephen.
  Negotiating transcultural relations in the early modern Mediterranean: Ottoman-Venetian encounters / by Stephen Ortega.
    pages cm. — (Transculturalisms, 1400–1700)
  Includes bibliographical references and index.
  ISBN 978-1-4094-2858-9 (hardcover: alk. paper) — ISBN 978-1-4094-2859-6 (ebook) — ISBN 978-1-4724-0557-9 (epub)
    1. Turks—Italy—Venice—History—16th century. 2. Turks—Italy—Venice—History—17th century. 3. Muslims—Italy—Venice—History—16th century. 4. Muslims—Italy—Venice—History—17th century. 5. Venice (Italy)—Ethnic relations—History—16th century. 6. Venice (Italy)—Ethnic relations—History—17th century. 7. Venice (Italy)—Relations—Turkey. 8. Turkey—Relations—Venice (Italy) I. Title.
  DG675.63.T87O76 2014
  305.894'35045309031—dc23

                                                                2014017432

ISBN: 9781409428589 (hbk)
ISBN: 9781409428596 (ebk – PDF)
ISBN: 9781472405579 (ebk – ePUB)

MIX
Paper from
responsible sources
FSC FSC® C013985
www.fsc.org

Printed in the United Kingdom by Henry Ling Limited, at the Dorset Press, Dorchester, DT1 1HD

to my wife Nancy and my daughter Ana

Contents

List of Figures

List of Ottoman Terms

ahdname	a treaty, political guarantee
askeri	soldier, non-taxpayer
aspri	a type of Ottoman currency
baş defterdar	chief treasurer
beylerbey	governor of a territory
çavuş	envoy, palace official
defterdar	treasurer
devshirme	Christian males brought to be trained as soldiers and officials at the Porte
Divan-I-Hümayun	imperial council
dizdar	castle warden
fetva	legal judgement
firman	edict from the sultan
hüccet	judicial ruling, agreement
hüküm	law or ruling
kadi	judge
kanun	traditional law
kadiaskers	chief judges
kapudan pasha	navy admiral
khul	slave or servant of the sultan
kitābü'l-kadis	exchange bill
mahr	mandatory payment to bride at time of marriage
müteferrika	member of the Ottoman cavalry
nişanci	court calligrapher
reaya	taxpaying subject of the empire
sadakāt	alms
sanjack	district
sanjack beyi	district governor

şeriat	religious law
silahdars	guards to the sultan
Şey-hü-islam	highest religious authority
spahi	cavalryman
süftece	exchange bill
voyvoda	local official

Acknowledgements

The list of people who have helped me with this project encompasses many people in many places. First, I would like to thank the people at the State Archives in Dubrovnik and Zadar in Croatia, the Başbakanlik archive in Istanbul, the Archivio General de Simancas, and the Casa dei Catecumeni archives and the Marchiana library in Venice. The people at these different archives and libraries were friendly, helpful and efficient in helping me find materials and in helping me photocopy, microfilm and digitize the documents that were so essential to this study. I would also like to express much appreciation to Himmet Taskomur who was a great help in assisting with the Ottoman Turkish documents. As I struggled to make meaning out of the wealth of Ottoman documents that I collected, he was a great source of support with particularly troubling paleography and a major help in deciphering subtle distinctions in linguistic interpretation that became so important to my analysis.

Second I would like to thank all those people who helped, encouraged, cajoled and supported me while I was in Venice. While the list is long I owe a special thanks to Karl Appuhn, Eric Dursteler, Maria Sofia Fusaro, Holly Hurlburt, Michelle Laughren, Stefanie Lew, Vittorio Mandelli, Francesca Trivellato, Andrea Vianello, John Visconti and Bronwen Wilson. When one spends close to two years away from home, a support network is essential, and these individuals were the core of this group. Without their help, this project would not only have been more difficult but also not as fun. I would also like to thank Michela Dalborgo, Sandra Sambo, and the staff at the Archivio di Stato. Their expertise and their assistance were essential in identifying the large number of different sources that I used.

Next I would like to express a great gratitude to all the people who have advised and supported me along the way: Cemal Kafadar for introducing me to the idea of working on "the Ottomans and Venice" (Cemal was very helpful in explaining to me the different available sources from the perspective of an Ottomanist), Guido Ruggiero for his invaluable guidance, sending me to Venice for the first time and encouraging me to take a broad view on interpreting sources, and Brian Pullan and Colin Imber for keeping me on task. This book comes out of a dissertation I wrote while at the University of Manchester, and Professors Pullan and Imber were fastidious in their reading and commentary on my work. Without their feedback, this project would have stalled a long time ago.

I would also like to thank my colleagues at the Department of History at Simmons College: Laura Prieto, Sarah Leonard, Laurie Crumpacker, Steve Berry and Zhigang Liu. Their support has been crucial to developing my scholarship and finishing the book. I would also like to thank Simmons College for funding some of my travel and Gretchen McBride for helping with editing when I could not do one more reading. I would also like to give a big thanks to my editor Erika Gaffney for being so kind, so informative and so patient.

In closing, my greatest thanks go to my wife Nancy and my daughter Ana. They have been there through all the ups and downs. They supported me emotionally and gave me the strength to forge on when doubt crept in and the project moved along slowly. Their love and their patience have become the pillars of the project, and with this thought, I dedicate the book to both of them.

Introduction

On June 28, 1597 the Papal Nuncio to Venice reported back to Rome that two Turkish merchants had quarreled in the Piazza San Marco. The Nuncio commented that one merchant had accused the other of wanting to become a Christian, whereupon the accused had pulled out a knife and stabbed his accuser in the side. The assailant was immediately arrested and held in the prison of the Council of Ten, before being released a few days later. The Nuncio was critical of the Venetians' decision, believing it politically dangerous to show such leniency towards the Turks.[1]

The incident on the Piazza San Marco is one example of the presence of Ottoman Muslims in Venice. While the Nuncio's correspondence indicates that these individuals had come to Venice to trade, other questions need to be asked about their contact with locals, their treatment by the Venetian judicial and political systems, their cross-cultural status and their power to influence events. The Papal Nuncio saw these merchants merely as Turks, not as individuals from a particular region, place, or social background. The merchants involved in the attack were connected to Venice in a variety of ways, some geographical, some linguistic, some commercial and some, perhaps, even personal. Their presence in the city was linked to a politics that transcended their encounter and transcended the power of the Council of Ten to act independently.

Individuals such as these two merchants were involved in a system that was influenced by a variety of different jurisdictions, courts, powerful people and mutual agreements. In adjudicating this type of case, the Venetians were not only dealing with the people standing in front of them, they were also responding to the people and to the institutions that supported them and gave them protection; thus, any decision represented a response to a set of extant power relations that existed across Venetian/Ottoman and Christian/Muslim boundaries and tied different people and institutions together in a variety of social and political contexts.

Muslims in the West

The study of Muslim influence in the West has been largely ignored in studies of cross-cultural contact between the Islamic world and Europe. In the final drive to push Muslims out of Spain in 1492 and in the marginalization of the Balkans as a field of European study, Muslims in Europe have been overlooked until

---

[1]   Archivio Segreto del Vaticano, Dispacci del Nuncio a Venezia alla Segretaria di Stato, filza 32, fogli 86V–87R, June 28, 1597. I would like to thank Brian Pullan for bringing this case to my attention.

their appearance as immigrants in the twentieth century.[2] A major reason for this lack of coverage has been the amount of attention given to the rise of the West and the European age of exploration.[3] These events have tended to overshadow other developments taking place at the time.[4] While East/West diplomacy and representations of the Turk have commanded a significant amount of attention,[5] only a handful of works have addressed the complex question of Ottoman/ European social relations.[6]

Currently, the book that represents the most definitive statement about Muslims in the early modern West remains Bernard Lewis's *The Muslim Discovery of Europe*. Using a wide variety of Muslim sources, Lewis posits that while Muslims had contact with Europe in a variety of different ways, until the French revolution, Muslim states and Muslim intellectuals, including the Ottomans, were not particularly interested in Western culture and Western ideas. Stating that while scattered groups of Muslim merchants did exist in European cities, in no way does the small number of Muslim travelers compare to the large number of Europeans who not only traveled to, but also at times settled in the Middle East. While Lewis's contention merits consideration, his reference to Ottoman

---

[2]   On Muslims in Spain post-1492 see Leonard Patrick Harvey, *Muslims in Spain 1500-1614* (Chicago: The University of Chicago Press, 2005). On the marginalization of the Balkans see Maria Todorova, *Imagining the Balkans* (New York: Oxford University Press, 1997).

[3]   The seminal work on the origins of the modern world system in the sixteenth century is Immanuel Wallerstein, *The Modern World-System: Capitalist Agriculture and the Origins of the European World-Economy in the Sixteenth Century* (New York: Academic Press, 1976). Wallerstein wrote four volumes on the workings of the Europeandominated system, addressing issues such as mercantilism, European expansion and the triumph of liberalism. See also Carlo Cipolla, *Guns, Sails and Empires: Technological Innovation and the Early Phases of European Expansion 1400–1700* (New York: Pantheon Books, 1965) and Fernand Braudel, *Civilization and Capitalism: The Perspective of the World* (Berkeley: University of California Press, 1992).

[4]   See Giancarlo Casale, *The Ottoman Age of Exploration* (Oxford: Oxford University Press, 2010).

[5]   On representations of the Turk see Alexandrine St. Clair, *The Image of the Turk in Europe* (New York: Metropolitan Museum of Art, 1973), Robert Schwoebel, *The Shadow of the Crescent: The Renaissance Image of the Turk in Europe* (New York: St. Martin's Press, 1967), Kenneth Setton, *Venice, Austria and the Turks in the Seventeenth Century* (Philadelphia: The American Philosophical Society, 1991), and Mustafa Soykut, *Image of the 'Turk' in Europe: A History of the 'Other' in Early Modern Europe 1453–1682* (Berlin: K. Schwarz, 2001). Also for a broader perspective see Daniel Goffman, *The Ottoman Empire and Early Modern Europe* (Cambridge, UK: Cambridge University Press, 2002).

[6]   On inter-communal connections see Eric Dursteler, *Venetians in Constantinople: Nation, Identity and Coexistence in the Early Modern Mediterranean* (Baltimore: John Hopkins Press, 2006). On people who facilitated imperial contact see E. Natalie Rothman, *Brokering Empire: Trans-imperial Subjects between Venice and Istanbul* (Ithaca: Cornell University Press, 2012).

Muslims who did come to the West and particularly to Venice is overly dismissive. Reference is made to an Ottoman merchant community in Venice who lived in their own residence, but no archival sources are included to shed further light on their business dealings or on their social connections. Undoubtedly, much of the reason for Lewis's position comes from his desire to relate the eventual decline of the Ottomans and ultimately the Muslim world to developments in the early modern period. This sort of teleology serves to homogenize the Ottoman Muslim experience in the West and also fails to recognize the important role of Ottoman Muslims in forms of cross-cultural exchange.[7]

Attempting to debunk the idea of an ongoing war between the Christian and Muslim worlds, Paolo Preto's *Venezia e i turchi* covers a large array of Venetian perceptions of Turks, ranging from contacts in Venice to depictions of Turks in political correspondences and literature. Preto theorizes that though the Venetians perpetuated negative stereotypes of Turks, actual relations between the two states and their respective subject peoples were characterized by conflict and cooperation. Preto's reliance on a wide variety of sources gives the work a broad perspective and allows him to comment about Ottoman Muslims in a variety of different situations. Yet classifying his study as a social history of the Ottoman presence in Venice is misleading; for while his work is useful in understanding the variety of different attitudes that Venetians had in regard to the Ottoman Empire and its subjects, Preto's book devotes only one chapter to Ottoman Muslims in the city, and this chapter does not point to social connections, to group solidarities or to Ottoman influence. In fairness to Preto, rather than trying to delve into Ottoman Muslims lives, he is more concerned with focusing on Venetian perceptions and attitudes writ large.[8]

If the works of Lewis and Preto represent broad attempts to understand cross-cultural relations, other studies break from the tendency to focus on Europeans in the Middle East and center more on the role of specific Ottoman groups who traveled to Europe. Much of the attention has been focused on Ottoman Christian and Jewish groups who came to Europe.[9] Emphasis has been placed on the connections they made with locals and on their natural proclivity for commerce. This tendency has had the effect of marginalizing Muslims' involvement in forms of exchange.

---

[7]   Bernard Lewis, *The Muslim Discovery of Europe* (New York: W.W. Norton, 1982).

[8]   Paolo Preto, *Venezia e i turchi* (Firenze: G.C. Sansoni, 1975).

[9]   James Ball, "The Greek Community in Venice: 1470–1620," (Ph.D. thesis, University of London, 1984), and Benjamin Ravid, "The Legal Status of the Jewish Merchants in Venice (1541–1638)," (Ph.D. thesis, Harvard University, 1973). For a broader work on Jewish merchants see Jessica Roitman, *The Same but Different?: Intercultural Trade and the Sephardim, 1595–1640* (Leiden: E.J. Brill, 2011). For an integrated history of East/West Mediterranean trade see Molly Greene, *Catholic Pirates and Greek Merchants: A Maritime History of the Mediterranean* (Princeton: Princeton University Press, 2010).

Yet more recent studies have developed a more balanced view. For instance, focusing on high-level Ottoman emissaries who came to Venice, Maria Pia Pedani demonstrates that given the lack of a permanent Ottoman ambassador in Venice, Ottoman envoys, the majority of whom were Muslims, were regular visitors to the city. By providing background information on these emissaries, Pedani not only differentiates between individual Ottoman Muslims, she also places them within the context of ongoing Ottoman/Venetian contact.[10] Also focusing on long-term contact, Cemal Kafadar's "A Death in the Serenissima" emphasizes the importance of the Anatolian Muslim merchant community in trade conducted in Venice. Supporting the argument that Muslims were more involved in Ottoman trade than has been generally been accepted, Kafadar points to the steady growth of Muslim trading activities across the Adriatic. In describing these activities, he demonstrates that Muslims were not only involved in regional commerce but were also important players in long distance trade. This role made them dynamic actors in a system that was based on cooperation and on trans-regional connections.[11]

Connected Histories

Pedani's and Kafadar's studies constitute attempts to illustrate what Sanjay Subrahmanyam calls "connected histories." Noting that the early modern world was integrated in a variety of different ways, Subrahmanyam argues that the "European voyages of discovery" were part of a larger pattern of movement across vast stretches of the world. He adds that "… a good part of the dynamic in early modern history was provided by an interface between the local and the regional. For the historian who is willing to scratch below the surface, nothing turns out to be quite what it seems in terms of fixity and local rootedness."[12] Local communities were culturally connected to distant places in a variety of ways. Upheaval from war and social and economic change from the Ottoman Empire to parts of England created a trans-regional interest in different types of love poetry.[13] Venice's close contact with the Islamic eastern Mediterranean led to some architectural forms from the Middle East becoming a mainstay of Venetian visual culture, and the

---

[10]   Maria Pia Pedani, In nome del Gran Signore: inviati ottomani a Venezia dalla caduta di Costantinopoli alla guerra di Candia (Venezia: Deputazione Editrice, 1994).

[11]   Cemal Kafadar, "A Death in Venice (1575): Anatolian Merchants Trading in the Serenissima," *Journal of Turkish Studies* 10, (1986), pp. 191–218.

[12]   Sanjay Subrahmanyam, "Connected Histories: Notes towards a Reconfiguration of Early Modern Eurasia," in *Beyond Binary Histories: Re-imagining Eurasia to c.1830* (Ann Arbor: University of Michigan Press, 1999), pp. 289–316. Quote p. 299.

[13]   Walter Andrews and Mehmet Kalpaklı, The Age of the Beloved: Love and the Beloved in the Early Modern Ottoman and European Culture and Society (Durham: Duke University Press, 2005).

luxury trade with Islamic world made a significant impression on artistic taste during the Italian Renaissance. [14]

These connections broke down boundaries and created territorial zones that were fluid and porous as people and materials traveled back and forth across Islamic/Christian boundaries. One of the ways in which the notion of fluidity has been used as means to explain relations between the eastern and western Mediterranean is through analysis of identity. Identity studies have grown increasingly important in giving a voice to under-represented groups and in breaking down reified categories. While terms such as Muslim and Christian and Ottoman and Venetian are certainly useful in explaining types of encounters, in other situations they lack the specificity to define certain types of relationships and social contacts. [15] Eric Dursteler comments that "(i)dentity in the early modern world did not possess 'an essential primordial quality', nor was it defined by a 'nuclear component of social and cultural characteristics.' It was not an object but rather a process, 'a bundle of shifting interactions'...." [16] While rigid characterizations serve as a way of dividing the world and in some way making it digestible, they also limit our understanding of how people saw themselves and how they entered into cross-cultural relationships.

If the idea of fixed geographical boundaries is an obstacle to better understanding the position of groups in transit, the concept of borderlands is an alternative way of thinking about how individuals from different places interacted with one another. The idea of borderlands rests on the supposition that people who live on frontiers are in many ways closer to one another than they are to people who live in centers. While much of the work in this field has been done on the American southwest and on interactions among Anglos, the Spanish and Native Americans, increasingly the Mediterranean has been seen as series of different borderlands. [17] Late seventeenth-century Crete was a place where Latin, Muslim and Orthodox culture both came into contact and also mixed freely; the high degree of contact along the Dalmatian coast between the border people of Ottoman and Venetian territories led to a high level of cultural understanding. [18] These areas were not only places Christians and

---

[14] Deborah Howard, *Venice and the East: The Impact of the Islamic World on Venetian Architecture* (New Haven: Yale University Press, 2000) and Rosamond Mack, *Bazaar to Piazza: Islamic Trade and Italian Art* (Berkeley: University of California Press, 2002).

[15] See Rothman, *Brokering Empire* and Dursteler, *Venetians in Constantinople.*

[16] Eric Dursteler, Venetians in Constantinople, p. 18.

[17] On the American southwest See James Brooks, *Captains and Cousins: Slavery, Kinship and Community in the Southwest Borderlands* (Chapel Hill: University of North Carolina Press, 2002). On Mediterranean borderlands see Linda Darling, "Mediterranean Borderlands: Early English Merchants in the Levant," in *The Ottoman Empire: Myths, Realities and 'Black Holes'*, eds. Eugenia Kermeli and Oktay Özel (Istanbul: Isis Press, 2006), 173–88.

[18] Molly Greene, A Shared World: Christians and Muslims in the Early Modern Mediterranean (Princeton: Princeton University Press, 2000), Wendy Catherine Bracewell, The Uskoks of Senj: Piracy, Banditry and the Holy War in the Sixteenth Century Adriatic (Ithaca, Cornell University Press, 1992).

Fig. I.1 Piri Reis, *Map of the Mediterranean*, fol 63b-64a (Kitab-ı-Bahriye: 1521–1525). The Walters Art Museum.

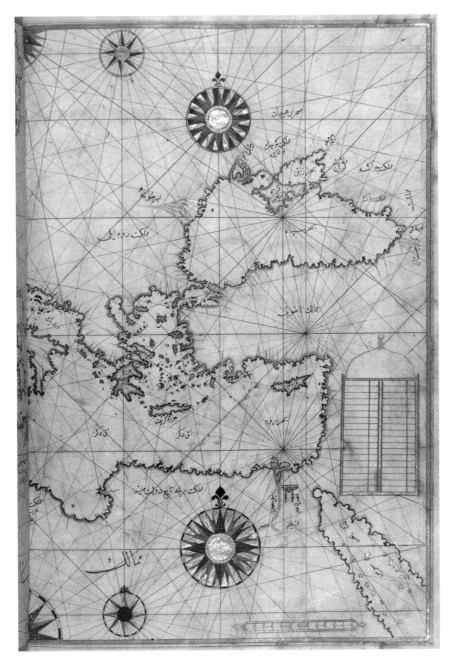

Fig. I.1   *Continued*

Muslims had frequent contact, but also sites where boundaries were blurred and constantly contested.

People moved between capital cities and their surrounding regions with some frequency and established social networks based on making contact with people in a variety of places. While these connections were not always apparent, particularly in regard to Ottoman Muslims in Venice, examples such as the Papal Nuncio's report that two Turks fought in what was recognized as the center of power and were quickly whisked off to the Council of Ten indicate that the two Turks either had contacts in Venice or were important enough people so that someone knew about them. Given this knowledge and familiarity, the case demonstrates that while the idea of borderlands is helpful in allowing us to go beyond fixed categories, we must be careful to assume that peripheral areas were natural contact zones and metropolitan centers were places characterized by anonymous encounters between people of widely divergent backgrounds. E. Natalie Rothman comments "that two cultures are disparate is not a pre-given fact but part of an ongoing process of boundary maintenance that unfolds in specific sites and institutions, through the efforts of those who purport to mediate and bridge them." Articulated and maintained by cultural mediators, these sites were both peripheral and metropolitan and led to the creation of boundaries that served and articulated different power interests. Rothman adds that while the Venetian empire has traditionally been thought of as diverse space that included people from a variety of different cultural, religious and linguistic backgrounds that embraced a certain type of multiculturalism, the notion of multiculturalism and tolerance obscures organizing principles that reflected imperial ambitions.[19]

Understanding Power in a Cross-Cultural Context

In the context of cross-cultural contact, these ambitions conformed to how a state managed its relation with people from other lands. Those thought to be foreign subjects needed to be watched, attended to and organized.[20] Michel Foucault notes that this form of organization can be thought of as "the way in which the conduct of individuals or groups might be directed...."[21] For communities from the Ottoman Empire, direction from the Venetians meant being told where to stay, how to be identified, with whom to come into contact, how to trade and how to file a grievance. This type of contact was managed by different institutions and conformed to Venetian political discourse. But this type of institutional order was just a blueprint for how the Venetians wanted relations to work, a theory for how inter-imperial contact should function. In practice, power relations were

---

[19]   Rothman, *Brokering Empire*, pp. 4, 14.

[20]   On the idea of subjecthood, see Rothman, *Brokering Empire*, p. 12.

[21]   Michel Foucault, "The Subject and Power," *Critical Inquiry*, vol. 8, no. 4 (1982), p. 790.

different. They were contingent, multilateral and inconsistent, originating from many different points of origin.

Foucault argues that "(e)very power relationship implies, at least *in potentia*, a strategy of struggle in which two forces are not superimposed, do not lose their specific nature, or do not finally become confused ... A relationship of confrontation reaches its term, its final moment, when stable mechanisms replace the free play of antagonistic reactions." [22] Conflict and resolution are two ways of understanding how different groups, communities and polities conduct negotiations and then build structures that address fundamental struggles over forms of control. The same was true in the early modern Mediterranean; conflict, negotiation and resolution between Muslim groups in Venice and the Venetians reflected struggles over different sites of power, similar to other conflicts in which people once thought to be completely marginalized, such as Jews, women, and members of the popular classes, participated in dialogs with elites, states and other established institutions.[23]

Not that we should think of individuals within these groups as naturally aligned with one other or always in direct opposition to those in power. When considering power relations, the study of any group or community needs to be understood within the parameters of a broad set of relationships, strategies and outcomes. The presumed absence of Muslims in European life has more to do with our expectations of how a community should behave than their actual place within trans-Mediterranean relations. In specific, Ottoman Muslims lack of a permanent presence in Venice does not reflect the power they wielded or the important connections they possessed.

In understanding these individuals' power and their connections, we must locate their presence within the context of movement that took place across the Mediterranean. Movement has been an important analytical tool in understanding how networks functioned, in comprehending how patronage worked and in considering how trade functioned.[24] These relationships have allowed us to think beyond conventional geographical boundaries and have emphasized the interconnectedness of certain cultural, economic and social spaces. With this understanding, part of the goal of this project will be to discern when Ottomans

---

[22]   Foucault, "Subject and Power," p. 794.

[23]   Many studies exist on those who have been excluded from traditional studies of power. See Benjamin Arbel, *Trading Nations: Jews and Venetians in the Early Modern Mediterranean* (Leiden: E.J. Brill, 1995), Michael Mullett, *Popular Culture and Popular Protest in Late Medieval and Early Modern Europe* (London: Croom Helm, 1987) and Leslie Pierce, *Morality Tales: Law and Gender in the Ottoman Court of Aintab* (Berkeley: University of California Press, 2003).

[24]   An excellent work on this subject is Francesca Trivellato, *The Familiarity of Strangers: The Sephardic Diaspora, Livorno, and Trade in the Early Modern Period* (New Haven, Yale University Press, 2009). For a different explanation of movement see Natalie Zemon Davis, *Trickster Travels: A Sixteenth Century Muslim between Worlds* (New York: Hill & Wang, 2006).

and their subjects used a similar logic to that of the Venetians and their subjects and when they diverged as they moved from Ottoman to Venetian territories. This approach will be taken not only to break down some of the barriers that have traditionally separated East and West, but also to better understand how people crossed boundaries. To date, lacking in most studies of East/West and Ottoman/ Venetian contact are inquiries into how individuals were able to fit in to a new place. Understanding the politics of different types of integration is important to gaining some sense as to how different Muslims were able to insert themselves into the daily practices and rhythms of Venetian life.

That is not though to give face-to-face contact primacy over other connections. While face-to-face contact explains how certain forms of negotiation, cooperation and conflict resolution worked, it does not necessarily explain why an individual acted in a particular way. An individual's actions, decisions and expression were also dictated by a variety of considerations. Lauren Benton, in her work, *A Search for Sovereignty*, talks about European empires being places that were subject to a variety of different legal realms and political influences. "As they moved, subjects performed legal rituals and acted as representatives of European powers, tracing pathways that became conduits for law and even corridors of jurisdiction."[25] Ottoman subjects acted in a similar fashion. As they crossed imperial boundaries, they moved through spaces that were not only connected by the implicit power relations of every encounter but also by the different juridical influences that subjects carried with them. Venice and Istanbul were not the only places linked, so were Venice and a court in Sarajevo, Venice and a governor in Egypt and Venice and an Ottoman sea captain.

The Parameters of the Study

In addressing these issues, the intention of this study is to focus on the presence of Ottoman Muslims in Venice during the period between the War of Cyprus in 1573 and the War of Candia in 1645. This was a period when the Ottomans and the Venetians avoided the major wars that had been fought between the two sides between 1463 and 1573 over territories in the Balkans and the Mediterranean such as Negroponte and Morea in Greece, Venetian Albania and Cyprus.[26] This was also a time when a significant numbers of Ottoman Muslims came to Venice to trade, and when other types of people connected to both the Christian and Muslim worlds stayed or transited through the city.

---

[25]   Lauren Benton, *A Search for Sovereignty: Law and Geography in European Empires, 1490–1900* (Cambridge, UK: Cambridge University Press, 2009), p. 31.

[26]   On Ottoman-Venetian wars see Peter Sugar, *Southeastern Europe Under Ottoman Rule 1354–1804* (Seattle: University of Washington Press, 1977), pp. 65–72 and Palmira Brumett, "The Ottoman Empire, Venice and the Question of Enduring Rivalries," in *Great Power Rivalries*, ed. William R. Thompson (Columbia: University of South Carolina Press, 1999), pp. 225–53.

The principal reason for this shift in trading patterns has been thought to be the Venetian nobles' decision to shift their economic activities away from trade to investments on the Venetian mainland. This decision brought more foreign traders to the city.[27] But this explanation does not address Ottoman interests or the changing nature of the Ottoman polity. The sixteenth century was a time characterized by Ottoman expansion into North Africa, the Fertile Crescent and the Indian Ocean. Ottoman trade, cross-cultural contact and political influence not only increased in these areas but in the Mediterranean as well. While many studies on Mediterranean trade and contact have focused on the importance of East/West commerce in an earlier period,[28] little has been said about the influence of the Ottomans in changing patterns of exchange in the late sixteenth and seventeenth centuries. In terms of contact with Europe, one notable development was the rise of Balkan cities such as Sarajevo as not just places of commerce but also as European centers of power with important connections across the Adriatic .[29]

So to gain a broad perspective, when appropriate and effective in illustrating a point, material will be used that falls outside of this time period. While the chronological parameters of this study are useful in terms of the amount of documentary evidence that is available, this choice of periodization does not mean that important practices and forms of conducting business between the two states and their subject peoples corresponded exactly to these dates. Some forms of contact both preceded and extended beyond this time period. Ottoman/Venetian relations formed in the fourteenth century and treaties and agreements that were established are important to understanding later developments. Along similar lines, evidence from developments after the period provides us with important insight into understanding particular patterns of contact and exchange.[30]

---

[27] Ugo Tucci, "The Psychology of the Venetian Merchant in the Sixteenth Century," in *Renaissance Venice*, ed. John Hale (London: Faber & Faber, 1973), pp. 346–78.

[28] David Abulafia, *Mediterranean Encounters: Economic, Religious, Political, 1100– 1550* (Aldershot England: Ashgate Press, 2000), Benjamen Kedar ed., *East-West Trade in the Medieval Mediterranean*, ed. (London, Varioum Reprints, 1986) and Jonathan Harris et al. eds., *Byzantines, Latins and Turks in the Eastern Mediterranean World after 1150* (Oxford: Oxford University Press, 2012).

[29] On Bosnia see Adem Handžić, *Population of Bosnia in the Ottoman Period: A Historical Overview* (Istanbul: Research Centre for Islamic History, Art and Culture, 1994), Stefka Parveva, *Village, Town and People in the Ottoman Balkans: 16th–mid 19th century* (Istanbul: Isis Press, 2009).

[30] For a discussion of Ottoman/Venetian relations in the fourteenth and fifteenth centuries, see Colin Imber, *The Ottoman Empire 1300–1650: The Structure of Power* (New York: Palgrave MacMillan, 2002), pp. 27–44, Halil İnalcik, "An Outline of Ottoman-Venetian Relations," in *Venezia centro di mediazione tra Oriente e Occidente, (-secoli xv–xvi: aspetti e problemi*, a cura di Hans-Georg Beck et al, vol. 1 (Florence: Olschki, 1977), pp. 83–90, and Marie Viallon, *Venise et la Porte Ottomane (1453–1563): un siècle de relations véneto-ottomanes de la prise de Constantinople à al mort de Soliman* (Paris: Economica, 1995).

Using this framework also does not limit the discussion exclusively to Ottoman Muslims who actually set foot on Venetian soil. The idea of an Ottoman Muslim presence in Venice constitutes an idea very different from just the numbers of individuals who came to the city. A presence indicates an ability to have influence and make an impact on decisions, events and relations; it also means a member of a Muslim community could have been involved with Venice from a distance, thus expanding the geographical boundaries of Ottoman/Venetian encounters. Fernand Braudel argued that the people and ideas that influenced life in the Mediterranean during the sixteenth century stretched far beyond the shores of the sea.[31] Rather than thinking of the Ottoman Empire as a place that was self-contained and subject to the machinations of outsiders, we must think about the ways that Ottoman knowledge and power manifested itself outside of the empire's boundaries.

Objectives and Structure

To capture the different ways in which power was expressed, negotiated and distilled, the book will be divided into five chapters. Themes rather than chronology will be used to designate different chapters. Part of the goal of covering a different theme in each chapter will be to analyze both micro and macro aspects of Ottoman/ Venetian contact. This approach will also be taken to explore the ways in which different manifestations and projections of power were connected to one another and reflected forms of contact that expanded from the local to the trans-imperial.

Chapter one will explore Ottoman networks, their living arrangements and attempts on the part of Venetian authorities to find a suitable housing solution for a Muslim population in its midst. This approach will be taken to examine how the Venetian state attempted to manage groups that were somewhat independent of state supervision. Although communities were dispersed throughout the city, they were active enough in local networks to challenge state power. Chapter two will build on the Venetian state's attempts at control and integration by examining the way in which local councils and magistrates served as mechanisms for assessing trade claims and as spaces of intercultural communication. This chapter will emphasize the ability Ottoman groups had to use a board such as the Venetian trade board, the Cinque Savi alla Mercanzia as portal for a dialog with the Venetian state. The issue of dialog will be examined further in the next chapter as the focus of the work shifts from contact in Venice to cases and conflicts that crossed boundaries and involved questions of social placement and cultural mediation. A principal focus of chapter three will be to address the ways in which conversion served as both a connection and a barrier between states and peoples. This chapter will also touch on how different forms of Ottoman power could be expressed in Venice and will serve as precursor to a larger discussion in chapter four on how individuals solicited backing from the Ottoman government to resolve conflicts

---

[31]   Fernand Braudel, *The Mediterranean and the Mediterranean World in the Age of Phillip II*, trans. Siân Reynolds (New York: Harper & Row, 1972).

involving the Venetians. Letters, imperial edicts and personal recommendations were expressions of inter-imperial communications that situated social actors and influenced decision-making. Much of the decision-making that took place, though, involved more than just a bilateral dialog and instead reflected power relations that were shaped by a variety of different actors throughout the Mediterranean and beyond. Picking up on this theme, chapter five will examine the ways in which different factions around the Mediterranean created integrated political spaces built on alliances of trans-cultural cooperation and strategic confrontation that included a complex triangulation of relationships between Venice, Spain and the Ottomans. While the discourse of fighting the "infidel" remained a powerful rhetorical device for the Spanish, the Ottomans and the Venetians, existing power relations necessitated participating in practices that were contingent on building relationships that challenged existing jurisdictional power and geographical control.

The Sources

In order to accomplish the task at hand, a wide variety of sources, including Venetian, Ottoman and Spanish, will be consulted in this project. To date most studies of Ottoman/Venetian relations have relied solely on European and primarily diplomatic sources. This has led to a view that is heavily skewed toward the attitudes and viewpoints of European governments. As is evident also in the works of Pedani and Kafadar, the obvious advantage of using Ottoman sources is that they give Ottoman Muslims a voice in their experiences and create an alternative to a Euro-centric point of view. Yet Ottoman documents are not the only means for gaining a wider understanding of Ottoman/Venetian relations. In Venice numerous criminal cases and Inquisition cases also shed light on issues that have not been addressed in other Ottoman/Venetian studies. These sources provide insights into the lives of members of the popular classes and also reveal important types of contact heretofore barely addressed.

While Ottoman sources have been included in this project, most of the sources are Venetian. The reason for this imbalance is threefold. First, Ottoman travelers did not leave travel accounts that, to date, have been found. Second, most of the Ottoman Muslims who did come to Venice probably stayed in Venice without the knowledge of the Ottoman government. Third, those people and incidents that are documented in Ottoman correspondences generally involve issues of diplomatic importance. This information, while helpful in supporting certain claims, does not provide information on the life of Ottoman Muslims on the streets that is comparable to Venetian sources.

While each chapter will address specific cases, information from these documents will also be included in other chapters as well. Much of the reason for this will be for purely practical. If the principal concern of this venture is both addressing the complex question of contact and also understanding how relations worked across boundaries, the ways a person presented himself or herself to both his or her own theoretical community and to the foreign community could have manifested itself in a variety of ways. Thinking of these cases and situations as texts, we must also consider that the different forms of analysis represented in the breakdown of the project into different chapters should also apply to the documents. Venetian, Ottoman and Spanish sources present different viewpoints that not only need to be understood in relation to one another but also need to be considered as different sites of power that had their own internal dynamics that were projected on to the larger Mediterranean political theatre.

Chapter 1
Scattered about the City: Ottoman Networks and Attempts to Control Them [1]

The year was 1574 and the War of Cyprus had just ended with the Ottomans gaining territory in the Eastern Mediterranean, including the island of Cyprus. While Venice in 1574 remained an important center of commerce, it was also going through a transformation. Venetian nobles had turned some of their attention away from trade to focus on other investments such as real estate and agriculture on the Italian mainland.[2] This shift contributed to the decision that long distance trade could no longer remain solely in the hands of Venetian nobles and resulted in a variety of foreign merchants, including those from the Ottoman Empire, coming to Venice.[3] A debate ensued on how to deal with groups of Muslim traders staying in the city.

On September 28, 1574, a Greek trade broker named Francesco Lettino[4] appeared before the Venetian senate, and asked that Ottoman Muslims be given a residence in the city. Lettino argued that Turks were living scattered about the city, having sexual relations with Christian women, and undermining Venice's good standing with God and Christendom.[5] Stating that he understood their customs and habits, he added that Turks should be given a place of their own to trade like the Jews had in Venice, and the Venetians had in the territories of the Ottoman

[1]   Material in this chapter is taken from Stephen Ortega, "Across Religious and Ethnic Boundaries: Ottoman Networks and Spaces in Early Modern Venice," *Mediterranean Studies: The Journal of the Mediterranean Studies Association*, vol. 18 (2009), pp. 66–89.

[2]   Brian Pullan, "The Occupations and the Investments of the Venetian Nobility in the Middle and Late Sixteenth Century," in *Renaissance Venice*, ed. John Hale (London: Faber & Faber, 1973), pp. 379–408.

[3]   See Ugo Tucci, "The Psychology of the Venetian Merchant in the Sixteenth Century," pp. 364–66.

[4]   Francesco di Dmitri's name is spelled both Littino and Lettino in various Venetian documents. I have chosen to use the spelling Lettino, because it seems to come up with greater frequency.

[5]   Ian Fenlon notes that Ottoman Muslims stayed in the house of Marc Antonio Barbaro at the time of the Battle of Lepanto. Ian Fenlon, *The Ceremonial City: History, Memory and Myth in Renaissance Venice* (Yale University Press: New Haven, 2007).

Fig. 1.1 Andrea (Michieli) Vicentino, *The Battle of Lepanto*, (1539-1614). Palazzo Ducale, Venice, Italy / Cameraphoto Arte Venezia / The Bridgeman Art Library.

Empire.[6] His proposal was accepted in 1575,[7] and in 1579,[8] with his family as custodians, a lodging for Ottoman Muslims from the Balkans was established at the *Insegna dell' Angolo* near the center of trade at the Rialto. Maintaining the custodial position throughout the sixteenth and seventeenth centuries, the family also supervised a larger residence for all Ottoman Muslims established on the Grand Canal in 1621.[9]

That Francesco Lettino would make this type of proposal does not seem strange. After the War of Cyprus ended in 1573, Ottoman Muslim merchants returned to the city. Housing them was a concern for Venetian authorities. German merchants had maintained a residence in Venice since the thirteenth century[10] and, as Lettino noted, the Venetians stayed in these establishments in Islamic lands. While his proposal reflected a feasible solution for housing Muslims, what does seem odd is that the Venetians would choose to put a person of Lettino's background and character in the position of custodian. A year prior, Lettino had been involved in an Inquisition case in Venice in which his connections to Muslims had raised suspicions.[11] Formed principally to stamp out Protestantism, the Inquisition in Venice was also interested in inquiring about and prosecuting Christians involved in Islamic or Jewish practices. In the case, Zorzi or Giorgio (his Italian name), a young servant of the Venetian noble Marcantonio Falier, who had been born Christian, became a Muslim, and had recently converted back to Christianity,

---

[6]   Archivio di Stato, Venezia (herein referred to as A.S.V.), Cinque Savi alla Mercanzia, nuove serie, busta 187, fascicolo 1, October 28, 1574. The Lettino case is also addressed in Rothman, *Brokering Empire*, pp. 29–35, 198–99. Rothman takes the view that the case reflects the connections and the activities of trans-imperial subjects. While I am in agreement with this assessment, I am interested in examining the way the case reflects a more extensive Muslim presence in the city than was once thought.

[7]   A.S.V., Cinque Savi alla Mercanzia, nuove serie, busta 187, fascicolo 1, May 17, 1575.

[8]   A.S.V., Cinque Savi alla Mercanzia, nuove serie, busta 187, fascicolo 1, August 4, 1579.

[9]   A.S.V., Cinque Savi alla Mercanzia, nuove serie, busta 187, fascicolo 1, December 11, 1620, March 11, 1621.

[10]   On the *Fondaco dei Tedeschi* see Henry Simonsfeld, *Der Fondaco dei Tedeschi in Venedig*, 2 vols. (Stuttgart: Cotta, 1887).

[11]   Paolo Preto notes that Francesco di Dimitri Lettino, who filed the petition to create a *fondaco*, could be the same person as the Demetrio Francesco who was incarcerated for a few days for harboring a young servant, Giorgio or Zorzi. Preto, *Venezia e i turchi*, p. 130, footnote 38. Upon closer examination of the trial, it is clear that the man in question was not Demetrio Francesco, but instead Francesco di Dimitri. (A.S.V., Sant'Ufficio, busta 35, testimony Francesco di Dimitri, 20 Augusto 1573). Further evidence that Francesco Lettino was the same man as Francesco di Dimitri in the Inquisition case is revealed in the fact that Giorgio or Zorzi, Francesco di Dimitri's son, testified in the Inquisition case, (A.S.V., Sant'Ufficio, busta 35, testimony Giorgio 20, Augusto 1573) and also later filed a petition regarding the fondaco. (A.S.V., Cinque Savi alla Mercanzia, nuove serie, busta 187, fascicolo 1, June 20, 1588).

made plans with three other young converts to leave Venice with some Ottoman merchants and return to the Ottoman Empire to be with his family. Needing a place to go, Zorzi chose to hide in Francesco Lettino's inn. Here, he changed his clothes, and shaved his head so as to appear like a Muslim. Unable to board the ship with the merchants, Zorzi was forced to stay in Lettino's inn. Compromised because of the change in appearance, Zorzi had no other choice but to continue to hide, until Lettino, out of fear, returned him to his master.[12]

A reading of Francesco Lettino's petition for a residence for "Turks" might lead one to the conclusion that Lettino was a loyal Christian subject who proposed a solution for the problem of housing Muslims in the city. The Inquisition case though reveals a different profile of Lettino. The case provides a picture of a man more on the margins than someone who was principally interested in maintaining boundaries between Muslims and Christians. His position reveals a person interested in putting forth contradictory narratives of integration and separation. Given these contradictions, questions need to be asked about the nature of community, about the existence of Muslim groups in unsupervised spaces, about the role of people like Lettino in working with Ottoman groups and about the decision to house all Ottoman Muslims in one place on the Grand Canal. Gaining a better understanding of these issues helps explain the gap between how group activities worked in practice and how they were presented in Venetian political discourse.

Ottoman Muslim Communities

In thinking about Lettino's situation and in considering the ways in which Ottoman Muslim merchants were housed in Venice, one issue that needs to be addressed is the nature of the Ottoman Muslim community or communities in the city. One of the claims that Lettino raised in his petition was that "Turks" were living scattered about the city. Broadly speaking, the term Turks was used to refer to the Muslim subjects of the Ottoman Empire. As early as 1419 Ottoman/ Venetian treaties not only guaranteed the rights of Venetian subjects in Ottoman territories but also the rights of Ottoman subjects in Venetian domains as well.[13] Sixteenth-century trading patterns had begun to change and the Venetians found themselves in an intense commercial competition with other ports such as Ancona and Livorno. No longer in a position to dominate trade the way it had in earlier centuries, the

---

[12]   A.S.V., Sant'Ufficio, busta 35. Lettino seems to realize the stakes involved and probably recognized the type of trouble he might create for himself by not turning over Zorzi. The Inquisition case indicates that the Inquisition board did not trust Lettino and let him off only after he had paid the large sum of 200 ducats, and the board was given a character guarantee by Dmitri Spatari.

[13]   George Martin Thomas, *Diplomatarium, veneto-levantinum sive acta et diplomata res Venetas Graecas atque Levantis (1351-1454)* vol. 2, (New York, B. Franklin, 1966), pp. 318–19.

Venetian government had to develop new ways of raising revenues and one of these was to attract more foreign traders to the city. In 1524 a law was passed that stated that "Subjects of the Turk are exempted from a law that prohibits foreigners from bringing their goods on Venetian galleys and ships from the Balkans, Alexandria, Syria and Istanbul to Venice and from Venice to its subject territories."[14] In the period after the War of Cyprus, the size of the Muslim merchant community in Venice continued to grow, and during this period its numbers were comparable to European trading groups.[15]

Yet to think of Turks or Muslims from the Ottoman Empire as a community requires further elaboration. While we do not want to dismiss religious identity as either a way that people defined themselves or as a way that people distinguished themselves from others, we do need to gain a better understanding as to how group consensus worked. From our perspective, the idea of a Turk represents a sociological term that defines people from a particular society, the nation-state of Turkey. [16] This way of thinking is based on the belief that Turks have a shared identity, and thus form an imagined community.[17] In the early modern period, though, the idea of the Turk represented a type of identification that was very different. References to Turks were largely connected to Europeans' attempts to define categorically their Muslim rivals. Turks represented a combination of what was reviled and what was feared. They served as the antithesis of what it meant be Christian, and thus formed in the minds of many a specific manifestation of the European "other."[18]

This categorical definition of Ottoman Muslims, though, obscures Ottoman cultural and social realities. While the Ottomans maintained a certain amount of central control, particular regions within the Empire could be very autonomous. Covering an area that stretched from North Africa to the Persian Gulf, the Ottoman Empire encompassed a territory that included people from a wide variety of different linguistic, religious and cultural backgrounds. Not all Muslims were Turks or even spoke Turkish. Arabic, Albanian and Slavonic were only a few of the languages spoken within the boundaries of the Empire. Significant cultural distinctions existed between those people who lived in the Balkans and those who

---

[14] A.S.V., Cinque Savi alla Mercanzia, Loro Regulazioni e Litigi, prime serie, registro.19, foglio 27. "Sudditi del Turco siano eccetuatti dalla prohibizione ch' hanno di foresteir di condur le loro robbe dalla Romania alta, e bassa, Alexandria, Soria, e Costantinopoli a' Ventia sopra Galere, e Navi Veneziane e da venetia ne'luoghi sudditi."

[15] Kafadar, "A Death in Venice."

[16] On Turkish nationalism see Masami Arai, *Turkish Nationalism in the Young Turk Era: Social, Economic and Political Studies of the Middle East*, vol. 43 (Leiden: E.J. Brill, 1992) and Hugh Poulon, *Top Hat, Grey Wolf and Crescent: Turkish Nationalism and the Turkish Republic* (New York: New York University Press, 1997).

[17] On nationalism as a type of imagined community see Benedict Anderson, *Imagined Communities: Reflections on the Origin and Spread of Nationalism* (London: Verso, 2006).

[18] See Soykut, *Image of the 'Turk,'* and Schwoebel, *The Shadow.*

lived in the Arab provinces of the Empire such as Iraq. These differences could lead to social divisions based on language and regional and local affiliation.[19]

One term that has been used to define these ethnic/linguistic groups is nations. In the early modern period, nations were not nations in the modern sense, nor did they constitute clearly defined ethnicities. Instead, they reflected a connection or a perceived association with a particular geographical or political entity. For instance, in Istanbul, the Venetians, the French, the Ragusans and the English constituted different nations.[20] The Venetians' desire to designate Muslims as separate nations reflected a line of thinking that resembled the way they differentiated Ponentine, Germanic and Levantine Jews.[21] As was noted above, the first residence for Muslims established near the Rialto only housed Muslims from the Balkans; Muslims from other parts of the empire still stayed in other parts of the city. In 1579, around the time that the site at Rialto was chosen, the issue was still under debate and the Venetians considered housing the different nations of the Ottoman Empire in a number of different places.[22] This dilemma continued to draw attention and at the time the decision was made to establish the *Fondaco dei Turchi* in 1621, Giacomo de Nores, the dragoman for Turks, commented that there would be two separate sections, one for Balkan merchants and the other for those coming from Asia. He believed that these two groups were fundamentally different in nature and in custom.[23]

Regional and linguistic ties were also expressed in the way that different Ottoman groups presented themselves in Venice. For instance, in 1582 two merchants from Bosnia had petitioned the Venetian government for more brokers on the Rialto who could speak Slavonic. Commenting that there were only four brokers capable of helping them with their business transactions, they argued that some of them were ill-intentioned and thus of no help.[24] While the merchants' principal concern was to argue that trade brokers who could speak their language were under-represented, their petition also reflected a certain geographical sensibility. Yet other individuals defined themselves in even more local terms. Following an Uskok attack on a Venetian ship in 1587, a group of merchants

---

[19]   For a discussion on Ottoman diversity see Uzi Baram and Linda Carroll, "The Future of the Ottoman Past," in *A Historical Archaeology of the Ottoman Empire: Breaking New Ground*, eds. Uzi Baram and Linda Carroll (New York: Kluwer Academic/Plenum Publishers, 2000), pp. 3–36 and Karen Barkey*, Empire of Difference: The Ottomans in Comparative Perspective* (Cambridge, UK: Cambridge University Press, 2008).

[20]   Dursteler, *Venetians in Constantinople*, pp. 23–40.

[21]   For a description of the different Jewish communities in Venice see Brian Pullan, *The Jews of Europe and the Inquisition in Venice* (London: I.B. Tauris, 1997), pp. 149–53.

[22]   Ennio Concina, *Fondaci: Architettura, arte, e mercatura, tra Levante, Venezia, Alemagna* (Venezia: Marsilio, 1997), p. 230.

[23]   A.S.V., Cinque Savi alla Mercanzia, nuove serie, busta 187, fasc. 1, March 29, 1621.

[24]   A.S.V., Cinque Savi alla Mercanzia, Risposte, prime serie, busta 138, foglio 68R, July 31, 1582.

signed their claim as residents of Sarajevo, as opposed to Bosnians.[25] In 1741, a ruling sent from an Ottoman judge in Galata to the Venetians listed the concerned parties as Ali beşe bin Hüseyn from Nauphlio, Baba Hasan bin Abdullah from Üsküdar, Hüseyn bin Abdullah from Mistra (Greece) and Hacı Mustafa bin Şaban from the han of Papasoğlu in Istanbul, to name a few.[26]

Signing the name of one's city or referring to a neighborhood symbolized a local allegiance that more closely mirrored one's sense of geographical loyalty. In the case of the murder of a local count in 1610, the citizens of two towns, one Ottoman, Risano, and the other Venetian, Perasto, stood opposed to one another not as Ottoman and Venetian subjects but as members of their communities.[27] In eighteenth-century Aleppo, people were quick to emphasize even small differences between themselves and other people throughout Syria.[28] Identity and attachment to place was more discernible at even more local levels than the city. Traian Stoianovich comments that "the Ottoman town was … an agglomeration of neighborhoods, a system of symbiotic arrangements:… each with its own set of fraternal and religious associations, its own tortuous alleys and dead-end streets."[29] In a *hüccet*[30] *issued by the kadi*, the judge, of Merzifon, the kadi mentioned that Isa and his sister were the only inheritors of Sergis, the son of Kaçeder, inhabitant of the quarter of Quoblan in the city of Merzifon, who had died in Venice.[31]

These differences were pronounced in the early modern era because local identity was expressed in a variety of different ways. In his study of the sixteenth-century miller Menocchio, Carlo Ginzburg demonstrates that Menocchio's understanding of the world and his identity were directly tied to the local agrarian culture of the Friuli.[32] In the early modern neighborhood of Ribera in Barcelona, identity was not based on territorial districts, but instead on memberships in guilds. When people signed their names, they also included their professions.[33]

---

[25] A.S.V., I Documenti Turchi, busta 8, fascicolo 953, November 1587.

[26] Maria Pia Pedani, *I documenti turchi dell'Archivio di Stato di Venezia* (Roma: Minestero per i beni culturali e ambientali, Ufficio centrale per I beni archivistici, 1994), p. 520.

[27] A.S.V., Quarantia Criminale, registro 134, fascicolo 202.

[28] Abraham Marcus, *The Middle East on the Eve of Modernity: Aleppo in the Eighteenth Century* (New York: Columbia University Press, 1989), p. 32.

[29] Traian Stoianovich, *Between East and West: The Balkan and Mediterranean Worlds*, vol. 2 (New Rochelle: Caratzas, 1992), p. 93.

[30] A legal document.

[31] A.S.V., I Documenti Turchi, busta 12, fascicolo 1308. Merzifon was a city in central Anatolia.

[32] Carlo Ginzburg, *The Cheese and the Worms*, trans. Ann and John Tedeschi (Baltimore: Johns Hopkins University Press, 1992).

[33] James S. Amelang, "People of the Ribera: Popular Politics and Neighborhood Identity in Early Modern Barcelona" in *Culture and Identity in Early Modern Europe: Essays in Honor of Natalie Davis (1500–1800)*, eds. Barbara B. Diefendorf and Carla Hesse (Ann Arbor: University of Michigan, 1993), pp. 119–37.

In medieval Marseille, notarial acts demonstrate that six categories were used to describe people: name, parentage or marital status, legal status, trade or profession, place of origin and address.[34] If listing one's trade was a way of differentiating oneself from members of other professions and guilds in Barcelona and if six categories were used as the parameters of identity in Marseille, then listing one's city must also have been a way of distinguishing oneself not only from Venetians, but also from other Ottoman Muslims.

Yet the listing of one's city was not only a social issue, but a political one as well. This type of geographical attachment made sense not only because of the need to distinguish oneself from a person from another city, but also because of the relative autonomy that many merchants had in relation to political structures. Other than the fact that connections to the state and to powerful individuals attached to the state could prove useful, connections based on broad territorial conceptions must have seemed meaningless. In fact, not only did these boundaries fail to evoke communal sentiments, but given that points of entry were used primarily for tax collection purposes, boundaries were to be subverted as opposed to respected. Palmira Brummett points out:

> While the energies of states like the Ottoman and the Portuguese were directed at garrisoning commercial entrepôts and transit points in order to collect customs taxes, the energies of individual traders were directed at circumventing the boundaries imposed by political overlords, and overcoming the limits posed by technology, by weather, and by predators whose only investment was in arms. State rationale was not necessarily merchant rationale. The organization of commercial activity was usually outside the immediate control of the state.[35]

While we must be careful not to assume that Ottoman Muslim merchants had connections to the Ottoman state or to large trading blocks, we must consider that Ottoman Muslim merchants were more independent than their European counterparts. As is well known, European merchants such as the Venetians and the Genoese had separate living quarters and formed very distinct communities in the Middle East.[36] These communities largely reflected very well-organized mercantile policies and the ability of these states to control long-distance trade.

Part of this had to do with the social make-up of the European city-state in comparison to the Ottoman Empire. Trading policies in Venice were established with the intention of protecting nobles who were engaged in trade.[37] The same was not true of the Ottoman Empire. The Ottomans did not have a noble class similar

---

[34] Daniel Smail, *Imaginary Cartographies: Possession and Identity in Late Medieval Marseille* (Ithaca: Cornell University Press, 1999), p. 195.

[35] Palmira Brummett, *Ottoman Seapower and Levantine Diplomacy in the Age of Discovery* (Albany: SUNY Press, 1994), p. 14.

[36] See Dursteler, *Venetians in Constantinople*.

[37] See Frederic Lane, *Venice: A Maritime Republic* (Baltimore: Johns Hopkins University Press, 1973) and Armando Sapori, *The Italian Merchant in the Middle Ages* (New York: Norton, 1970).

to that of the Europeans, nor did their elites seek to control trade. Thus, while long distance trade at times may have involved officials of the state and at other times may have necessitated state intervention, commercial activity was not directly tied to the state. Much of the reason for this autonomy and independence had to do with the inability of the state to impose its will on merchant activities. Rhoads Murphey posits that while the state had a communications network along the Via Egnatia, the principal trading route across the Balkans, it would be a mistake to assume that the state maintained a high degree of control over it. He adds that "the flow of traffic along and near state routes such as the Via Egnatia was determined to a very large extent by autonomous economic forces that had their origin in the locality." Though Murphey does acknowledge that Ottoman authorities had better control over ports, this type of authority would not necessarily have affected the local trader or regional trading networks that existed between the Balkans and Venice.[38]

The Ottoman Muslim Presence in Venice

Taking the different Ottoman group loyalties and connections into account is important in thinking about efforts to house Ottoman Muslims in Venice and in considering Ottoman/Venetian spatial politics. As was noted, developments led to the establishment of a residence for Ottoman Muslims from the Balkans in 1579 and ultimately resulted in the creation of a *fondaco* for all Ottoman Muslims in 1621. In the interim, many other attempts were made to house Muslims in one place. While these attempts were unsuccessful, they reflected a continued uneasiness about the presence of a Muslim population.[39]

One way of thinking about the introduction of the idea of a location for Muslims is that it represented the actions of a more intrusive state. As means of gaining better control, the creation of this type of residence was an attempt to house scattered groups of Muslims all in one place and was connected to other developments in which institutional attempts were made to control women, the poor and certain marginal social elements.[40] Muslims were seen as outsiders, a social grouping that needed to be institutionally located, identified and supervised.

---

[38]   Rhoads Murphey, "Patterns of Trade along the Via Egnatia in the Seventeenth Century," in *The Via Egnatia Under Ottoman Rule: Halcyon Days in Crete II: A Symposium held in Rethymnon 9–11 January 1994*, ed. Elizabeth Zachariadou (Rethymnon: Crete University Press, 1996), pp. 190–91.

[39]   On the evolution of the fondaco in Venice see Concina, *Fondaci*.

[40]   On attempts at social control in the sixteenth century see Sandra Cavallo and Simona Cerutti, "Female Honor and the Social Control of Reproduction in Piedmont between 1600 and 1800," in *Sex and Gender in Historical Perspective: Selections from Quaderni Storici*, eds. Edward Muir and Guido Ruggiero (Baltimore: John Hopkins University Press, 1990), pp. 73–109, Sherrill Cohen, *The Evolution of Women's Asylums since 1500: From Refuges for Ex-Prostitutes to Shelters for Battered Women* (New York: Oxford University Press, 1992) and Brian Pullan, *Rich and Poor in Renaissance Venice: The Social Institutions of a Catholic State to 1620* (Cambridge MA: Harvard University Press, 1971).

This development was also connected to changing social conditions in the sixteenth and seventeenth centuries in which urban elites, when faced with the increased arrival of new communities, thought of new ways to shape urban spaces. Thus, a residence for Muslims constituted an "imposed enclosure" that was similar to the Ghetto and represented a structure that focused on ethnic differences.[41]

Yet to think of the segregation of Muslims as the only way of understanding the social and political dynamics of situating Ottoman Muslims in Venice fails to recognize other reasons that fondaci and ethnic spaces were considered suitable forms of housing. Merchant residences in Venice were similar to other types of residences that existed in the Islamic world and other parts of the Mediterranean. They represented concrete evidence of the importance of trade, of cooperation and of cross-cultural contact. Reflecting a region-wide sensibility, these residences were adapted from place to place as a means to help integrate a foreign population.[42]

The first suggestion about creating a residence for Muslims actually arose in August 1573 when the Papal Nunzio Giambattista Castagna commented that the Turks had requested a proper location for their trading activities similar to the Ghetto.[43] Although we do not know the origins of the people who initially approached the Venetian government, the very existence of this request indicates that a certain group or groups of Ottoman Muslims had the power to ask for their own trading facility. That Castagna would comment that Turks were advocating for a trading location similar to the Ghetto also demonstrates that at least some Ottoman Muslims wanted to be segregated from the local Christian population. Their request suggests that a residence was not imposed on Ottoman Muslims but instead involved a negotiated process. In the context of the late sixteenth century, a residence in the city would have put them on par with other merchant groups and given them a permanent seat in the city.[44]

Historically, groups of Arabs, Turks and Slavs had stayed in different parts of the city, and in the fourteenth and fifteenth centuries small groups of these individuals could be found in fifteen different parishes. These living arrangements held true for other groups as well. Though members of Levantine communities were concentrated in certain areas from the middle of the fifteenth to the beginning of the sixteenth centuries, people from the Eastern Mediterranean and the Balkans

---

[41]   Donatella Calabi, "Foreigners and the City: An Historiographical Exploration for the Early Modern Period," *Fondazione Eni Enrico Mattei Working Papers*, Paper 15 (September, 2006), http://www.researchgate.net/publication/5023555_Foreigners_and_the_City_An_Historiographical_Exploration_for_the_Early_Modern_Period

[42]   Olivia Constable, *Housing the Stranger in the Mediterranean World: Lodging Trade and Travel in Late Antiquity and the Middle Ages* (Cambridge, UK: Cambridge University Press, 2003).

[43]   Preto, *Venezia e i turchi*, p. 130. Ennio Concina contends that the idea of creating a specific location especially for Turks also relates to the Greek request for a church and seat made at the beginning of the sixteenth century. Concina, *Fondaci*, p. 221.

[44]   Concina, *Fondaci,* pp. 22–3.

were still dispersed throughout the city.[45] In essence the type of living arrangements that attempted to place people in specific spaces existed side by side with another more open and less structured way of lodging foreigners that was characterized by the inns that accommodated them. Springing up more organically, they were scattered throughout the city and acted both as temporary residences and as taverns.[46]

Even given Lettino's rhetoric and even given the fact that Muslims were not permitted to go out past a certain hour, the type of residence that Lettino was advocating for more closely resembled the other types of *hosterie* and lodgings that existed in the city. Milanese, Luccans, Greeks and Balkan Slavs all had designated places to stay and institutions to support their activities.[47] The space that was chosen for Muslim merchants from the Balkans at the *Insegna dell'Angolo* was located in the heart of the trading center close to the *Fondaco dei Tedeschi*; thus, as a residence, it conformed to the other ethnic spaces that were set up to place merchants in the city center.[48]

Other Muslim groups continued to live in other parts of the city. These spaces were defined by other relationships and by other network connections. While evidence is scant on this issue, at the time of the creation of the *Fondaco dei Turchi* on the Grand Canal, an edict listing fourteen inns stipulated that these inns were no longer allowed to receive Ottoman Muslims as guests. Each of the inns listed was either in San Marco or Rialto.[49]

One characteristic of these inns was that they catered to people of different religious backgrounds and, thus, represented a different social geography than enclosed spaces. When asked by the Inquisition authorities if Christians had stayed with them, Giulia, Lettino's wife, commented that "the day the Turks came a group of Greek merchants from Zante had left."[50] A similar situation was described in another Inquisition case in 1581 in which Paulina Briana (she is also referred to as Briani), a woman who ran an establishment that housed Turks, was accused of sleeping with a Turk named Hüseyn. In response to the inquisitors' question as to whether Muslims and Christians had stayed together in her residence, Paulina denied that they had interacted with one another but did acknowledge that Turkish

---

[45]   See diagrams in Brunehilde Imhaus, *Le minoranze orientali a Venezia 1300–1510* (Roma: Il Veltro, 1997), pp. 223, 225.

[46]   For information on taverns and inns see Lina Urban, *Locande a Venezia* (Venezia: Centro Internazionzle della Grafica, 1989).

[47]   Donatella Calabi, "Gli stranieri nella capitale della repubblica Veneta nella prima età moderna," *Mélanges de l'Ecole francaise de Rome, Italie et Méditerranée*, vol. 111, no. 2 (1999), p. 722.

[48]   Ibid.," pp. 722, 726 and Concina, *Fondaci*, pp. 225–7.

[49]   A.S.V., Cinque Savi alla Mercanzia, nuove serie, busta 187, fascicolo 2, November 13, 1621.

[50]   A.S.V., Sant'Ufficio, busta 35, August 27, 1573. "in quel giorno che zonse i Turchi si ha partido i marchidani Grechi da Zante."

and Greek merchants had stayed with her at the same time.[51] Other Christian servants and slaves also stayed in these types of residences. When asked if other Christians had come to the house with hopes of becoming Muslims, Lettino replied that "children of Christians came to my house to socialize with Turks, but they were Turkish slaves of other merchants."[52] Gregorio, a young Armenian who was found in the house of Paulina, testified that he had spent a month in Venice with a Turk by the name of Moola.[53] In fact, these living situations persisted long after Lettino's original petition, and in 1596 the procurator of San Marco Leonardo Donà noted that the locations in which Turks lived also housed Christians and thus must be changed.[54]

Paulina Briana's and Francesco Lettino's houses were in the district of Santa Maria Formosa, an area close to the central business district at Rialto and the center of public life in San Marco.[55] This district was populated during the sixteenth century by one of the largest contingents of Christians from the Levant.[56] The heterogeneous character of the neighborhood was revealed in one of the denunciations against Paulina, in which her accuser claimed she had had a daughter by a Turk.[57] While this accusation clearly could have been fabricated, the interesting sidelight is that one of the people to make the allegation was a Muslim cavalryman. The cosmopolitan and international nature of Santa Maria Formosa must have contributed to more contact and probably a greater openness to foreigners.[58]

This type of openness and the mixing of communities existed in different cities in the Ottoman Empire as well. While it would be a generalization to state that Ottoman cities conformed to a prescribed set of social relations between different ethnic and religious groups, evidence exists that traveling merchants coming from Ottoman cities and towns must have been exposed to integrated communities and integrated social spaces. For instance, in the sixteenth century in Sarajevo the principal mosque, the Gazi Beg Husrev mosque, the main Orthodox church and the most important synagogue were in close proximity to one another.[59] In sixteenth-century Jerusalem while many Muslims, Christians and Jews did live in

---

[51]   A.S.V. Sant'Ufficio, busta 47, November 12, 1588.

[52]   A.S.V. Sant'Ufficio, busta 35, September 9, 1573. "Ho detto che in casa mia vengano fioli di Cristiani pratticar con li turchi ma altri turchetti schiavi de altri merchandanti."

[53]   A.S.V., Sant'Ufficio, busta 47, January 2, 1581.

[54]   Frederico Seneca, *Il Doge Leonardo Donà* (Padova: Antenore, 1959), p. 205.

[55]   In one of the testimonies against Paulina the point was made that corte nova was in Santa Maria Formosa. See A.S.V., Sant'Ufficio, busta 47, December 30, 1581.

[56]   Imhaus, *Le minoranze*, map p. 222.

[57]   A.S.V. Sant'Ufficio, busta 47, December 30, 1581.

[58]   That is not to say that other neighborhoods were not cosmopolitan. This comment only reflects observations on Santa Maria Formosa.

[59]   András Riedlmayer, "From the Ashes: Bosnia's Cultural Heritage," in *Islam and Bosnia: Conflict Resolution and Foreign Policy in Multi-Ethnic States*, ed. Maya Shatzmilller (Montreal: McGill's-Queens University Press, 2002), p. 103.

particular quarters, segregation was not enforced and Muslims did end up buying houses in Jewish neighborhoods.[60] In the latter half of the century, a large number of Jews moved to the Temple Mount, where they were subject to the Muslim *shayk al-haram*, the local head of the quarter.[61] Galata, across the Golden Horn from Istanbul, also contained a varied population, and in the mid-seventeenth century the traveler Evliya Çelebi claimed that this location contained seventeen Muslim districts, seventy Greek districts, three Frankish districts, one Jewish district and two Armenian districts.[62]

If these types of neighborhoods represented contact zones between Christians and Muslims, so did the integrated spaces that were frequented by travelers. The Ottoman traveler was exposed to a variety of different types of inns.[63] For instance, in a crossing near the Marizza river, in what is now Bulgaria, the anonymous chronicler traveling with the Venetian ambassador Jacopo Soranzo to Istanbul in 1575 commented that

> ...next to the Marizza river at 3:00 in the afternoon we arrived at the bridge of Mustafa which is a very good place, and here we stayed in a caravansaray.... This was built by the sultana, wife of Sultan Selim with a mosque close by and a little hospital where the ambassador stayed to escape the smell and the heat of the caravansaray. ... the building is for the comfort of travelers, she endowed it with enough regular income to pay the expenses for three consecutive days and, this was adhered to inviolably, because no one passed without receiving bread, water, rice soup and meat....Moreover many poor people come for the alms that are continually distributed, and are given equally to Christians and Jews.[64]

---

[60]   Dror Ze'evi, *An Ottoman Century: The District of Jerusalem in the 1600s* (Albany: SUNY Press, 1996), p. 23.

[61]   Amon Cohen, "On the Realities of the Millet System: Jerusalem in the Sixteenth Century" in *Christians and Jews in the Ottoman Empire: The Functioning of a Plural Society*, vol. II, eds. Benjamin Braude and Bernard Lewis (New York: Holmes & Meier, 1982), p. 9.

[62]   Robert Mantran, "Foreign Merchants and Minorities in Istanbul during the Sixteenth and Seventeenth Centuries," in *Christians and Jews in the Ottoman Empire*, vol. 1, eds. Benjamin Braude and Bernard Lewis (New York: Holmes and Meier, 1982), p. 129.

[63]   On the different types of lodging facilities in the Middle East see Constable, *Housing the Stranger*.

[64]   *Diario de viaggio da Venezia a Constantinopoli fatta da M. Jacopo Soranzo al Sultano Murad III in compagnia di M. Giovanni Correr bailo alla porta ottomana*, descritto da anonimo che fu al seguito del Soranzo (Venezia: n.p. 1856), p. 52. "accanto il fiume Marizza, ed alle 15:00 arrivammo al ponte di Mustafa ch'è bonissima terra, e qui allogiamneto in una caravanserá…...fabbricato dalla moglie di Sultan Selim, con un mosche quivi vicina ed uno ospitaletto, ove allogió il signor ambasciatore per fuggir la puzza e il caldo de caravaserá…la fabrica per comoditá de viadanti, gli ha applicato tanta entrato ferma che a chiunque passa di qui facesse le spese per tre giorni continui, il che viene osservato inviolabilmente, perché non passa nessuno di qui che non abbia pane, acqua, minestra di riso e carne…Oltre questo molti poveri vengono per limonsina che loro fatta continuamente dandone tanto a Cristiani ad Ebrei."

While the lodging site near the Marizza River was seen through the eyes of a Venetian observer, this account also gives us an indication of the different types of spaces a traveler encountered. The *caravansaray* catered to different types of people. Located on a trade route, it was open to members of different faiths who needed lodging. While we must be careful not to assume that a Muslim merchant would have been incapable of drawing very strict boundaries in regard to contact with Christians in Venice, we should not be surprised that those who left home were used to integrated spaces. Along similar lines, the Habsburg ambassador to the Porte, Ogier Ghiselin de Busbeq noted in his travels across the Ottoman Empire in 1555, "I sometimes lodged in a Turkish khan. … No one is refused admittance, whether Christian or Jew, rich or poor; the door is open to all alike."[65] The road was a very unique place, and the spaces that people stayed were governed by a different logic than the segregated spaces of Venice.[66]

Beyond catering to different merchants, mixed ethnic and religious spaces were undoubtedly more favorable locations for groups of Muslims traveling with Christian servants or slaves. For example, in January of 1591 a man named Andreas Negroni told the Inquisition authorities that a Turk was staying with a man who claimed to be a Christian. After investigating, the tribunal found out that the person in question was a man by the name of Pietr who had been born and baptized in Russia. Brought to Venice, Pietr contended that he had tried to escape from his master on many occasions, claiming that his principal wish was to return to living as a Christian.[67]

Pietr's living situation was probably quite common. An Ottoman merchant who traveled needed servants to transport goods and to attend to belongings. In Venice, these living arrangements could lead to conflicts between visiting merchants and local authorities. For instance, when authorities discovered in Paulina Briana's inn that the young Armenian named Gregorio was staying with the Muslim merchant Hüseyn, the church with the help of the state took Gregorio away from his master, forcing Hüseyn to file a petition demanding his servant back. Hüseyn pointed out that Gregorio had come to Venice as the servant of another Turk named Achmed. Achmed had turned Gregorio over to Hüseyn for the sum of 20 ducats and Hüseyn wanted Gregorio returned so that he could recoup this investment.[68] Though the authorities were afraid that Gregorio would become a Muslim, they were also aware that Hüseyn had a legitimate claim to ask for his servant back. The dispute raised the complicated question of where a Christian should be allowed to stay.

Other contacts between Muslims and Christians that the Venetians found unsuitable also took place in *hosterie*. Mustafa Balirai was brought before the

---

[65]   Ogier Ghiselin de Busbeq, *The Turkish Letters of Ogier Ghiselin de Busbeq*, trans. Edward Seymour Forster (Oxford: The Clarendon Press, 1927), p. 18.

[66]   On travelers during the early modern period see John Hale, *The Civilization of Europe in the Renaissance* (New York: Atheneum, 1993), pp. 153–84.

[67]   A.S.V., Sant'Ufficio, busta 67, January 15, 1591.

[68]   A.S.V., Sant'Ufficio, busta 47, December 30, 1581.

Inquisition board in August of 1586 on charges that he had become a Christian and had then attempted to reconvert to Islam. Balirai had been the servant of a Genoese master who attempted to convert him to Christianity. Although he rebuffed his patron's attempts, he soon fell in love with a woman and in hopes of securing her affections decided to convert. Subsequently, this relationship failed and he ran away, traveling across Italy in Christian clothes and entering churches to pray. While in Venice, Balirai encountered a group of Turks willing to provide him with assistance in leaving. Accompanied by these individuals, Balirai went to the residence of Muslim merchants where they changed his clothes and gave him a turban. [69]

Balirai's story gives us insight into the assistance that groups of Ottoman Muslims could provide to people who straddled the Christian and Islamic worlds, and it shows us how these connections could undermine Venice's social order. The contact that Balirai made with Ottoman merchants indicates that Muslim networks existed that provided people like Balirai with assistance. A similar network connected Zorzi to the Ottoman Muslims who were staying at Lettino's inn.

Establishing this type of contact was related to a sense of responsibility that a Muslim traveler felt towards other religious members in need. In 1588, in the case heard before the *Quarantia*, concerning a Venetian ship that was attacked by Uskoks, a man by the name of Francesco De Paulo from Sabioncello commented that "two men had come from the galley {to the merchant ship} to tell the Turks that some of the slaves had requested alms" at which point "two Turks went to the galley and they brought a little bread, a little rice and some money." [70] One of a Muslim's responsibilities to poor fellow Muslims was to donate a certain amount of wealth as charity. This responsibility was not only true in an institutional setting, but also in an impromptu sense as well. Alms called *sadakāt* were given voluntarily while those referred to as *zakāt* were considered obligatory. Such donations attracted a certain degree of good will and were thought to expiate one's sins and ward off the afflictions of this world.[71] Norman Stillman points out that in the Islamic world, "(n)atural inequality was mitigated by the religious injunction not to rebuff the beggar and by the Muslim secular ideal of politesse, which makes a certain human courtesy de rigueur even to the lowliest beggar."[72] This type of alms giving was particularly recommended as a good source of protection for those who traveled.[73] Given the sorts of dangers that existed on the road, if a

---

[69] A.S.V., Sant'Ufficio, busta 57, August 8, 1586.

[70] A.S.V., Quarantia Criminale, busta 99, processo 47, foglio 19R. "Doi della gallea venero a dir alli turchi, che erano alcuni schiavi che dimandavano limonsena." "Et doi turchi andorno in galea et le portorno un poco de pan, de risi, et soldi."

[71] On *sadakāt* and *zakāt* see C.E. Bosworth et al., eds., *The Encyclopedia of Islam*, New Edition, vol. 8 (Leiden: E.J. Brill,1994), pp. 105–15.

[72] Norman Stillman. "Charity and Social Service in Medieval Islam," *Societas: A Review of Social History*, Spring 1975, p. 114.

[73] Bosworth, *Encyclopedia of* Islam, pp. 105–15.

Muslim were to come in contact with someone in need, a goodwill gesture could only enhance his or her position in God's eyes.

The Venetians clearly understood Ottoman Muslims' desire to assist fellow Muslims. In 1593 a letter was sent from the Senate to the *provveditore*, administrator, in the Gulf of Venice, ordering that the vessel that was to bring the representative of the pasha of Bosnia to Venice should not carry any Muslim slaves.[74] Part of the Venetians' fear was connected to a realization that Ottoman Muslim contact with Muslim slaves might lead to attempts at liberation that closely mirrored their own efforts. Marino Cavalli, the Venetian *bailo*, chief representative in Istanbul, commented in his *Relazione* to the Senate in 1560 that the Venetians had irritated the Ottoman government, not only by helping Spanish slaves to escape, but also by assisting them to travel to Christian lands.[75] In 1586, responding to an offer from the sultan to sell back a number of slaves, many of whom were Venetian, the Venetians decided to find ways to raise the money to ransom them and other slaves in the future.[76] By 1619 alms collecting obligations had expanded beyond Venice and the *terraferma* to include Venetian governors in the overseas territories of Istria, Dalmatia, the Ionian Islands and Crete. The Venetians enlisted these individuals to help significant numbers of slaves escape surreptitiously from the Ottoman Empire.[77]

Forbidden Practices

Given the attempts that were made to search for people considered to be fugitives, one way that both Balirai and Zorzi integrated themselves into Muslim networks was by changing their appearance. The change in appearance represented a subversive act in that clothes, like spaces, constituted a way of classifying people in a world where race did not serve as the basis of identity.[78] While neighborhoods were used to define the particular ethnic and religious spaces of the city, clothes and appearance were attached to individual souls. They ignored norms that penetrated beyond mere conscious sensibilities and represented fundamental truths. In this regard, one's religious identity was not something that was negotiable. One's appearance was a way of ensuring that these boundaries were maintained.[79] For

---

[74]   A.S.V., Senato, Deliberazioni Constantinopoli, registro 7, foglio 103 R–V.

[75]   Eugenio Alberi, ed., *Relazioni degli ambasciatori veneti al senato*, series 3, vol. 1, (Firenze: Società Editrice Fiorentina, 1840), p. 287.

[76]   Robert Davis, "Slave Redemption in Venice," in *Venice Reconsidered: The History and Civilization of an Italian City-State, 1297–179,* eds. John Martin and Dennis Romano (Baltimore: Johns Hopkins University Press, 2000), p. 456.

[77]   Ibid., p. 466.

[78]   For a discussion on the importance of clothes in distinguishing different communities see Bronwen Wilson, *The World In Venice: Print, the City and Early Modern Identity* (Toronto: University of Toronto Press, 2005), pp. 120–27.

[79]   Ibid.

instance, hats were important in distinguishing Jews and Christians, and Jews were expected to wear yellow or red hats.[80] In trying to determine if Giuseppe Struppiolo had alleged Turkish sympathies, Venetian Inquisition authorities were interested in the fact that he wore Levantine pants and a red cap, had a tuft of long hair in the middle of his head, and most importantly of all, sported a large mustache and beard.[81]

The symbolic meaning of clothes in relation to religious identity probably did not seem that strange to the Ottoman visitor. Ottoman authorities also used clothes as a way of distinguishing between Christians, Muslims and Jews. *The Şey-hü-islam*[82] *Ebussuûd issued a fetva* in the mid-sixteenth century in which he stated that if a non-Muslim changes his clothes and then out of fear answers that he is Muslim, he should be considered a Muslim.[83] In an edict issued by the authorities in 1577 (985 AH) to the *sanjack beyi* and the kadis of the Albanian towns of Skopje, Vulçitrin and Prizren, the Porte ordered that the aforementioned authorities stop Jews from wearing Christian clothes.[84] Similarly, in another edict sent the next year to a kadi of Bursa, the Porte stated that non-Muslims had not only been selling wine to Muslims but also were wearing Muslim clothes. The Divan warned these practices would not be tolerated and must cease immediately.[85] In the early modern period the language of nationalism had not yet appeared either as a unifying or an exclusionary practice and hence communal identity could be fostered through something as simple as clothes.[86]

While changing religious clothes represented a challenge to fixed religious identities, another difficulty for Venetian authorities was that in places where boundaries were ambiguous, Muslim visitors had the power to engage Christians in practices that were considered too intimate, such as sharing meals. In the case against Lettino, prosecutors were interested if Zorzi had eaten with the Muslim guests.[87] The inquisitors asked a young Armenian, Arahiel, one of the people who testified in the case against Paulina, "Do you know or have you heard if the aforementioned Turk {Hüseyn} did anything unseemly with the Armenian Christian {Gregorio}, in particular by making him eat meat on the days it was

---

[80]   Moses Avigdor Shulvass, *The Jews in the World of the Renaissance* (Leiden: E.J. Brill, 1973), p. 187.

[81]   Preto, *Venezia e i turchi*, p. 119.

[82]   Chief Islamic jurisprudent.

[83]   M. Ertuğrul Düzdağ, *Şeyhülislam Ebusuûd Efendi Fetvaları* işğinda 16 asır Türk hayatı (Istanbul: Enderun Kitabevi, 1972), p. 89, fetva 362.

[84]   Başbakanlik arşivi, Mühimme Defteri cilt 31, sira 698.

[85]   Başbakanlik arşivi, Mühimme Defteri, cilt 35, sira 91.

[86]   On the importance of clothes as a component of identity see Ulinka Rublack, *Dressing Up: Cultural Identity in Renaisssance Europe* (Oxford: Oxford University Press, 2012).

[87]   A.S.V., Sant'Ufficio, busta 35.

prohibited?"[88] While Gregorio may not have eaten meat at forbidden times, for nobody actually caught him in the act, it still must have troubled not only the Inquisition board but others in power that Gregorio could be seated at the same table with a Turk.

Allowing Ottoman Muslims to share meals with Christians presented number of problems. First, the issue of dietary laws created a need for the Venetians to separate Muslims and Christians. As was noted in the case of Gregorio, the servant of Hüseyn, authorities feared that if Muslims and Christians ate together Christians would break dietary laws and eat foods forbidden on Friday or Saturday. The Church and the inquisitors were so preoccupied with making sure that Christians did not break these laws that in order to ensure that German inns maintained these standards, they took over from the Patriarch the task of inspecting the inns' kitchens on Fridays and Saturdays.[89] Similar circumstances existed elsewhere. In early centuries in Spain, dietary restrictions separated Muslim, Christian and Jewish communities, and while theoretically Christians were not prohibited from eating anything that "God had created," countless ecclesiastical councils imposed prohibitions on Jews, Muslims and Christians dining together.[90]

While we have no way of knowing how often Muslims in Venice may have tempted Christians in this regard, we do know that even in a space as controlled as the Ghetto, Christians could be tempted into breaking their dietary habits. For example, an Inquisition case reveals that during a Lenten soirée at the house of a man in the Ghetto named Lieberman, Christian guests danced to the fiddle, while they were entertained and given forbidden foods, including meat and butter.[91] The activities that took place at Lieberman's house present an alternative view to the church's and the state's sense of order. While no Muslims were present, we do gain some sense that shared meals did not present much of a problem for those at the party. In the trial against Paulina Briana, Gregorio was taken from Hüseyn when it was speculated that he had broken Christian dietary practices and threatened to go to the Ottoman Empire allegedly to become a Turk. Hüseyn rebutted these charges, claiming that he had made sure that Gregorio had observed Christian dietary practices. He contended that Gregorio lived according to Christian law, as did many other Christian men and women who lived in the houses of Jews and were given wages and food. Eating together was practical for those who shared a house: it was hardly surprising that though Gregorio and Hüseyn were of different religious persuasions, they should end up at the same table.

---

[88]   A.S.V., Sant'Ufficio, busta 47, December 30, 1581. "Se sa o ha inteso a dire che detto turcho con detto christiano armeno habbi tenuto vita deshonesta et particularmente fatoli magnar carne nelle di prohibiti."

[89]   Pullan, *Jews of Europe*, p. 13.

[90]   David Nirenberg, *Communities of Violence: Persecution of Minorities in the Middle Ages* (Princeton: Princeton University Press, 1996), p. 169.

[91]   Pullan, *Jews of Europe*, p. 166.

Other social practices also took place in open spaces that the Venetian government and the Church considered to be scandalous. For one, Muslim men might engage in sexual relations with Christian women. The mere accusation of having illicit sex in Paulina's case indicates that sexual relations between Muslims and Christians were not only on people's minds, but also a practice that had to be stopped. The denunciation emphasized that Paulina not only had had intercourse with Turks, but that she was also involved with Marc Antonio, a broker on Rialto, to bring other prostitutes to the house to have sex with Hüseyn, the Muslim merchant.[92] Lettino knew that The Venetians feared this type of contact, and in his petition, he stated emphatically that one of the principal reasons for creating a *Fondaco dei Turchi* was that some Turks were having carnal relations with Christian women and others residing with women of ill repute.[93] These types of encounters preoccupied Venetians long before the arrival of significant numbers of merchants as seen in 1508, when the Venetian diarist Marino Sanudo found it worth recording that three women had been brought before the *Collegio* on charges of sleeping with Turks.[94]

One fear was that sex between Muslim men and Christian women threatened Venetian social order. Venice had a highly stratified social hierarchy that attempted to maintain certain forms of segregation between different social groupings. Consisting of estates or orders that were given specific privileges, and corporations that specialized in certain economic practices, Venice was a highly regulated society in which non-Christians such as Jews were considered to be of lower in status than other social orders.[95] While Ottoman Muslims were outsiders and thus not officially a part of the social order in Venice, they did form a part of a social world that was subject to certain norms and expectations.

Sexual relations between non-Christian men and Christian women created the fear that Venice's social hierarchy was breaking down. This form of disorder had a number of consequences. While in a city committed to trade a certain amount of mixing between Christians and non-Christians was tolerated, sex between Muslim men and Christian women was more problematic. Such behavior brought acceptance to people thought to belong to an inferior religious group. As was noted above, allowing Christians and Muslims to eat together produced fears that Christians would break certain dietary laws and threatened to confer equality on people such as Muslims and Jews. In a more trenchant way, the same applied

---

[92] A.S.V., Sant'Ufficio, busta 47, denunciation.

[93] A.S.V., Cinque Savi alla Mercanzia, busta 187, fascicolo 1, October 28, 1574 and May 17, 1575.

[94] Giovanni De Lorenzi, *Leggi e memorie venete sulla prostituzione* (Venice: M. Visentini, 1872), p. 256. On fear of contact see Belgin Özkaya, "Theaters of Fear and Delight: Ottomans in the Serenissima," in *Thamyris/Intersecting Place, Sex and Race: After Orientalism: Critical Entanglements, Productive Looks*, vol. 10, ed. Inge Boer (New York: Rodopi, 2003), pp. 45–61.

[95] Pullan, *Jews of Europe*, p. 146.

to sexual relations. Sexual relations between Muslim men and Christian women gave Muslim men power over Christian women. This practice was unacceptable, and although Venetians accorded Ottoman Muslims a certain degree of respect because they were subjects of the sultan, given that they were not Christians, they had to be treated as outsiders. Thus, intimate personal relations such as eating and, more importantly, sex were off limits.[96]

The Venetian authorities' view of adultery presents an interesting comparison to their attitude to Muslim/Christian sexual relations. From the patriarchal perspective the male adulterer was seen as the outsider who was breaking into the family unit and taking the adulteress away. The victim was the husband and the male adulterer was the only one who could be prosecuted because punishing the wife would dishonor the family unit.[97] One can surmise that in his petition, Lettino was proclaiming that the city represented the metaphorical family that had been dishonored, and the reason for this loss of honor was that Muslim men had become too familiar with Christian women. Only by attending to the problem could the honor and the integrity of the city be restored. Like an adulterous affair, sexual relations between a Muslim man and a Christian woman threatened Venetian male dominance over the private spaces of Venice.

The spaces of Venice were divided into public and private realms. While San Marco as the center of political power and Rialto as the center of trade constituted male spaces, other spaces such as the local parishes and convents constituted female spaces.[98] Venetian masculinity was reinforced by the notion that men protected these areas and prevented unspeakable acts such as sex between Christians and non-Christians. If a Muslim were to enter the realm of Venetian private spaces and have carnal relations with a married Venetian woman, the honor of the woman would not only have been tarnished, but the status of the man could have been damaged as well.[99] While theoretically the Muslim was the outsider breaking into family unit, because he received protection as an Ottoman trader, the only person to punish was the woman.

In considering this issue, the principal focus, therefore, should not be to concentrate on how the Venetian justice system handled Muslim offenders, but instead to consider what type of sexual contact the Venetian government was willing to tolerate. While the claim that the broker Marc Antonio was responsible for bringing young women to the house of Paulina may have only been a ploy to incriminate Paulina, it also indicates that people believed that brokers acted as intermediaries between Muslim merchants and local prostitutes. The Venetian

---

[96]   The ideas in this paragraph come from discussions with Brian Pullan.

[97]   Guido Ruggiero, *The Boundaries of Eros: Sex Crime and Sexuality in Renaissance Venice* (New York: Oxford University Press, 1985), p. 54.

[98]   Dennis Romano, "Gender and Urban Geography of Renaissance Venice," *Journal of Social History*, vol. 23, no. 2 (1989), pp. 339–53.

[99]   On the question of honor and the control of women see Ruggiero, *Boundaries of Eros,* pp. 17–19.

government may even have thought it useful to allow people such as Marc Antonio to offer these types of services. First, prostitution was legal in Venice and considered an acceptable though not a commendable social practice. Sex outside marriage was seen as a necessary activity in a city that needed sexual outlets for people who did not fit into the legitimate social order.[100] Second, the Venetians clearly made prostitutes available to foreign merchants by concentrating trade and prostitution in the same area around the Rialto.[101] In 1429, when a Jewish man was charged with having sex with a Christian prostitute, the punishment he faced was six months in jail if the offense took place in and around the Rialto and a year if it took place elsewhere.[102] Similarly, in May 1514 one of the principal concerns of the Venetian government in the case of a Jewish man by the name of Simeon was that he had sex with a Christian prostitute in the district of Santa Maria Mater Domini. The Venetians believed that such an act polluted a Christian neighborhood, and they proposed a penalty of two years in jail and a fine of five hundred ducats.[103]

While sex between non-Christians and Christian women was unacceptable in certain situations, in other situations contact between prostitutes and Muslim men was deemed if not acceptable, tolerable. Here, the Venetians had to decide how to maintain a balance between those practices that should be allowed and those that should be prohibited.

Empowering Intermediaries and Control of Networks

Factoring in these interests and thinking in terms of the different and sometimes contradictory needs that the Venetians had to consider in hosting Ottoman Muslims, we can begin to understand why Francesco Lettino's petition for a fondaco was accepted and why he was chosen as the residence's 's custodian. While the Venetians needed to guard against different types of contact, they also needed to recruit an intermediary who understood different types of cross-cultural contact and needed to empower someone who could take into consideration both Venetian and Ottoman interests and who could gain access to Muslim social networks.

Jobs for intermediaries existed at a number of levels. First, there were the dragomans or the state-appointed interpreters.[104] Considered important in

---

[100] See Ruggiero, *Boundaries of Eros*, p. 153.

[101] Annibale Alberti and Roberto Cessi, *Rialto: l'isola, il ponte, il mercato* (Bologna: Nicola Zanichelli, 1934), p. 277.

[102] De Lorenzi, *Leggi e memorie venete*, p. 40.

[103] Ibid., p. 262.

[104] On Dragomans see S.G. Marghetitch, *Étude sur les fonctions des dragomans des missions diplomatique ou consulaires en Turquie,* Constantinople n.p. 1898, reprint (Istanbul: Isis Press, 1993). Rothman, *Brokering Empire*, pp. 165–86. On brokering Ottoman/Venetian relations see Arbel, *Trading Nations*, pp. 77–94. These two chapters are on Solomon Askenazi, the Jewish doctor who was very influential in Venetian/Ottoman relations.

matters of diplomacy and trade, dragomans acted as important intermediaries in negotiations between Venice and the Ottoman state and its subjects. In fact, they were considered so important in these matters that the Venetians established a policy of sending young men to Istanbul to be trained in this capacity.[105] Second, there were people like Lettino who worked as brokers on the Rialto. Establishing a presence in the city, brokers or *sensali* were given the authorization to form a guild in June 1487.[106] In their role as middlemen, they were expected to record transactions and ensure that trades were conducted in a manner that was fair to all parties. While the numbers of brokers assigned to the Turks fluctuated over time, as Turkish trade increased their numbers grew larger from 15 to20 in 1587 to seemingly over 30 by 1621.[107] Though these numbers may seem small in comparison to other fields, brokers, dragomans and other intermediaries played a very important role in a city that was still dependent on revenues generated from foreign trade.[108]

Even given his transgressions, Lettino was the type of intermediary that could be enlisted by the Venetians to monitor contact. When asked by the inquisitors if he knew what ceremonies Turks performed when someone converted to Islam, Lettino replied that "I don't know what to say to you,... I have put my life and possessions in danger for having conveyed out of Patras a Turk with his wife and four children and had them baptized on 5[th]April 1551."[109] His claim indicates that though his loyalties were questionable, he did have dealings in Muslim/Christian affairs, and he did have experience in contact zones, areas where both Muslims and Christians congregated.

While the Venetians were looking to segregate spaces, by hiring intermediaries who lived between the Muslim and Christian worlds they were also trying to find ways to integrate people who understood these contact zones.[110] For example, during the 1580s, commenting on the people who found jobs as brokers, the *Cinque Savi* stated that some of the brokers on the Rialto were Turks and Jews who had

---

[105]   Preto, *Venezia e i turchi*, p. 104.

[106]   Giorgio Vercellin, "Mercanti turchi e sensali a Venezia," *Studi Veneziani* 4 (1980), p. 50.

[107]   Ibid., p. 63.

[108]   Referring to a document drawn up sometime around 1674–75 and described as 'Nota delli sanseri della Cittá,' Giorgio Vercellin notes that there were 25 brokers who worked with the Turks. This was in comparison to 30 who were affiliated with the *Fondaco dei Tedeschi,* 36 who were assigned to grain, 25 for matters relating to exchange, 40 for wine, 24 for the Ghetto. Vercellin, "Mercanti turchi," p. 61. Rothman argues that intermediaries were at the center of trans-imperial exchange. While I agree with this assessment, my principal concern in this this section is to look at the ways intermediaries represented Venetian interests. Rothman, *Brokering Empire*, pp. 29-61, 165–89.

[109]   A.S.V., Sant'Ufficio, busta 35, September 9, 1573. Non vi so dir....ho messo la mia vita et faculta in pericolo per haver condotto fuori di Petrasso un Turco, con sua moglie con 4 figli et li ho fatto battizar a 5 Apti del 1551."

[110]   Rothman, *Brokering Empire*, pp. 11–15.

become Christians.[111] The Venetian dragoman Michele Membre, who was born in Cyprus of Circassian descent, commented in his *Relazione di Persia* that

> I ... was raised in the house of the magnificent Benedetti and their children ... and many times they sent me to Turkey and Syria in his (Benedetti's) name ... knowing well that I associated with all of the foreign merchants that came from these parts and with those that spoke the language.[112]

Along similar lines, born to a Greek mother and a father from the Dalmatian coast who had worked as a cobbler, Michel Cernovic became the Venetians' chief dragoman to the Ottomans in Istanbul because of his command of Turkish, Italian and Slavonic.[113] Clearly, the practice of employing these types of individuals existed in Venice ever since the arrival of important Ottoman dignitaries in the city. In 1497, Teodoro Paleologos, a member of the former Byzantine ruling family who had been a lieutenant pasha in the service of the Ottomans, came to Venice and also ended up as a dragoman.[114]

Well-connected elites were not the only people in a position to serve as intermediaries. In 1573 Julio Torquatto petitioned the Venetian government to become a broker on the Rialto, reporting that while he was a slave of the Turks he had learned the Turkish language and the art of business negotiations. While his stated purpose for returning to Venice was his desire to return to Christianity, he realized that he had something to gain from the time that he spent as a Muslim.[115] Undoubtedly, Torquatto's skills and his experience could have been considered of great value to the Venetians. With a growing number of Ottoman merchants trading in Venice after the War of Cyprus, the Venetian government needed a wide variety of people who could not only communicate, but also understand the cultural and business practices of the people who were coming to the city. Nicolò Merendis fulfilled a similar role. Captured and made a slave in the war against the Turks in 1537, he lived in Ottoman territories for a number of years where he learned to speak Turkish and read its literature. Freed in the same year as Torquatto, he also came to Venice hoping that the Venetian government would grant him the position

---

[111] Vercellin, "Mercanti turchi," p. 49.

[112] Michele Membre, *Relazione di Persia*, ed. Gianroberto Sarcia (Napoli: Instituto Universitario Orientale, 1969), p. 3 "....perche io preditto servitor vostro Micael Membrè mi son arvelaro in casa delli ditti magnifici Benedeti e con sui figilioli, e molte volte mi hanno mandato in Turchia e in Soria per suo nome, ...sapendo bene che io practicava con tutti quelli foresieri marcandanti che venivano da quelle bande e con quelli che sapevano la lingua...."

[113] Michel Lesure, "Michel Cernovic 'explorator secretus' a Constantinople (1556–1563), " *Turcica: revue d'etudes turques,* Tome 15 (1983), pp.132–4. Cernovic's story is an interesting one for while working as dragoman for the Venetians in Istanbul he was also spying for the emperor Ferdinand I.

[114] Pedani, *In nome del Gran Signore*, p. 42.

[115] A.S.V., Collegio, Risposte di Dentro, filza 5 foglio 202, October 4, 1573.

of a broker on the Rialto so that he could support his family and have his daughter married. Similarly, while his stated position was that he had come to Venice in order to live as a Christian, he clearly realized that he was a valuable asset to a state that needed people to work as brokers.[116]

Although there is no indication as to what became of either of these requests, we have some evidence that the Venetians may have been amenable to giving such individuals this type of work. First, the Venetians were anxious to have Christians who had become Muslims reconvert to Christianity. Converting back to Christianity was an important issue in what the Venetians felt was a battle over souls and may have been a way of compensating someone whom the Venetians regarded as a forced convert.[117] Torquatto and Merendis understood this need and constructed their arguments to emphasize that they had been forced to convert. Broker positions could be awarded to individuals who were not *cittadini originari* as was required in many other positions. The only stipulation was that an individual should have resided in Venice for a period of five years. Even this regulation did not apply to brokers of wheat, jewels, and exchange; these positions could be awarded directly to foreigners.[118] Evidence exists that the Venetians were even willing to select Muslims to make sure that these positions were filled. In 1593 a Moor failed to obtain a position of broker by only one vote. Some of his support came from the fact that a Turk had been willing to speak in the Collegio in his favor.[119] Muslims were suggested for other positions as well and in 1692 Giambattista Donà, the ambassador in Istanbul, suggested that Ibrahim Ahmed, an Albanian convert with a long history of service at the Porte, be allowed to teach Middle Eastern languages to the younger members of the ducal chancellery.[120]

Undoubtedly, the Venetians were anxious to utilize a valuable resource, consisting of people who moved between the Christian and Islamic worlds. The fact that men such as Ibrahim Ahmed were able to speak a number of different languages was clearly an asset in a city that attracted so many foreign visitors.[121] Second, intermediaries were also well-traveled and undoubtedly culturally flexible, like the Rialto broker who worked with Muslims, Giovanni Battista Bonaventura. While ultimately the charges that he had eaten meat on Friday, blasphemed against the Christian faith and expressed a desire to go to the Ottoman Empire were dropped, the circumstances of his life reflect a man who lived on the boundaries between different worlds. Born to Jewish parents in Damascus, Bonaventura had been taken by Turks at the age of 14 in Jerusalem and, in order to save his life, had converted to Islam. His conversion, though, was only temporary,

---

[116] A.S.V., Collegio, Risposte di Dentro, filza 5, foglio 299, December 13, 1573.

[117] On attempts on the behalf of the church to reconvert people from Islam to Christianity see R. Davis, "Slave Redemption in Venice," pp. 454–87.

[118] Pedani , *In nome del Gran Signor*, p. 173, footnote 168.

[119] Ibid.

[120] Preto, *Venezia e i turchi*, p. 106.

[121] Pedani, *In nome del Gran Signore*, pp. 29–30.

for within an unspecified period of time he left the eastern Mediterranean and made his way to Venice where he decided to become a Christian. Undoubtedly aware of his linguistic skills and his experiences in the Ottoman Empire, the Venetian government allowed him to become a broker for Muslims on the Rialto.

While we might assume that given his past, Bonaventura might have been ill-disposed to interact with Ottoman Muslims, the opposite appears to be true. Testifying in the case, Francesco Spinola of Genoa stated that on different occasions Bonaventura came to his tobacco shop in the company of a group of Turks.[122] Spinola's testimony indicates that Bonaventura was part of a steady flow of people that passed back and forth between the Christian and Islamic worlds, facilitating social and cultural contacts between East and West.

One advantage of such people was not only their cultural flexibility or linguistic capability, but also their ability to establish good relations with foreign guests and their capacity to gain access to personal spaces and important networks. Commenting on a gathering to celebrate the appointment of a local leader during his trip to the Persian court in the 1540s, Michele Membre stated that he and other members of the court drank alcohol freely until finally retiring to sleep at the house of Nerangi Sultan.[123] While Michel Cernovich's loyalties were suspect, given that he worked for Venice and spied for Spain at the Ottoman court, his value to his employers was tied to his ability to understand Ottoman court culture. This type of access was also tied to other connections, and some of an intermediary's appeal to an Ottoman subject may have resulted from a sense of shared ethnic backgrounds. The Ottoman envoy to the Porte at the time of the war of Cyprus, Kubad, felt close ties with Membre at least partly because both had Circassian origins.[124] Although we have no way of knowing how much this fact shaped their relationship, their similar backgrounds and Membre's familiarity with the language and culture of the Ottoman court created an atmosphere of at least limited trust.[125]

More than just a translator, Membre did the bidding of various groups of Turks with the Venetian government.[126] He was a source of information and sometimes even a confidant. The Polish convert to Islam, Ibrahim Strasz, sent a letter to Membre asking him to ensure that the goods being sent by his adopted father Mustafa Çelebi should not be subjected to Venetian taxes. Ibrahim was

---

[122] Pier Cesare Ioly-Zorattini, *Processi del S. Uffizio di Venezia contro ebrei e giudaizzanti*, vol. 9 (Firenze: L.S. Olschki, 1985), pp. 147–208.

[123] Membre, *Relazione de Persia*, p. 44.

[124] Pedani, *In nome del Gran Signore*, p. 29.

[125] Pedani points out that in 1567 during an earlier visit Kubad asked that Membre be present while a surgeon bled him. Pedani, *In nome del Gran Signore*, p. 35.

[126] The notion of a local doing the bidding of a foreign group had a parallel in the Middle East where local Christians asked on behalf of Venetian, French and English and other European traders. On this subject in a later period see Ali İhsan Bağış, *Osmanlı Ticaretinde Gayri Müslimler, Kapitülasyonlar-Beratlı Tüccarlar, Avrupa, ve Hayriye Tüccarları (1750–1839)* (Ankara: Turhan Kitabevi, 1983).

not only counting on Membre's goodwill, but also expected Membre to use his influence with the people who made these types of decisions.[127] It may well have been customary for Membre to enter into negotiations on the behalf of Ottoman Muslims. In 1583 an Ottoman visitor named Hasan Ağa asked the Venetians that Membre be allowed to conduct his negotiations with the French ambassador because he believed Membre was the only person that could be trusted.[128]

Trust for an intermediary was also an important factor in an incident in 1603 involving another Venetian dragoman, Giacomo de Nores.[129] Assigned to find out why an emissary from the Shah of Persia had arrived in Venice, de Nores proceeded to the house of the emissary's agent, Christoforo Suriano, where arrangements had been made for the emissary to stay. Here, de Nores discovered that an Englishman named Don Antonio had harassed the Persian emissary. Aware that the emissary had brought silk to Venice to trade, Don Antonio expressed interest in making a trade and, after being rejected, proceeded to try to intimidate the emissary. Obviously feeling threatened and fearing for his life, the emissary turned to de Nores, who immediately went to the Senate and asked that the Venetian government do something about the situation.[130]

The case demonstrates that a person as important as the emissary of the Shah of Persia could not act on his own, but instead was reliant on de Nores to help him find protection. Clearly, de Nores had intervened in what amounted to a personal conflict. He commented that, while the Persian was in negotiations with the Milanese merchant Lucillo Fossato, the Englishman had shown up with twelve men bearing swords, threatening that if the Persian were to continue the negotiations he would be in great trouble. Fearing for his life, even Suriano refused to venture out to finish the transaction. It was only the next day, after de Nores arrived and was informed of what had happened, that someone appeared before the Senate to ask that they do something to remedy the situation.[131] Obviously a person such as de Nores was expected to intervene in different situations involving important visitors, and this intervention necessitated him gaining the confidence of the emissary.

The emissary also relied very heavily on Christoforo Suriano, the man referred to as his agent. Suriano was the person assigned to conduct negotiations for the emissary during his stay in Venice. Whose interests did he represent? Can we assume that one who housed the Persian emissary was only acting as a middleman or should we think of him as a more personal representative? We must be careful not to think of these situations in a modern context. The fact that a person served

---

[127] Alessio Bombaci, "Una lettera turca in caraterri latini del dragomanno ottomano Ibrahim al veneziano Michele Membre (1567)," *Rocznik Orjentalistyczny* 15 (1948), pp. 129–44. See Chapter 4 for a discussion of the letter.

[128] Pedani *I documenti turchi*, pp. 232–3.

[129] On de Nores's background see Rothman, *Brokering Empire*, pp. 173–8.

[130] A.S.V., Quarantia Criminale, busta 114, fascicolo 142.

[131] A.S.V., Quarantia Criminale, busta 114, fascicilo 142, March 19, 1603.

in an official role did not prevent him from sharing common interests. Nor did it mean he could not switch sides.[132]

The nature of these individuals' roles raises a number of different points. First, if a state was to gain information about another state, it had to use people whose loyalties were not decidedly obvious.[133] In traveling to visit the Shah of Persia, Membre had to receive a recommendation from the Venetians, because the ship's captain seemed to believe that "I was a subject of the Turk."[134] His ambiguous identity must have helped him gain the confidence of the people that he was going to see. Familiarity not only helped in terms of language, but also in terms of acceptance. Second, the tendency to look at persons such as Membre or Giacomo de Nores as merely interpreters or functionaries fails to take into consideration the fact that the Venetian government counted on them to act as advisors on Ottoman affairs. The Venetian government was well aware of Membre's knowledge of matters relating to the Islamic world. His relazione on Persia was a tract on how relations with Persia could be developed. His insights served as important contributions to Venetian policy. De Nores also performed a similar function. He went to the house where the emissary was staying with the stated purpose of "fully understanding the reason that he had come"[135]

Lettino fulfilled a similar role as an informant. Even given his ambiguous loyalty, gaining the service of a person like him must have been important in controlling the movements of Muslims throughout Venice. Lettino had a first-hand understanding of the activities of Muslim guests and by allowing him to become the custodian of residence for Muslims traders, the Venetians were assigning him an identity and offering him an incentive not to collaborate in these types of capers. In a world where the necessity of these arrangements must have been well understood, Lettino could not only act as an intermediary, but he could also control the sorts of mischievous activities that were taking place. If the incident involving Zorzi was a mark against him, the opportunity to enlist someone to prevent this type of incident from happening in the future must have made him an asset. He was an insider, a person with knowledge about the Turks and any smuggling that was taking place. Robert Jütte notes that in border areas people "found in smuggling an important subsidy to a precarious livelihood."[136]

---

[132] Patrick Monahan argues that the Venetians made it a common practice to host foreign diplomats, including Ottoman envoys, in residences on Murano and the Giudecca. While this practice may have existed as official policy, undoubtedly other unofficial residential arrangements also existed. Patrick Monahan, "Sanudo and the Venetian Villa Surbana," *Annali di architettura* 21 (2009), pp. 46–8, 51, 52.

[133] On the question of the question loyalties of particular dragomans see Dursteler, *Venetians in Constantinople,* pp. 36–7.

[134] Membre, *Relazione di Persia*, p. 7.

[135] A.S.V., Quarantia Criminale, busta 114, fascicolo. 142, March 3, 1603.

[136] Robert Jütte, *Poverty and Deviance in Early Modern Europe* (Cambridge, UK: Cambridge University Press, 1994), p. 15.

Smuggling included the transit of people, and the Venetians needed somebody to work for them to address this problem. A financial incentive must have been at the core of the matter for Lettino and his family, and any lost income from assisting Muslim merchants could be recovered by working in the service of the Venetian state. The Lettino family chose this option, becoming permanent figures in the Venetian surveillance network and remaining custodians of the Muslim residence even after the location was switched from its location at the *Insegna del' Angolo* to the Grand Canal.[137]

Creating a Supervised Space on the Grand Canal

If the role of intermediaries was important in supervising a foreign population, the move of the residence for Muslims from the Ottoman Empire to the Grand Canal constituted a more ambitious desire to control the activities of Ottoman Muslims and represented a further attempt to define Christian/Muslim relations. Yet, why did the Venetians make the change at this time? For a significant period of time large numbers of Muslim merchants had stayed elsewhere and had lived in integrated spaces. What took place to provoke the Venetians to act when they did? One explanation that has been given for the move is that it represented the natural outcome of a process that began with Lettino's petition. This view sees the move as part of a continuum that finally led to the placement of all Ottoman Muslims in the same place, and the creation of the fondaco on the Grand Canal as a coordinated effort to address a problem that ultimately produced a solution over time. Even after the creation of the residence in 1579, debates persisted on where and how to house Ottoman Muslims. On June 5, 1588 a petition was filed with the Venetian government suggesting that diverse nobles had offered their houses as a residence for "Turks."[138] Fifteen days later, Zorzi Lettino, the son of Francesco, petitioned the Collegio, complaining that an adversary of the Lettino family was trying to wrest control away from his family who had been designated by the Senate as custodians.[139] This debate continued and in 1602 an anonymous petition submitted to the Senate argued vehemently against the creation of a space for Muslims.[140]

Yet in understanding these discussions, one must also consider how the change of venue in 1621 was more closely tied to the politics of the time. The inn had changed hands in June of 1620, and the new owners declared that they wanted to

---

[137] A.S.V., Cinque Savi alla Mercanzia, nuove serie, busta 187, fascicolo 1, March 11, 1621.

[138] A.S.V., Cinque Savi alla Mercanzia, nuove serie, busta 187, fascicolo 1, June 5, 1588.

[139] A.S.V., Cinque Savi alla Mercanzia nuove serie, busta 187, fascicolo 1, June 20,1588.

[140] Biblioteca Museo di Correr, Codice Cicogna 978, fascicolo 17.

Fig. 1.2   Franceso Guardi, *Grand Canal with a View of the* Fondaco dei Turchi (18th century). Private collection, sold by Kollerauktionen.

restore the building to an inn or receive higher rent.[141] This point was reiterated on December 11, 1620 when Giovanni Battista Lettino, a descendant of Francesco Lettino, and one of the current custodians of the residence for merchants from the Balkans at the *Insegna dell'Angolo*, went to the Cinque Savi and stated that the proprietors of the residence wanted to return the inn to its former status.[142] On March 11, 1621 the Senate responded by stating that since the Venetian government's intention had always been to house all Ottoman Muslims in one place, they had had found a palace on the Grand Canal that would serve this function.[143] Different clues emerge in regard to what happened. First, the decision does not appear

[141] Benjamin Ravid, "The Religious, Economic and Social Background and Context of the Establishment of the Ghetti in Venice," in *Gli Ebrei e Venezia: secoli XIV-XVII: Atti del convegno internazionale organizzato dall istituto di storia della società e dello stato veneziano della Fondazione Giorgio Cini*, ed. Gaetano Cozzi (Milano: Edizioni Comunità, 1987), p. 239.

[142] A.S.V., Cinque Savi alla Mercanzia, nuove serie, busta 187, fascicolo 1, December 11, 1620.

[143] A.S.V., Cinque Savi alla Mercanzia, nuove serie, busta 187, fascicolo 9, March 11,1621.

related to financial concerns. If there was a shortage of Muslim merchants coming to the fondaco, why was no attempt made to force the other Muslim merchants that Giovanni Lettino claimed were still living around the city to live in the residence? All indications are that housing Turks remained a potentially profitable business. Two years earlier a controversy had developed between the Lettino family and a certain Domenico Borello as to who should have control if a new residence for Turks was created.[144] This disagreement indicates that the fondaco still must have produced sufficient revenues.

Instead the change in plans seems related to a series of incidents alleged to have taken place at the church close to the *Insegna dell'Angolo.* In March 1620, two months before the owners voiced their desire to change the function of the residence, a petition was filed with the Senate, complaining about the behavior of Muslims in and around the church of San Matteo. The petitioners stated that Muslim merchants living in the nearby inn would pass by the church laughing and ridiculing the Christian religion and its practices. The worst abuse occurred the previous September, when it was alleged that, on the church's feast day of Saint Matthew, Muslims fired their arquebuses into the church, expressing even greater ridicule and causing great danger to the worshippers. The petitioners concluded that the correct course of action was to move Muslim merchants from their present location to another residence that was not close to any church.[145]

While there is no direct evidence that the new owners decided to return the inn to its former status because of these incidents, the fact that the petitioners believed that Muslim merchants should be moved instead of expelled is revealing. Previously the idea was introduced that the possibility of Christians and Muslims dining together or Muslim men having sex with Christian women provoked demands that Muslims and Christians should be separated and social barriers constructed. Fear of this type of contact created the need for physical boundaries that could both be identified and maintained. The proximity of the residence to the church of San Matteo also served as a reminder that the church was a place that needed to be protected and to be defended against certain types of abuses from "outsiders." The series of alleged incidents served as the catalyst for new ways of defining communities.

The importance of an event or events in generating discussions about redefining communal boundaries had historic precedents in many different places. In 1445, Nice's Christian population complained that Jews should not be allowed to live with Christians because Jews had dropped water and refuse on the Eucharist when it was carried through the streets.[146] In 1462 Pius II's ruling that Jewish homes in

---

[144] A.S.V., Cinque Savi alla Mercanzia, nuove serie, busta 187, fascicolo 1, December 5, 1618.

[145] A.S.V., Cinque Savi alla Mercanzia, nuove serie, busta 187, fascicolo 1, March 12, 1620.

[146] Shlomo Simonsohn, *The Apostolic See and the Jews,* vol. 7–8 (Toronto: University of Toronto Press, 1991), p. 144.

Frankfurt should be transferred from the area around the church of St. Bartholomew was due to the fact that the proximity of Jews to the cemetery allowed them to view Christian religious ceremonies and listen to Christian prayers.[147] Similar logic applied to religious spaces in the Ottoman Empire. In 1560, a report was sent to the sultan informing him that a group of Christians had built houses on the site of a former church that was very close to the Umayyad mosque in Damascus.[148] After the matter was investigated a Damascus judge was asked to order all Christians and Jews in the vicinity of the mosque to sell their houses to Muslims. Regulations concerning the sale of alcohol also had a bearing on attempts to separate Muslims and Christians. In an edict sent by the Porte in the late sixteenth century to a local kadi, the authorities commented that they had heard that Christians had opened up taverns between Muslim residences and must be stopped.[149]

These types of events explain how the discourse of separation can be put into practice. The event or events at the church necessitated a new spatial conceptualization as to where and how Muslims should be housed. The shift to the fondaco on the Grand Canal constituted a reordering of the Venetian social and economic landscape. Ottoman Muslims were expected to stay in the fondaco; it was no longer just a residence for merchants from the Balkans.[150] The fondaco was far removed from the commercial and administrative centers of the city at San Marco and Rialto. In this regard, it occupied a position similar to that of the Ghetto and lessened the probability of encounters such as the one at the church of San Matteo.[151] That is not to say that the fondaco was solely an attempt to marginalize Muslim merchants. The palace that was used as the fondaco had been awarded to the Marquis of Ferrara in 1381. In the early sixteenth century, the papal legate resided there. In 1602, the residence was sold to the Venetian senator Antonio Priuli for the not insignificant sum of 24,000 ducats, and in 1608 the Priuli family rented the palace to the imperial ambassador of Venice. In no way was the palace in a fringe location or considered a marginal residence.[152]

The location on the Grand Canal was also situated in a place where goods could be brought in and out very easily. In a list of suggestions made to the Cinque Savi, Giacomo de Nores noted that Muslim merchants had a difficult time loading

---

[147] Ibid., p. 145.

[148] Muhammad Adnan Bakhit, "The Christian Population of the Province of Damascus in the Sixteenth Century" in *Christians and Jews in the Ottoman Empire*, vol. 2, eds. Benjamin Braude and Bernard Lewis (New York, Holmes & Meier, 1982), p. 26.

[149] Başbakanlik Arşivi, Mühimme Defteri cilt 39, sira 120.

[150] A.S.V., Cinque Savi alla Mercanzia, Nuove Serie busta 187, fascicolo 1, December 11, 1621, March 29, 1621.

[151] Concina, *Fondaci*, p. 232.

[152] Jürgen Schulz, *The New Palaces of Medieval Venice* (University Park: Pennsylvania State University Press, 2004), pp. 134, 136, 139.

and unloading their goods at the Rialto location.[153] The new space contained an adequate amount of space for merchants to store their goods as well.[154] This function made the merchants less dependent on keeping their goods on the premises of brokers who could both take advantage of them and the Venetian government.[155]

By separating Muslim merchants and informal contacts, official intermediaries of the state gained power over Muslim visitors and at the same gave them a prestigious trading entrepôt on the Grand Canal. As was noted earlier, the Venetian state relied on intermediaries who lived and worked in the liminal spaces between Christian and Muslim communities. The state was willing to ignore Lettino's transgression because he could be co-opted into supervising the activities of Muslim merchants in the city. Assigning him this role aligned his interests with those of the Venetian state. Now, over forty years later, the Lettino family had become an integral part of the surveillance network designed to monitor contact between the two religious groups. An industry of dragomans, brokers and other assorted intermediaries such as the Lettino family benefited as official representatives of the Venetian state. In 1618, Giovanni Battista Lettino came before the Venetian government and argued this point specifically stating that his family should be the only ones who had the right to be landlords for a residence for Turks. The dragoman de Nores played a major role not only in negotiating the move to the Grand Canal, but also in determining how living arrangements in the fondaco worked.

For these individuals, championing the discourse of separation and moving the whole Ottoman Muslim community to one residence led to a more concentrated attempt to eliminate inns and other institutions that facilitated cross-cultural contact. Integrated residences and informal contacts stood for competition, and they represented unsupervised activities. Both official intermediaries and the Venetian state understood that a single residence directed Muslims to one place where they could be accounted for, forced to pay custom dues and separated from Christians and sacred sites.

Yet did this surveillance network and the fondaco perform their functions? Complaints were still filed that Muslim merchants were living scattered around the city.[156] While these complaints indicate that the Venetian government had a difficult time forcing all merchants to live in the fondaco, other evidence suggests that a space like the fondaco served as a good location for the Venetians to monitor their activities so that local and assorted other Christians could be prevented from

---

[153] A.S.V., Cinque Savi alla Mercanzia, Nuove Serie busta 187, fascicolo 1, March 29, 1621.

[154] A.S.V., Cinque Savi alla Mercanzia, Nuove Serie busta 187, fascicolo 1, March 29, 1621.

[155] The question of brokers taking advantage of merchants came up periodically. The most informative source on this was a document issued by the Savi on March 10, 1586 in the Senate. A.S.V., Cinque Savi alla Mercanzia, nuove serie, busta 187, fascicolo 1, March 10, 1586.

[156] See A.S.V., Compilazione delle Legge, busta 366, July 13, 1679.

making connections with Ottoman groups. For instance, in May 1631, three men from Spain with connections to merchants in the *Fondaco dei Turchi* were charged by the Holy Office in Venice with turning away from the Christian faith in order to become Muslims.[157] One of those tried, Muhammed or Juan Fecondo (his Christian name), after stating one day earlier that he was a Muslim, claimed that he had really been born to Christian parents and baptized as Stefano in the cathedral of Barcelona. At fourteen, deciding to travel, he set out for Rome in the company of a friar. Unable to reach Rome and separated from his traveling companion, he arrived in Venice, and desperate to find someplace to stay, he tried to gain lodging in the monastery of Santo Stefano. This effort proved to be futile, though, for those in charge of the monastery were suspicious of him and turned him out into the streets where he was forced to sleep. Hence, pleading that he had no place to go and persuaded by the exhortations of another of the accused named Juan Lopez, he went to the Turks and told them that his parents were Muslims and that he wanted passage to Istanbul. Willing to help, the Turks brought him into the *Fondaco dei Turchi* and cut his hair to make him appear more like a Muslim. From there he hoped to depart on a merchant ship due to set sail across the Adriatic.[158]

The third of the accused, Mustafa, otherwise Bartolomeo Derrera, (his adopted Christian name in Spain) like Juan Fecondo first claimed that he was a Muslim, and then recanted, claiming that he had been born a Christian in Fimena.[159] Before deciding to leave, he set out for Verona where he met up with the aforementioned Juan Lopez. Together the two of them headed east and proceeded to Venice where they arrived dressed as Christians. Here they must have been separated because Juan Lopez added that, forced to sleep in the streets, he met a Jewish man under the columns of San Marco who brought him to the *Fondaco dei Turchi*, where he was reunited with Bartolomeo. Planning to help them conceal their former identity, the Turks cut each man's hair and dressed Bartolomeo in Turkish clothes, guaranteeing each man passage to Istanbul.[160]

The Inquisition case gives us a good deal of insight into how these three Spaniards were able to integrate themselves into a network in Venice, and into how the Venetians were able to monitor these activities. First the connections that the three Spaniards made were dependent on making contacts with Ottoman Muslims. While we don't know how Juan Fecondo or Bartolomeo was introduced to the Ottoman merchants, we do know that Lopez was introduced to Muslims in the fondaco through a Jewish intermediary. This individual provided support much in the way that Lettino and the other servants had helped Zorzi establish relations with Ottoman merchants. He acted as the facilitator that Lopez needed to establish

---

[157] A.S.V., Sant'Ufficio, busta 88. For another reading of this case see B. Wilson, *World in Venice*, pp. 123–4.

[158] A.S.V., Sant'Ufficio, busta 88, May 22, 1631.

[159] We can discern from Bartolomeo's testimony that Fimena was in Castille.

[160] Information on these two individuals taken from testimonies, A.S.V. Sant'Ufficio, busta 88, May 24, 1631; May 27 1631; June 5, 1631; June 12, 1631.

a relationship with merchants staying at the fondaco. In entering the fondaco and changing their appearance, Lopez and his two companions transformed the space. A space that had been designated as a residence for Muslims had become, like many of the other integrated places in Venice, a place where Muslims and Christians could live together and also a place that could secretly serve the types of networks that existed in contradistinction to the strict segregation that was represented publicly by the fondaco. In essence, a controlled space had turned into a networked space.

Yet in realizing that these types of networks utilized this space, the Venetians also relied on their own networks and informants to prevent this kind of encounter. A barber from Apulia named Francesco made the denunciation against two of the defendants. He had learned from a guard at the *Fondaco dei Turchi*, from a Neapolitan doctor and from a Neapolitan tailor who worked in San Marco, that two of the defendants, a priest and a soldier from Spain, dressed in Muslim clothing, had left the *Fondaco dei Turchi* accompanied by a group of Turks and had gone to the merchant galley to leave for the Ottoman Empire. Francesco probably knew at least a couple of the defendants because in his denunciation he was able to identify them by name. [161]

The testimony illustrates a few different points. First, the fact that the guard at the *Fondaco dei Turchi* had informed Francesco about the Spaniards indicates that the Inquisition had some power to deter people who attempted to go to the fondaco to change their religion. While informants were also important in the cases involving Francesco Lettino, Paulina Briani and Mustafa Balirai, the control that could be exercised through the presence of a designated space and thorough surveillance conducted by individuals hired to act as guards was more thorough and more consistent. Any attempt by a Christian to enter the fondaco, to which all Muslim merchants had now been directed, constituted a breach of the regulations governing cross-cultural contact and residential spaces. Boundaries between religious groupings and networks could, at least in theory, be managed more efficiently.

Other evidence exists that individuals not only respected these boundaries, but also went to the Venetian government as opposed to locals to address residence-related issues. In November of 1621, a Muslim merchant named Mehmed petitioned the Cinque Savi alla Mercanzia to be allowed to stay with his Christian friend outside of the fondaco because of his arthritic condition. [162] Though Mehmed had a friend in Venice, he accepted that under normal circumstances the fondaco was the only place for a Muslim merchant to stay. Why else would he have asked the Venetians for permission? Even prominent Ottoman Muslims approached these types of concerns in a similar manner. In 1624 an Ottoman sanjack beyi appeared before the Collegio with a group of merchants complaining that they

---

[161]   A.S.V., Sant'Ufficio, busta 88, Francesco, May 22, 1631.

[162]   A.S.V., Cinque Savi alla Mercanzia, Nuove Serie, busta 187, fascicolo 3, November, 1621.

did not want to stay in the fondaco because the building was poorly maintained, it was a long way from the Rialto, the closing hours were unduly restricted and locals insulted them.[163] The Venetians did not honor their request but were quick to agree to address the problems. While these two incidents illustrate cases in which individuals attempted to leave the fondaco, they also demonstrate that at least some Muslim merchants did not make surreptitious attempts to leave their assigned housing space, but instead applied for permission from the Venetian government.

Edhem Eldem comments that the Ottomans' reception of Christian subjects from foreign lands in Istanbul represented a "'degrading hospitality,' a strange mix of hospitality and privilege on the one hand, and exclusion and insult on the other."[164] Similar attitudes toward outsiders were present in Venice. While Muslim merchants needed to be protected, they also needed to be sequestered. With the opening of the *Fondaco dei Turchi* on the Grand Canal, this new spatial arrangement was a physical manifestation of this belief. New procedures were put in place; intermediaries were assigned new responsibilities to monitor the activities of foreign travelers such as Ottoman Muslim merchants, and magistrates such as the Cinque Savi alla Mercanzia were asked to make decisions regarding the request of someone such as Mehmed who desired to stay outside of his assigned location.

---

[163] Preto, *Venezia e i Turchi*, p. 136.

[164] Edhem Eldhem, "Foreigners at the Threshold of Felicity: The Reception of Foreigners in Ottoman Istanbul," in *Cites and Cultural Exchange in Europe, 1400–1700* (Cultural Exchange in Early Modern Europe), vol. 2 , eds. Donatella Calabi and Stephen Turk Christensen (Cambridge, UK: Cambridge University Press, 2007), pp. 119–20. Eldhem also notes that we have little understanding of the "shadowy world" of Istanbul, where cultures mixed and people challenged these traditional boundaries. Here one can surmise these sections of Istanbul probably looked very similar to the integrated spaces of Venice.

Chapter 2
Negotiating with the Venetian Bureaucracy: Paths of Integration

The petition of the Muslim merchant Mehmed to address his medical condition reveals more than just a particular individual's desire to stay outside of the *Fondaco dei Turchi*. The petition also illustrates one of the ways in which an Ottoman subject could communicate and could negotiate with the Venetian state. In this particular instance, Mehmed's request was referred to the Cinque Savi alla Mercanzia,[1] the Venetian trade magistrate; thereby, the petition serves as evidence that this group was responsible for at least some diplomatic dealings with Ottoman merchants. Other requests and complaints in Venice were heard by the *Avogaria di Comun*, an important judicial body that handled investigations and tried both civil and criminal cases. In addition, the *Quarantia* or the Forty and the *Consiglio de Dieci* or the Council of Ten were two of the most important deliberative bodies in the Venetian government, and one of their principal functions was to deliberate over matters of state involving foreign subjects. The Forty served as the final court of appeals, while the Council of Ten handled conspiracies and cases of treason related to state security. At the level of neighborhoods, the Signori di Notte also meted out justice.[2]

To understand negotiations that the Venetian government had with foreign subjects, we must examine the relationship between these different Venetian government functions and investigate how Ottoman Muslims were able to interact with the Venetian system. While some of these courts and advisory boards were subordinate to other functions of government, they did have the ability to provide advice to the Venetian Senate and to try certain cases involving Ottoman subjects. The Venetians took a variety of approaches to the handling of disputes and conflicts and weighed each case in relation to different factors such as the status of the individuals involved and the different interests that were at stake. These complex political dynamics demanded flexibility not only in regard to negotiations with foreign subjects, but also in regard to how matters were deliberated internally.

Politics were based on different forms of communication between various social groups. According to Felippo De Vivo, political communication represented

---

[1]   Can be referred to as the Cinque Savi or just the Savi.

[2]   For a discussion on law in Venice see Edoardo Rubini, *Giustizia veneta: lo spirito neele leggi criminali della Repubblica* (Venezia: Filippi, 2003), Gaetano Cozzi, *Repubblica di Venezia e Stati italiani: politica e giustizia dal secolo XVI al secolo XVIII*, (Torino: G. Einaudi, 1982) and Gaetano Cozzi, "Authority and Law in Renaissance Venice," in *Renaissance Venice*, ed. J.R Hale (Totowa NJ: Rowman & Littlefield, 1973).

a "circulation of information and ideas concerning political institutions and events." This communication took place at many levels including patricians, "their secretaries and clients, foreign ambassadors and their agents" and other assorted people on the margins of Venetian society.[3] Decisions were not just handed down from the top. In coming before different magistrates, courts and other parts of the Venetian government, Ottoman Muslims did not exist as outsiders: instead, they participated in "an exchange." Both cooperative and contentious, this exchange, as illustrated in the case of Mehmed, was based on attempts to sustain dialogue and to reach a mutual undertanding.

Approaching the Venetian Government

To understand the nature of Ottoman/Venetian communication, we must first comprehend how the Venetian state functioned. The structure of Venice's government in the early modern period can best be thought of as a pyramid with the office of the Doge, the head of state, at the top and the Great Council, (*Maggior Consiglio*), made up of leading families, at the bottom. Given the size of the Great Council, which grew to 1100 members, many decisions regarding foreign policy, taxation and laws were debated in the Senate, a smaller body in the middle of the pyramid. Originally comprising sixty people, over time the Senate expanded to incorporate the Forty and a group of sixty senators referred to as the *zonta*. Ultimately, the number of the Senate grew to 300 people of whom 230 were allowed to vote.[4]

While a significant amount of power was concentrated in the office of the Doge and his council, a number of the deliberative functions of government were handled by the *Collegio*. The Collegio comprised the Doge, his six counselors, the three heads of the Quarantia and sixteen advisors or Savi.[5] The relationship to other councils placed the Collegio at the center of the Venetian government's decision-making process and gave it an important role in a variety of negotiations.[6] While technically the Collegio did not have the power to render decisions, it did have the power to decide how information should be passed on. No measure could be voted on in the Senate that had not been vetted first by the Collegio. This function of the deliberative body was especially important in negotiating conflict because a resolution needed to be established before information was passed on to the larger councils. At times, this political dynamic resulted in the Collegio framing issues

---

[3]   Filippo De Vivo, *Information and Communication in Venice: Rethinking Early Modern Politics* (Oxford, UK: Oxford University Press, 2007), pp. 2–3.

[4]   Lane, *Venice: A Maritime Republic*, p. 254. See also Robert Finlay, *Politics in Renaissance Venice* (New Brunswick: Rutgers University Press, 1980), chaps. 2, 3.

[5]   Anon, *Description ou traictié du gouvernement ou régime de la cite et seigneurie de Venise* (Perret, 1896) pp. 270–74. cited in David Chambers and Brian Pullan, *Venice: A Documentary History* (Oxford, UK: Blackwell, 1992), p. 43.

[6]   Finlay, *Politics in Renaissance Venice*, p. 40.

Fig. 2.1   Joseph Heintz the Younger, *The Interior of the Sala Maggior Consiglio* (17th century). Private Collection.

in a way that made it difficult for the Senate to disagree with the consensus that had already formed.[7]

The Collegio also represented the first point of contact with the Venetian government for many foreign groups, including Ottoman subjects. Meeting in the hall of public audience,[8] the group would gather in the morning to hear petitions, read dispatches and greet foreign envoys and delegations from subject cities.[9] On a raised dais, the Doge would sit with his counselors and the heads of the Forty. This group would greet visitors and hear petitions for about an hour before being joined by the Savi. Certain important individuals were granted a private audience with the Doge. Generally, matters everyone agreed on were responded to immediately while other affairs in which a disagreement existed were passed along to the Senate. All correspondences that were dispatched by the Collegio needed to be signed by at least four of the Doge's counselors. Other issues were passed onto the

---

[7]   De Vivo, *Information and Communication*, p. 38.

[8]   Marino Sanudo, *Laus urbis Venetae*: BCV ms. Cicogna 969, ff 8 V–19r cited in Chambers and Pullan, *Venice*, p. 16.

[9]   Lane, *Venice: A Maritime Republic*, p. 256.

Savi so that they could provide written explanations as to what should be done in the interests of the state.[10]

While in theory petitioners and the members of the council were expected to maintain formal relationships and work through bureaucratic channels, in practice relationships between foreign subjects and Venetians were more complicated. For instance, in 1481 the Council of Ten issued a report that certain individuals from the Collegio, the Senate and secret councils were discussing important government business with foreigners in locations throughout the city, including private residences. The Council was stern in its warning that these practices should not be allowed to continue and that if any individual was caught conferring with a foreigner about state business, he would be subject to a 1,000 *ducat* fine and two years in exile.[11] The Venetian heads were determined to maintain strict boundaries between government officials and foreign subjects.

Petitioning

In contrast to the ritualized ceremony that characterized these diplomatic encounters, Mehmed's relationship to the Venetian state and his place in the Ottoman/Venetian social order were defined by his petition to the Cinque Savi. Petitions were one way the Venetian government established non-elite forms of contact and control. A petition was a form of communication that gave the government the ability to weigh in on matters that were considered important. A petition constituted a demand for a favor or a complaint of injustice and could be filed for a variety of reasons. A petitioner might denounce a particular individual, ask for concessions from the state or request a ruling on a dispute between groups.[12]

Different types of petitions existed across Europe. *Gravamina* were collectively written petitions submitted by estates to lords on the occasion of an assembly. They came to represent the collective voicing of grievances.[13] In contrast, Cecelia Nubola notes that supplications were more diverse and were used to express a variety of different "requests, demands and complaints." Many supplications filed by individuals appealed to the state's sense of grace.[14]

---

[10]   Anon., pp. 270–274, cited in Chambers and Pullan, *Venice*, p. 44.

[11]   *Capitular delli Inquisitori di Stato* (Romanin, 1853–61, VI, 116–177) cited in Chambers and Pullan, *Venice*, p. 80.

[12]   Lex Heerma Van Voss, "Petitions in Social History," in *International Review of Social History*, ed. Lex Heerma Van Voss, vol. 46, supplement 9 (Cambridge, UK: Cambridge University Press, 2001), p. 1.

[13]   Andreas Würgler, "Voices from Among the 'Silent Masses': Humble Petitions and Social Conflicts in Early Modern Central Europe," in *International Review of Social History*, ed. Lex Heerma Van Voss, vol. 46, supplement 9 (Cambridge, UK: Cambridge University Press, 2001), p. 14.

[14]   Cecilia Nubola, "Supplications between Politics and Social Conflicts in Early Modern Europe," in *International Review of Social History*, ed. Lex Heerma Van Voss, vol. 46, supplement 9 (Cambridge, UK: Cambridge University Press, 2001), p. 35.

Both Gravamina and supplications were advantageous to governments in different ways. First, they allowed certain members of a government to form an alliance with a group of petitioners. These alliances were important in establishing interest groups that were involved in the building of modern states. Second, petitions acted as a guarantee both against certain clandestine activities and against conflicts in the streets by giving an individual or a group the opportunity to make a claim directly to the government with the guarantee of an audience.[15]

In her work on early modern France, Natalie Davis argues that petitions made to the King reflected particular narrative strategies. Petitions were shaped, crafted and molded into stories that were designed to win the favor of court officials. While constituting a certain type of fiction, they also represented the ways in which people dealt with power.[16] Ottoman subjects used petitions in a variety of ways to make their claims. In September 1572, during the period that Ottoman envoy Mehmed Bey was held in detention in Verona during the time of Lepanto, five individuals characterized as poor Turks and claiming to be part of Mehmed's entourage petitioned the Collegio for food and clothes. Left with no more than twelve *soldi* among them and fearful of the approaching winter, they turned to what might have been the only place they felt they could find relief.[17]

The petition of these Ottoman subjects raises a number of interesting points concerning strategies used by the petitioners. First, the fact that these individuals presented themselves as destitute would have resonated with a Venetian desire to provide relief to the poor. At the beginning of the sixteenth century, governments became increasingly aware of the issue of poverty and took it upon themselves to address this problem more seriously. Even the most destitute members of society were targeted by these efforts.[18] Due to the public nature of poverty relief, the members of Mehmed Bey's entourage seemed to have understood the willingness of the Venetian government to provide assistance. That they mentioned the approaching winter also indicates that the idea of freezing in the cold could engage the sympathy of those who might be in a position to help. Interestingly, no mention was made of the individuals' names. This omission demonstrates that their connection to Mehmed Bey was more important than their individual roles or positions and indicates that they wanted the Venetians to know that they had a powerful patron. Earlier, these same Turks had petitioned to visit with Mehmed Bey.[19] Establishing this connection served as another notice that these individuals had an important patron.

Not all Muslim groups who were anonymously identified by the Venetians included documented connections to specific patrons. In August of 1587, a group

---

[15]   Van Voss, "Petitions in Social History," p. 4.

[16]   Natalie Davis, *Fiction in the Archives: Pardon Tales and Their Tellers in Sixteenth Century France* (Stanford: Stanford University Press, 1987), pp. 3–6.

[17]   A.S.V., Collegio, Risposte di Dentro, filza 5, foglio 86, September 25, 1572.

[18]   Pullan, *Rich and Poor*, p. 216.

[19]   A.S.V., I Documenti Turchi, busta 6, fasc. 813, Italian translation fasc. 814.

of merchants approached the Venetian government looking to resolve their business dealings with a man named Zuane Buonaventura. The merchants stated that because of the troubles they had experienced with Buonaventura, they were unable to live off of their business transactions.[20] Indications are that the individuals may have represented a sizable contingent because the next January the Senate acknowledged that a large number of Ottoman subjects had experienced problems with Buonaventura.[21] In this case, the anonymity of the Ottoman subjects in the Venetian documents points less to the routine nature of the claim and more to the collective power of the Ottoman community and to the negative reputation of Buonaventura.

Hearing petitions also allowed the government to acquire information that provided a means of understanding what a particular claim entailed. On May 20, 1598 Süleyman, an Ottoman subject, petitioned the government to reclaim wool that was being held by the captain of the armada.[22] While the information that can be gleaned from this petition is limited, it does tell us that the government may have had no way of identifying the owner of merchandise or of returning his or her goods without a supplication.

These supplications were particularly important in providing the Venetians with information about inheritance issues. On March 8, 1587 Urem of Skopje and Mahmud from Plezarin appeared before the Collegio with translated copies of the wills of Ahmed and Agi Hüseyn. Ahmed's will consigned his goods to Urem with the stipulation that the goods should be sold and a portion should be sent as alms to Mecca, while Agi Hüseyn's will stated that his goods should be given to his companion Mahmud so that Mahmud could take the goods to Hüseyn's children.[23] An untimely death was a distinct possibility for a trader in the early modern world, and governments not only had to be prepared for this type of occurrence, they also had to be ready to cope with the claims of another state's subjects.

In contentious cases, petitions included corroborating documentation from witnesses and other supporters. In a petition to the Doge in the 1560s, two Muslim merchants, Ahmed and Piri from Castelnuovo, asked that the goods and ship of Ahmed, which had been taken and held by the fleet commander, Pandolfo Contarini, be returned to Ahmed. Testifying on behalf of the Muslims' claim were the captain of the ship, Giacomo Mazzolao, and a group of other Italians.[24] Ahmed and Piri buttressed their claim by soliciting a letter from the governor

---

[20]   A.S.V., Senato Mare, filza 96.

[21]   A.S.V., Cinque Savi alla Mercaniza, Regulazioni et Lititgi, prime serie, registro 16, p. 29.

[22]   A.S.V., Cinque Savi alla Mercanzia, Regulazioni et Litigi, prime serie, registro 19, p. 35.

[23]   A.S.V., Cinque Savi alla Mercanzia, Risposte, prime serie, busta 139, March 8, 1587.

[24]   A.S.V., I Documenti Turchi, busta 6, fascicolo 764, Italian translation .

of Cattaro, Marino Pisani. In the letter Pisani testified that Ahmed and Piri had always maintained good relations with Christians. [25]

Although in the end the Venetian government did receive a letter from the Porte asking that the Venetians restore the goods of the two merchants, the petition the merchants filed contains some important considerations.[26] For one, their request demonstrates that the two merchants grasped the political protocol involved in having their goods returned. That they approached the Venetian government directly indicates that they possessed the ability to undertake their own diplomacy and, at the same time, understood that the incident was more than just a local matter and so required the intervention of officials. In an attempt to influence these officials, the merchants made use of certain conventions. For instance, they solicited the testimonies of the ship's captain and some Italians on the ship. Finding witnesses to testify was one component in a strategy a Muslim merchant could use in staking a claim and asking for reparations or other concessions. Similarly, it was not unusual for the Venetians to use Muslim witnesses as signatories. Having these individuals on record was an important part of convincing Ottoman authorities that a dispute had been handled in a fair manner.[27]

Including accounts of witnesses with a petition was one tactic used to establish credibility. Another tactic was to present a group petition as was filed by the merchants who had a claim against Bonaventura. These individuals were able to pressure the Venetian government into giving them a hearing. Credibility was also established when a group or an individual made it known that a connection existed to a prominent individual. Any Ottoman merchant trading along the Dalmatian coast who was interested in demonstrating to the Venetian government the worthiness of a claim would have attempted to receive the assistance of a local Venetian official or proxy. A letter from Governor Pisani not only guaranteed Ahmed and Piri's good character, it also validated their right to trade in Venetian territories. Castelnovo and Cattaro were very close to one another and if an Ottoman merchant had been harmed or had his goods stolen, it would have behooved him to prove to the Venetians that his standing warranted a fair hearing. States and state officials were in the business of facilitating commerce, and legal protection existed at a number of levels. The dangers posed by local officials, brigands and other attackers were significant, and host governments, therefore, understood the necessity of creating arrangements that gave guarantees to traders and other important people.[28]

---

[25]   A.S.V., I Documenti Turchi, busta 6, fascicolo 765.

[26]   A.S.V., I Documenti Turchi, busta 6, fascicolo 766, Italian translation fascicolo, 767.

[27]   A.S.V., Senato, Deliberazioni Constantinopoli, registro 7, foglio 33R, March 27, 1586.

[28]   Braudel points out that "police records of the city pale beside the bloodstained history of banditry in the Mediterranean, banditry on the land that is, the counterpart of piracy on the sea, with which it had many affinities." Braudel, *The Mediterranean*, vol. 2, p. 743.

Facilitating Communication and Delivering Guarantees

In reflecting on how a petition was handled by the Venetian government, and on how it was circulated to a particular court or magistracy, we must consider how legal and political guarantees related to protection. On March 19, 1574 in a case presented to the tribunal of the Avogaria di Comun, the magistracy responsible for hearing both civil and criminal cases, two Ottoman Muslims by the names of Hassan and Mustafa, envoys of the grand vezir, the sultan's representative and regent, angrily called on the Venetian government to do something about the sort of unacceptable treatment that they had received just the day before.[29] Testifying first, Mustafa claimed that the evening before, without any provocation whatsoever, a group of men from the *terraferma* had taken up arms and hit him right in front of the proprietor of the hosteria in which he and Hassan were staying. In the subsequent testimony, other abuses were revealed. Hassan added that while he had been standing on the balcony of the hosteria people passing beneath on the street began calling him a series of very unpleasant names such as "goat," "horned cuckold," "Jew" and "dog." Hassan complained that the experience was so unsettling that not only did he and his companion feel as though they had to avoid going on the street, they also had to abstain even from standing on the balcony.[30] Adamantly, they demanded that justice should be served, the guilty punished and measures taken to prevent these sorts of incidents from happening in the future. Anxious to appease their guests, the Venetians were very quick to respond, and a day later, at the behest of the Avogaria di Comun, a notice was put up at the Rialto publicly stating

> that no one, whoever he may be, may presume in any way by words or deeds to injure, or offend or cause to be offended or use words injurious or other words against the subjects and the representatives of the sultan, who should rather be well treated and cherished, on pain of five years of service in the galley of the condemned and hoisted three times on the rope in public, and if unfit for the galley, they should spend the same amount of time in a closed prison. If they are women or children they shall be lashed from San Marco to Rialto and banned from the city for a period of ten years, and other more severe penalties may be imposed at the discretion of the court.[31]

---

[29]   No further background is given as to where these individuals came from other than they signed as two subjects of the Sultan.

[30]   A.S.V. Avogaria di Comun, Miscellenea Civile, busta 278, March 19, 1574.

[31]   Ibid. "Che niuno et sia si voglia no ardir, per lacun modo forma over ingegno cosi in parolè, come in fatti inguiriar, ne offender, ne far offender, o usare parole di qual si voglia sorte inviriose o altramentè contra li sudditi et representanti il Ser. Signor Turco, ma quelli ben trattar et accarezar, sotto pena, di servir per anni cinque in galia de condennadi, et tratti tre di corda in pubblico, et non essendo boni da Galia di star per ditto tempo nella preson forte et essendo donne over putti, da esser frustadi, da San Marco a Rialto, et non di possendo haver nelle forze della giustizia di anni diese di bando di questa città et destretto et altre piu severe pene ad arbitrio giustitia."

Abusers were forewarned and the penalties were stiff.

The response of the Venetian government indicates that protection was a guarantee that the Venetians had to offer Muslim visitors. The language of the edict and the potential of punishment indicate the willingness of the state to intercede at a moment's notice. Men who roamed the streets and insulted Turks threatened public order. In the statement that they filed with the Avogaria the two aggrieved Ottoman subjects mentioned that the sort of behavior they had been subjected to was not uncommon in the inn where they were staying. Given that the hostilities had just ceased in the War of Cyprus, there might have been a certain amount of popular hostility toward Ottoman subjects. During the war, Ottoman subjects in Venice had been put into detention, as had Venetian merchants in Istanbul, including the bailo in Istanbul.[32] Fearing reprisals from the local population during a period of political tension, the Venetians had to be careful that no harm came to their guests. Mustafa and Hassan were quick to point out that they had a powerful backer in the sultan. While the Venetians' motivation for the intervention probably was to prevent news from getting back to the Porte, their action also reflected the legitimate workings of the bureaucracy.

This type of problem must have come up periodically, for in 1594, responding to the complaints of a group of Muslim and Jewish merchants, the same body issued a decree that anyone who abused the Turks either by word or by deed would be banned, put in the galley or put in prison.[33] The repetition of the demand indicates that mechanisms were in place that not only greased the wheels of trade, but also gave Muslim merchants legal access.

Support for these guarantees and access to legal bodies was granted for a wide variety of cases involving protection. In 1592, directed to the Avogaria by a Jewish man, a Muslim merchant, Haydar, claimed that when traveling on a ship from the gulf of Neretva[34] to Venice, he had left behind a chest containing a variety of goods and the sum of 3,400 *tolleri* that had been stolen after the boat was shipwrecked at Malamocco. Alleging that the money had been stolen by some of the sailors on the ship and a group of local peasants, Haydar demanded that the Avogaria restore his goods and ensure the rendering of justice.[35]

---

[32] A.S.V. *Senato Deliberazioni Constantinopoli Registro 4*, Foglio 26R, April 4, 1570. Benjamen Arbel notes that it was not until the Sultan found out that his subjects had been put in detention in Venice that he decided to have Venetian merchants in Istanbul arrested. Prior to that the Sultan had only ordered that the bailo be confined to his mansion. Other Venetians were allowed to trade and move freely throughout the city. See Benjamen Arbel, *Trading Nations: Jews and Venetians in the Early Modern Mediterranean* (Leiden: E.J. Brill, 1995) p.70. On the bailo's internment see Deborah Howard, *Venice Disputed: Marc'Antonio Barbaro and Venetian Architecture, 1550–1600* (New Haven: Yale University Press, 2011), pp. 81–82.

[33] A.S.V. *Senato Deliberazioni Constantinopoli*, registro 8, p. 156R.

[34] The Gulf of the Neretva is north of Dubrovnik along the Dalmatian coast.

[35] A.S.V., Avogaria di Comun, Miscellanea Penale, busta 211, fascicolo 11.

Certain points emerge that are important to understanding the options that the Venetian government made available to Ottoman Muslim subjects. First, the Jewish man who advised Haydar to go to the Avogaria played an important role as a middleman in expediting an issue between Muslim merchants and the government. Informing Ottoman Muslims as to how to handle a situation and directing them to the correct legal body, as noted in the first chapter, was one of the functions of middlemen or cultural intermediaries. In this regard, they were able to help the merchants work within the Venetian legal system. These middlemen were sometimes necessary because Ottoman Muslims did not have a means for dealing with the Venetian government in the same way as Jews: they had no consul and no councils and did not form a *università*, a corporate body.[36]

Second, though the case involved the claims of one individual, the charges were considered a very serious matter by the government and guaranteed the injured party the full protection of Venetian law. Replacing a system in which different families negotiated disputes between themselves based on tradition, Venetian communal law dated back to the middle of the thirteenth century when Doge Jacopo Tiepolo and a group of nobles compiled a series of guidelines and regulations for the commune to follow that were largely based on Roman law. In the fifteenth century, as Venice expanded its maritime and territorial ambitions, these statutes became more comprehensive and more expansive.[37] Many of the reasons for these statutes had to do with the necessity of incorporating the interests of a variety of different noble families and with the need of taking into consideration diplomatic relations with subject peoples and other states. Gaetano Cozzi points out that "for the Venetian aristocracy, law was not something extrinsic or imposed; it was the expression of themselves, of their own will and nature, the highest and most representative form of self-expression, the most ingrained in their own political and civil experience...."[38] The law in this regard ensured that the noble class, embodied in the state, could conduct its business.

Part of the state's business in this case involved giving legal access to widely diverse groups of people. On the one hand, Haydar, whose chest and money were stolen, received a hearing because he was part of group of merchants who came regularly to Venice to trade; on the other hand, the sailors, as members of the crew, and the local peasants from Malamocco, as Venetian subjects, also had a voice. While Ottoman merchants were clearly important guests in the city, in cases involving different parties, the Venetians had to take into consideration how a verdict might impact their own subject population. Many points of contact existed between the Venetian subject population and the subjects of the Ottoman Empire,

---

[36]   On Jewish self-government in Venice see David Joshua Malkiel, *A Separate Republic: The Mechanics of Venetian Self-Government, 1607–1624* (Jerusalem: Magnes Press, 1991).

[37]   Gaetano Cozzi, *Stato, Società e Giustizia* (Roma: Jouvence 1980), p. 21.

[38]   Cozzi, "Authority and the Law," p. 306.

and it was not unusual for the law courts of the Venetian government to weigh in on an issue that had taken place in another location.

In the case initiated by Haydar, protecting a person of status must have been a factor in not only the decision of the Avogaria to investigate the matter, but also in how the deliberations progressed. [39] The same logic applied in the case of the two envoys from the grand vezir who were harassed by people in the street. Life on the streets could be quite violent, and the Venetian government was committed to controlling the violence of individuals categorized as "outlaws."[40] In the same manner that nobles enacted laws to discipline people who were inclined to direct violence against their class, by the sixteenth century and possibly even earlier, Venetian elites with the aim of protecting trade created a set of legal practices that guaranteed this protection to foreigners, including Ottoman Muslims.

While commercial, legal and political cooperation did form between Ottomans and Venetian subjects, it would be inaccurate to think of these shared interests as an indication of the existence of an international elite similar to the one that is present today. These types of connections may have existed within the court culture and amongst elites of Europe, but to state that these ties extended to the Muslim population of the Ottoman Empire would be overstating the point.[41] In cases such as the one involving Haydar, the Venetians did not really have any idea what type of person they were dealing with. An inquiry gave the Venetians the opportunity to find out what had happened and also allowed them to gain more background information on an individual or a group. Through the hearing, the government could assess potential problems and outcomes. Aware of the potential political complications of any case, the legal system provided the Venetians with a mechanism to recognize the social dynamics of a dispute.

In attempting to understand status, the Venetians used a variety of different strategies in identifying the social background of an individual or a group. As was noted earlier, the surveillance network that the Venetians created allowed them to keep tabs on Ottoman visitors who had come to the city. This approach worked well in attempts to monitor what was going on in the street. The Venetians also had an elaborate spy network across the Mediterranean that kept the government informed about Ottoman politics and that provided them with intelligence on Ottoman dignitaries.[42] Other means were also at their disposal.

---

[39] Guido Ruggiero argues that in the fourteenth century the Venetian state, recognizing the presence of a certain class tension, used the law as a bureaucratic means for preventing lower-class violence and aggression against their social superiors. Guido Ruggiero, *Violence in Early Modern Venice* (New Brunswick NJ: Rutgers University Press, 1980), p. 148.

[40] Cozzi, "Authority and the Law," p. 294.

[41] On connections between different courts see Christine Isom-Verhaaren "Shifting Identities: Foreign State Servants in France and the Ottoman Empire," *Journal of Early Modern History* (2004), pp. 109–34.

[42] On spies and spying see Preto, *I servizi segreti*.

The *Cinque Savi alla Mercanzia*

As the Venetian state became more bureaucratized, different magistracies and councils were entrusted with the responsibility of sorting through different political and social matters. From tax collection to blasphemy to inheritance, the state assigned certain magistrates the task of upholding the law and investigating cases relevant to their jurisdiction. Within this framework, the task of protecting Ottoman Muslim merchants and hearing their grievances was placed in the hands of the Cinque Savi alla Mercanzia. The Savi was an advisory board established in 1506 to deal with a number of issues related to trade that arose after the Portuguese had discovered a route to India around the tip of Africa that bypassed the Mediterranean. Manned by five nobles experienced in international commerce who were elected annually, the Savi were expected to handle a number of issues ranging from the supervision of some guilds to tariffs. This responsibility was expanded to Ottoman traders as well, and the Savi became so central to these merchants' affairs that none of the other magistracies was able to dispute one of their decisions.[43]

The Savi's central role in both commercial and Ottoman affairs made the board very influential with the Venetian Senate. The channeling of information and recommendations from the board to the Senate was representative of how the Venetian bureaucracy functioned. In March 1586 the Senate announced that the Savi had informed them that Ottomans, including Muslims, were being cheated by brokers on the Rialto. Because of these irregularities, brokers must write details regarding each transaction in their account books and must ensure that Ottoman buyers received their goods. The decree demonstrates the willingness of the Senate, on the recommendation of the Savi, to support the interests of Ottoman merchants. The Senate pointed out that "the [Ottoman] merchants and others who transport merchandise to this city are not to be hindered, molested nor in any way cheated by means of illicit payments, harassment or extortion."[44] Protecting the collective interests of the Ottoman community in Venice, the Venetian government chose to enter into a dispute that involved brokers. Though, as was pointed out in the previous chapter, brokers could be of dubious backgrounds, they did constitute a guild and an interest group and the decision to back the claims of the merchants indicates the willingness of the Savi to protect foreign interests.[45]

In cases like this one, the Cinque Savi were not asked to make decisions but instead to give the Senate advice. Advice was given with the understanding that

---

[43]   Maria Borgherini-Scarabellin, "Il magistrato dei Cinque Savi alla Mercanzia dalla istituzione alla caduta della republica," *Miscellanea di storia Veneto-Tridentina*, Vol. 2 (Venezia: Deputazione *di storia* patria per le Venezie, 1926), pp. 14–19.

[44]   A.S.V., Cinque Savi alla Mercanzia, nuove serie, busta 187, fascicolo 1, November 10, 1586. "Li mercanti et altri che conducono mercnazie in questa città non siano impediti, molestati, ne in altro modo perturbati per via de pagamenti illeciti angarie estorsioni."

[45]   Ibid.

information in Venice was passed along on a number levels, some more official than others.[46] That the Savi were chosen to provide advice on Ottoman affairs indicates that the Senate was willing to accept their interpretation of a particular case and to act upon this counsel. The Senate had confidence in the magistracy because the Savi were well versed in commercial matters and could consider different sides of a dispute. In December 1619, a group of Muslim merchants demanded that their goods be returned by the people of the hamlet of Pastorvich[47] who removed them from a frigate destined for the port of Antivari.[48] The people of Pastorvich contended that they had taken the goods because in the past months when they had gone to Ottoman territories in Albania to buy grain, they had been told that they could not export it. Deciding instead to try to smuggle grain out, they were discovered and were punished for their actions. Although the Cinque Savi may have been sympathetic to the retaliatory measure that the people of Pastorvich had taken, the board told the Senate that not all the merchandise on the ship belonged to the Muslims from this territory. Some of the other goods belonged to merchants from other Ottoman cities. While they did not make any further suggestions, their recommendation indicates that what was essentially a local matter should not be allowed to turn into a larger dispute.[49] The other merchants may have had important connections, and their complaints to authorities could have affected Venetian merchants in Ottoman territories. In deliberating the matter, the Savi clearly understood that the guarantee of protection extended beyond a merchant's physical well-being and also included the trader's merchandise.

The responsibility of weighing in on long distance commercial matters also related to credit issues, and in July of 1614 the board considered a claim made by an Arab, Agir Cara. In their investigation, the Savi found that the bailo in Istanbul had received word that Agir Cara claimed that he was entitled to the 804 *piastres,* which his brother, who was murdered in Venice in 1611, was owed by heirs of Alfonso Rotta. The board surmised that the case was indeed complicated for the contested money was tied to a series of events that took place over a number of years. In 1605 an Ottoman subject, Fogia, had come before the Cinque Savi as a creditor of the said Rotta and demanded that Rotta repay a debt of 4,428 ducats. Since he was unable to pay, the Venetians were left with no alternative but to sentence Rotta to prison where he was forced to spend the five years between 1605 and 1610. Yet the case was by no means closed. On September 10, 1610, Rotta petitioned the Venetian government, asking that the 804 piastres that he had paid in Aleppo in regard to an outstanding lawsuit be transferred to Venice so that he could pay his debt to Fogia and thus be liberated from prison. The complications in verifying the information that Rotta had provided made an immediate decision difficult. However, on March 28, 1611, the Senate, on receiving word that the

46   De Vivo, *Information and Communication*, p. 3.

47   Pastorvich was a small hamlet on the Montenegran coast.

48   Antivari was a port just south of Pastorvich.

49   A.S.V., Cinque Savi alla Mercanzia, Risposte, prime serie, busta 145, foglio 48V.

lawsuit had been terminated, agreed that Rotta or one of his representatives could receive the 804 piastres in Syria. Claims on the money still remained outstanding, though, for before Rotta's representatives arrived to collect the money, the brother of Agir Cara was killed in Venice and his relatives announced their claim in accordance with his last will and testament. Nonetheless, as far as the Savi were concerned the case was closed and the relatives of Rotta, who had died in the interim, had correctly received the 804 piastres.[50]

The Savi were forced to deliberate on a sequence of events involving legal issues that stretched beyond local jurisdiction. The sanctity of the contract and accompanying credit was essential for Mediterranean trade. Bills of exchange and their Islamic equivalent kitābü'l-kadis and *süfteces* functioned as written proof of long-distance commercial transactions.[51] Different forms of credit existed that facilitated these transactions. In medieval Venice, the *colleganza* was an agreement that was made between an investor and a traveling merchant. The investor put up the capital for a shipment of goods and was entitled to ¾ of the profit.[52] Venice also had a very diverse credit market in which banks, private lenders, foreigners, pawnbrokers and other assorted individuals supplied credit to both governments and private individuals alike.[53] In the Ottoman Empire, credit was available in a variety of different forms. Though from an Islamic perspective interest was not seen as permissible, small lenders charged varying degrees of interest for different types of loans, and large lenders found other ways to circumvent this prohibition.[54] *Vakufs*, pious foundations, also used their cash assets to provide important sources of credit, and frequently they also charged interest.[55]

All of these credit mechanisms functioned to expand trade and to circulate money. Frederic Lane comments:

> If a merchant in Venice had sufficiently good standing with an agent in Bruges,
> … and if he was hard up for cash, the Venetian partner might draw on a bill
> for his partner in Bruges. He would sell that bill for cash to someone in Venice
> who would send it to Bruges for collection. When the bill arrived in Bruges, the

---

[50]   A.S.V., Cinque Savi alla Mercanzia, Risposte, prime serie, busta 144, foglio 8R.

[51]   On the use of kitābü'l-kadi and süfteces see H. Sahillioğlu, "Bursa kadı Sicillerinde İç ve Dış Ödemeler Aracı Olarak 'Kitabü'l-kadı' ve 'Süftecele'ler," in *Türkiye İktisat Tarihi Semineri: Metinler/Tartışmalar* (8–10 Haziran 1973) ed. O. Okyar (Ankara: Haceteppe Universitesi, 1975), pp. 103–41.

[52]   Reinhold Mueller, "The Procuratori di San Marco and the Venetian Credit Market: A Study of the Development of Credit and Banking in the Trecento" (Ph.D. thesis, Johns Hopkins University, 1969).

[53]   Rheinhold Mueller, *The Venetian Money Market: Banks, Panics and the Public Debt: Money and Banking in Renaissance Venice*, vol. 2 (Baltimore: Johns Hopkins University Press, 1997), pp. 570–73.

[54]   Şevket Pamuk, *A Monetary History of the Ottoman Empire* (Cambridge, UK: Cambridge University Press, 2000), p. 79.

[55]   Ibid., p. 81.

partner there, in order to get the money to pay it, might sell in Bruges a new bill drawn on Venice.[56]

This system of credit relied on long distance trust and the reputation of a network or an individual. If creditors were to allow merchants and agents to buy goods without cash in hand, the system could only function if this trust was preserved.[57] That Alfonso Rotta was able to secure the loan from Fogia must have meant that Rotta was a part of a network in good standing. The fact that the relationship extended beyond kinship and communal boundaries must have also meant the lender was secure that the borrower would pay him back.[58] While credit relations between members of different religious groups and states were not unheard of, logistical difficulties and cultural differences must have contributed to a higher standard of trust. A breach of this trust, as we see in the case of Rotta, necessitated that the state step in and restore the confidence of the injured party.[59]

Maintaining trust involved putting mechanisms in place that guaranteed creditors restitution, and in an Ottoman/Venetian treaty of 1595, the agreement stated that any Venetian who came to Ottoman territories to do business and slipped away fraudulently, defaulting on his obligations, would have his or her case heard before an Ottoman tribunal. The Ottoman court was given the power to decide what amount of money must be repaid. Similarly, these terms also applied to Ottoman subjects coming to Venice. If an Ottoman merchant was to leave Venice owing money to someone, the Venetians had the right to decide the amount of money owed. To this stipulation was added the provision that if an Ottoman subject or a Venetian subject who owed a debt or was charged with a particular crime escaped to the other's territories, he or she would not be given a safe haven nor a reprieve from paying back the said monies.[60] In 1576 Sultan Murad III sent a letter to the Doge Alvise Mocenigo asking that the Jewish Ottoman subject Baruh Crespi, a resident of Venice for six or seven years, repay the 248,700 *aspri* that he owed the Jewish merchant from Istanbul, Salomone di Giacobbe.[61] The debt not only constituted a breach of contract, but given that Crespi was an Ottoman subject, Ottoman officials had legal grounds for claiming that Crespi was not

---

[56] Lane, *Venice: A Maritime Republic*, pp. 146–7.

[57] On the issue of trust and credit see Craig Muldrew, *The Economy of Obligation: The Culture of Credit and Social Relations in Early Modern England* (New York: St. Martin's Press, 1998), pp. 4–5.

[58] Charles Tilly makes the point that, as the depersonalized market expanded, kinship, neighborhood and religious ties became more important in trading relations. Charles Tilly, *Trust and Rule* (Cambridge: Cambridge University Press, 2005), p. 15.

[59] Kate Fleet, *European and Islamic Trade in the Early Ottoman State: The Merchants of Genoa and Turkey* (Cambridge, UK: Cambridge University Press, 1999), p. 127.

[60] Par M. Belin. "Relations diplomatiques de la République de Venise avec la Turquie," *Journal Asiatique*, Novembre-Décembre 1876, p. 413. French translation of treaty of December of 1595, section on evasion of debts.

[61] Pedani, *I documenti turchi*, p. 212.

entitled to the protection of the Venetian state.[62] This scenario was also true in the case of Alfonso Rotta. By not paying his debt, Rotta had violated one of the principal tenants of Ottoman/Venetian trade relations and thus the Savi must have felt that Fogia was due his owed monies.

To state, though, that Fogia understood how the inner mechanisms of the Cinque Savi worked would be an exaggeration. No evidence supports this view, nor does any proof exist that he had personal relationships with anybody on the board. The absence of these connections, though, does not mean that the board did not have a clear sense of the ramifications of a particular situation, the interests involved and the impact on the Venetian government. In July 1605, an Armenian, Amurat, came forward to claim that his brother Simon had been murdered and had 2,000 *cecchini* of his money stolen by two Turkish merchants currently staying in Venice, Musli and Seffer of Skopje.[63] The government sought the advice of the Cinque Savi because Amurat wanted to recover the money that he alleged had been stolen by the two Turks. In recounting the story, Amurat commented that Ottoman officials had sentenced Musli to death,[64] but Musli had subsequently escaped to Venice to avoid being caught. Undoubtedly, Amurat hoped that the Venetians would be anxious to uphold a decision handed down by the Ottoman judge. The fact that Simon was murdered might also have factored into the way the Savi thought about the case. Yet the case also hinged on other factors; three Armenians and two Turks claimed that Musli was not a fugitive from justice, but instead a legitimate merchant who had come to Venice with two shipments of goods. While the Savi were conflicted as to how to resolve the respective claims of these Ottoman subjects, they felt that given the circumstances of the case and the accompanying evidence, the need to protect the Muslim merchants' interests outweighed other concerns.[65]

Weighing the interests of different parties was closely tied to attempts to assess the long-term interests of the Venetian state. In the case involving the people of Pastorvich, the Savi recognized the local community's justification in taking action against the local Muslims but were cautious about supporting the people of Pastorvich outright for fear of alienating the long-distance Muslim merchants who had had their goods confiscated. Even when standard Venetian practices were challenged, the Savi thought carefully about the specifics of a particular case. For instance, in 1612, Bechin and Risvan, two Bosnian merchants, contended that after failing to sell their goods, which consisted of 28 bales of treated leather, they should only be responsible for paying the previous tax. The merchants complained

---

[62]   In fact, this understanding must have applied much earlier for in 1530 Sultan Süleyman sent a letter to the beys of Egypt and the kadi to open an investigation into the claims that Venetian merchant Giovanni Badleto made against a Jewish custom officer. See Pedani, *I documenti turchi*, p. 70.

[63]   A.S.V., Cinque Savi alla Mercanzia, Risposte, prime serie, busta 141, foglio 145R.

[64]   No indication is given as to whether Seffer was also tried and sentenced.

[65]   A.S.V., Cinque Savi alla Mercanzia, Risposte, prime serie, busta 141, foglio 145R.

that if they had sold their goods, they would have had to settle for a price that would have been eight *lira* less per bale than they had received in the past. The board responded that given that these merchants came to Venice every year to sell a large quantity of goods and were unaware of the new tax, they should only be required to pay the former tax.[66]

Obviously, the board felt that it was important to maintain this relationship. While there is no way of knowing what the difference in tax might have been, clearly, the Savi thought it was important to reward traders who were regular visitors. In responding to their complaint, the board also recognized that in cities such as Livorno and Ancona other trading options existed for Ottoman merchants who wanted to trade their goods in Italy.[67] Market conditions must have weighed heavily in their recommendation.

Many cases, though, were more complicated politically and involved more than personal reputation and more than the present market conditions. Venice's relationship to Muslim merchants was built on historical precedents that had been established over a period of time and involved legal arguments that referred to prior events. For instance, on February 17, 1592, both Ottoman Muslims and Christian merchants bringing wool from the port of Alessio complained that they should not be subjected to the *mezzi noli*, an insurance tax that been imposed on merchants coming from Split. They reasoned that in the preceding April another group of Muslim merchants had made the same request and their wishes had been granted.[68]

Different points bear consideration. First, historical precedent was just one of the criteria the Cinque Savi used in judging particular cases. While the board understood the importance of standard policies, it also recognized the unique nature of each case. In framing their response to the Senate in these terms, the Savi felt that the Venetian government should be careful in offering a concession to one group and not to another. This thinking demonstrates that in certain cases the Savi could think of Ottoman groups in corporate terms and yet also frame their recommendation to the government in a way that emphasized the importance of making certain exceptions. While the complaint reflected both trans-chronological and trans-religious connections of Ottoman groups, to think of this case in immutable terms misses the complexity of their association. In all likelihood these groups' collective identity was based on specific interests. Group identity was ephemeral and many of the alliances probably dissolved when the reason that the participants had rallied together had disappeared. In some cases one's chance of succeeding must have been enhanced by thinking in corporate terms. Why else would the Muslim merchant Şeyhi have filed a protest in the name of the Turkish nation in regard to the tax advantages that the Venetians had in conducting trade

---

[66] A.S.V., Cinque Savi alla Mercanzia, Risposte, prime serie, busta 145, foglio 47V. The traders were expected to pay an exit tax even though they had not sold their goods.

[67] See Kafadar, "A Death in Venice."

[68] A.S.V., Cinque Savi alla Mercanzia, Risposte, prime serie, busta 140, foglio 189R.

out of Ottoman Syria? The effectiveness of group solidarity resonated strongly with the Venetians. In fact, in regard to Şeyhi's protest, one of the Savi, Zuane Correr stated:

> I am sure that our Venetian merchants would suffer greatly if (as they responded to us in both speech and writing) the Turks were to be treated on a par with our own merchants and pay only one percent, for a venue who would then be opened up to all the Jews and other Turkish subjects, who on this pretext ask for the same favour.[69]

The nature of the petition indicates that Şeyhi's claim of be a part of a community of Muslim merchants gave him a sense of empowerment when he petitioned the Venetian government. This point is reinforced by Correr's concern that agreeing to Şeyhi's demand would have the effect of providing all Muslims with the same tax advantage.

One reason for Şeyhi's decision to present his petition in this manner must have had to do with his knowledge that the trade board not only assessed petitions but also had a favorable relationship to foreign traders. Not only did this relationship raise the status of the traders, it also the enhanced the position of the board. Benjamin Ravid believes that one reason Levantine Jews received favorable treatment from the Savi was because the board attempted to protect its jurisdiction over foreign merchants.[70] In this respect, the Savi were both vulnerable to the lobbying efforts of Muslim merchants and also anxious to protect their own stake in negotiations between different parties. In May 1631, a group of Muslim merchants petitioned the board asking that they be allowed to sell their leather to anyone who was interested in buying it. The board surmised that the problem stemmed from the restrictions that had been enacted by the *mercanti da cordovani*, limiting the number of buyers of hides to between four and six. This development presented many problems for Turkish merchants and for the Venetians as well. The board feared that, since "Turks" were the principal importers of leather, if these problems were to persist, the Muslim merchants would be likely to take their business to a port that was more amenable to their needs. To alleviate these problems, the Savi suggested that anyone who wanted to buy the leather be allowed to enter the guild without being subjected to a vote of the guild's members, but instead be required to pay four ducats. At the time of the petition, the plague of 1631 was devastating the city and attempts to turn traders away obviously could have disastrous consequences for all concerned. In fact, Muslim merchants had actually filed two petitions, one on

---

[69]   A.S.V., Cinque Savi alla Mercanzia, Riposte, prime serie, busta 138, foglio 66V.
Io son sicuro, che cio aporterrebe grandissimo danno a nostri merchanti venetiani, se come ne hanno resposta boccâ et in una sciturra presentata a noi et se essi turchi dovessero esser trattati al pari di nostri nel pagar solamente uno percento se venirá ad aprir una strada a tutti li hebrei et altri sudditi Turcheschi che per questa via dimandiarano l'istessa gratia.

[70]   Ravid, *Legal Status of the Jewish Merchants*, pp. 188–9.

March 13 and the other on April 2 and the board did not render their opinion until May 27 of the same year. This delay may indicate the difficulty they had in coming to a decision. In the end the board concluded that opening up the guild to more members would not only alleviate the Muslim merchants' concerns, but it would also increase the amount of business that came through the guild.[71]

The case certainly points to the complexity of managing the interests of different groups. Clearly, the decision to rule in the favor of one faction should not be seen strictly along religious or state lines. In deciding to emphasize the necessity of allowing Turkish merchants to do business with the buyers of their choice, the board placed itself in opposition to a powerful interest group in Venice, the mercanti da cordovani. The Council of Ten had recognized the mercanti da cordovani as a separate guild on March 8, 1585.[72] They were given the right to buy and to sell leather but not to manufacture items such as shoes. Growing in stature, the guild tried to continue to consolidate its power, and in 1616 the *Collegio delle arti* granted the mercanti da cordovani the right to restrict its membership to the sons of individuals currently in the guild.[73] In 1663 the Venetian government turned down the request of the mercanti da cordovani to have an exclusive monopoly on the leather trade, and by the eighteenth century the guild had gained an increasingly dominant role in the sector.[74] Andrea Vianello notes that "(a)n important limit to the control exercised by the merchants over the tanners and on the internal market of hides for shoes was protected by an ancient right enjoyed by members of the guild of the shoemakers and cobblers who could buy from Turkish, Bosnian and other merchants."[75] Understanding the severe consequences that could result from the withdrawal of Turkish hide traders from the city, the Savi realized that they had to challenge a guild that had become increasingly more powerful not only to protect the interests of Muslim traders but also to guarantee the welfare of other guilds in Venice.

The degree of government protection that a guild could expect was an important concern for the early modern state. In his study of guilds in sixteenth- through eighteenth-century Bologna, Carlo Poni notes that if two guilds could not negotiate

---

[71] A.S.V., Cinque Savi alla Mercanzia, Risposte, prime serie, busta 148, foglio 161V. For another reading of this case see Stephen Ortega, "Shaping Legal Decisions: Power across borders in the Early Modern Mediterranean," *Interpreting the Past: Essays from the 4th International Conference on European History,* Eds. Kenneth E. Hendrickson & Nicolas C.J. Pappas (Athens: Atiner, 2007**)**, pp. 205–14.

[72] Andrea Vianello, *L'arte dei calegheri e zavateri di Venezia tra XVII e XVIII sec*olo (Venezia: Istituto veneto di scienze, lettere *ed* arti, 1993), p. 48. "Un importante limite al controllo esercitato dai mercanti sui conciacurame e sull'interno mercato delle pelli da tomaia in città era representato da un antico diritto goduto dai membri dell'Arte dei calegheri e degli zavateri, i quali potevano comprar da mercanti turchi, bossinessi e altri mercanti."

[73] A.S.V., Cinque Savi alla Mercanzia, Risposte, prime serie, busta 148, foglio 161V.

[74] Vianello, *L'arte dei calegheri*, pp. 49–50.

[75] Ibid., p.49.

a particular agreement, the state would intervene either on the request of one of the parties or on their own initiative. Citing an example of a dispute between the tanners' guild and the butchers' guild in 1637, Poni points out that the once the tanners' guild refused to pay the increase in prices that the butchers' guild wanted for hides, the butchers took this an opportunity to obtain a ruling from the Bolognese Senate and the Cardinal Legate that allowed them to sell to a wide variety of buyers. One of the butchers' strategies was to sell to the journeymen of the tanners, thus putting them in competition with their superiors.[76] Ottoman guilds were closely controlled, at least in theory, because of the state's need for specific provisions. Thus, at least in some cases, the state was directly involved in deciding certain guild leaders and in regulating guild practices. While, given the diversity of the empire, a single standard for all guilds did not exist, guilds that were closely aligned with the state enjoyed a good amount of government support and protection.[77]

Although the mercanti da cordovani perceived the Savi's actions as hostile to their interests, the Savi argued that increased trade would actually increase business opportunities for the guild. In essence, the Savi was arguing that business growth and the inviolability of the market were standards that needed to be maintained if the Venetians were to prosper. This type of thinking demonstrates that competition at the time of petition was seen, at least from the perspective of the Savi, as good for everybody. The Savi argued for a market standard in what amounted to a dispute between two groups. They believed that the Venetian state would benefit in terms of increased revenue and other commercial groups would gain from expanded business activities.

The idea of a level playing field appealed to other groups as well. In March 1578 Venetian merchants argued that an additional payment that had been adopted by the government put them at a disadvantage in regard to Jewish, Turkish and Greek merchants who were trading in the city.[78] In the end, while hoping to assuage

---

[76] Carlo Poni, "Local market rules and practices: Three guilds in the same line of production in early modern Bologna," in *Domestic strategies: Work and Family in France and Italy 1600–1800*, ed. Stuart Woolf (Cambridge: Cambridge University Press and Editions de la Maison des Sciences de l'Homme, 1991), pp.77–78. On guilds also see Richard Mackenney, *Tradesmen and Traders: The World of the Guilds in Venice and Europe* (London: Croon Helm, 1987).

[77] On guilds in the Ottoman Empire see Amnon Cohen, *The Guilds of Ottoman Jerusalem* (Leiden: E.J. Brill, 2004), *Andre Raymond, Artisans et commergants au Caire au XVIIIeme siecle* (Damascus: Institut Francais de Damas, 1973), Charles L. Wilkins, *Forging Urban Solidarities: Ottoman Aleppo 1640–1700* (Leiden: E.J. Brill, 2010), chap. 4, pp. 205–86. Eujong Yi, *Guild Dynamics in Seventeenth Century Istanbul: Fluidity and Leverage* (Leiden: E.J. Brill, 2004).

[78] One of the reasons that the import and export taxes that Ottoman merchants paid were different from those paid by Venetian merchants was because of the number of different taxes that existed. In fact, the problem attracted the attention of the government, and in 1579 the Savi was asked to standardize the tax structure. See Borgherini-Scarabellin, "Il magistrato dei Cinque Savi alla Mercanzia," p. 50.

the merchants' fears that they had been put in a disadvantageous position in regard to the payment, the board did point out that the presence of foreign merchants not only helped bring in extra revenues, but also kept these traders away from competing ports such as Ancona.[79]

Yet the board did not always rule in favor of Ottoman market demands. In the event that Ottoman subjects filed a petition that threatened to reduce state revenues, the Cinque Savi were reluctant to rule in their favor. In August 1635 Ottoman Muslims from Modon and Coron requested that they be allowed to carry empty bottles that were used to transport oils. Fearful that they would take them to Apulia and sell them to Spanish and Portuguese merchants who would avoid coming to Venice, the Savi recommended that these bottles should not be given to Ottoman merchants. Consistent with their decision not to force Ottoman merchants to pay more tax, the Savi anticipated the loss of revenues that could occur if merchants chose to transact business elsewhere.[80]

The determination of the Savi to protect Venetian revenues also applied to situations involving powerful Ottomans, and in 1613 in response to the request of the grand vizir Nasuh not to pay taxes the board replied that

> this new practice of not paying excise duties on merchandise brought to this city would do great damage to the public good, because if merchandise were to be exempted at the request of the leading Turkish ministers all goods would henceforth be said to belong to them. Hence your customs revenue would, every day, be diminished by similar requests. So we do not believe that any such damaging steps should be taken that prejudice the public good, but recommend that, in order to make this business go smoothly, your lordships should as a favor make some kind of donation to the representatives of the grand vizier when he comes with his merchandise to Venice.[81]

Even in a case where one of the most powerful members of the Ottoman court had made a request, the risk of setting a precedent made the Venetians think twice about giving in to the grand vezir's demands.

More importantly the issue of a tax break touched on very complicated cross-cultural expectations. While, as a member of the Ottoman elite, the grand vezir may have thought that he should not have to pay taxes, the Venetians were worried

---

[79] A.S.V., Cinque Savi alla Mercanzia, Risposte, prime serie, busta 136, foglio 104V.

[80] A.S.V., Cinque Savi alla Mercanzia, Risposte, prime serie, busta 150, foglio 70R.

[81] A.S.V., Cinque Savi alla Mercanzia, Risposte, prime serie, busta 144, foglio 166R–V. "…come questa introduttione de non pagar datii delle mercantie che vengono condotte in questa città sarebbe una introduttione, che apportarebbe molto maleficio al pubblico, poiche sotto questa coperta di essentar le mercantie ad istanza de principali ministri Turcheschi, tutte le mercantie da giu avanti, per diverse vie, si fariano di ragione di questi suggeti ondi li suoi Datii resterieno molto aggravati ogni latro giorno da simili instanze, et peró noi non sentimo che in alcuna maniera sia dato principio a far questo foro tanto pregiudiciale al per temperamento di questo negotio fosse da VV fatto qualche gentilezza di donativo a gli intervienti di detto Signor Visir. Quando capiterá con sue mercantie a Venetia."

about protecting an increasingly important source of revenue. This issue persisted over time because in 1546 Sultan Süleyman complained in a letter sent to the Doge Francesco Donà that Ağa Bey, a Muslim merchant, had been unjustly put in prison for refusing to pay the customs tax. The issue of taxes was one on which the Ottomans felt they could convince the Venetians to recant.[82] As members of the privileged estate in the Ottoman Empire, Ottoman officials were not accustomed to paying taxes. Ottoman society was divided into two distinct groups: one was the *reaya* or the segment of society that was expected to pay taxes, and the other the *askeri* or the military class and the bureaucrats who were not obliged to do so.[83] Tax issues with the Venetians must have been both contentious and politically charged. In an order sent to an official in Dubrovnik in 1590 from the Porte, the Porte asked the official not to charge Zaim Mustafa any tax on the silk that he was bringing to Venice. In the absence of a gift, tax concessions were payments that were culturally acceptable on both sides and could be handled in such a way as to avoid other complications.[84]

In cases such as these power politics entered into the equation as much as anything else. Differences were mediated through a cultural exchange that involved constant negotiations over standards, laws and practices. The Venetians understood that while they wanted to maintain control over tariffs and trade rights, they also had to grant many exceptions. Venetian traders in the eastern Mediterranean were no longer numerous enough to sustain Venetian import and export requirements; the Venetians were also dependent on Ottoman Jewish and Muslim traders who had powerful backing. This dependence and the realization of the necessity of accommodating Ottoman traders in Venice created a set of circumstances that allowed Ottoman Muslims to insert themselves into Venetian society and allowed them to petition the Venetian government with the counsel of the Cinque Savi alla Mercanzia in matters involving conflict.

The Uskok Attack: Mediating Potential Conflict

On the November 22, 1587 one of these conflicts arose. The Venetian Senate announced that it had been informed by the count of Lesina[85] that a Venetian ship carrying the goods of a number of Muslim merchants and assigned protection by the galley ship of Giovanni Battista Calbo had been attacked by Uskoks. In a very somber tone, the Senate proclaimed that these types of attacks must not be permitted and that without further delay an investigation must be launched to determine what had happened. Rumors abounded that Calbo and his crew had been lax in their defense of the merchant ship and some even went so far as to suggest

---

[82]   Pedani. *I documenti turchi*, p. 154.

[83]   For an overview of this subject see Halil Inalcik, *The Ottoman Empire: The Classical Age* (London: Weidenfeld & Nicholson, 1973), chap. 9.

[84]   Başbakanlik Arşivi Mühimme Defteri, cilt 67, sira 20.

[85]   Lesina was an island north of Ragusa and across from the mouth of the Neretva.

that Calbo had been in league with the Uskoks. At a time when the promise of protection of foreign merchants had great economic and political importance, the accusations against Calbo caused the Venetian government great concern.[86]

The case raised not only the issue of Venetian law and treaties, but also the question of protection, an issue central to Ottoman/Venetian relations. Because of the importance of the matter the Quarantia investigated the case. The Quarantia had the power to overturn cases that had been tried in lower courts and also to conduct inquiries and investigations, but in this case, they seemed more interested in gathering information and questioning witnesses.

In his testimony, the galley ship's captain Giovanni Calbo declared that en route to the mouth of the Neretva he had stopped at San Zorzi, the chief port of Liesna. At about four in the morning a contingent of Uskok ships and a number of people from the land had launched a raid against the merchant ship and Calbo's galley. Quickly subduing the merchant ship, the Uskoks made a swift escape with Calbo in pursuit. Arguing that he had done everything that he could, Calbo claimed that he had followed the attackers to a place called Proprochvenil. At this point, convinced that he could not pursue the attackers any further on land, he gave up his chase, found the abandoned merchant ship and returned to Lesina.[87]

The captain of the merchant ship, Marco Scuro, added that his ship had been carrying 15 Turkish and some other Jewish merchants. They had embarked from Venice to go to the mouth of the Neretva, but for convenience had stopped in Ancona. To protect them against Uskok attacks, Muslim merchants had requested a galley. Accompanied by the galley, the merchant ship crossed the Adriatic and proceeded to their destination. In support of Calbo, Scuro stated that after the Uskoks had taken control of the ship, they sailed to the island of Barazzo with the galley in pursuit. Somewhere along the way, the galley had abandoned the chase and the Uskoks had taken their Muslim prisoners ashore. Given that three Muslims had been killed and two had possibly escaped, he thought that about ten people had been taken captive in total.[88]

This raid corresponded to standard Uskok attacks. Two men, Luca and Bertoldo, who had come into contact with Uskoks prior to the attack, asserted that during the raid the Uskoks had cried out to Calbo that they were interested in attacking Muslims, not Christians.[89] The principal aim of the Uskok raiding activities was to seize the goods of Jews and Turks. Frequently, Uskoks boarded ships and declared that the Christians on the ship had nothing to fear because the attack was directed specifically against the enemies of Christendom. In some instances, Christian seamen even assisted the attackers.[90]

---

[86]   A.S.V., Quarantia Criminale, busta 99, fascicolo 47.
[87]   A.S.V., Quarantia Criminale, busta 99, fascicolo 47, foglio 3R.
[88]   A.S.V., Quarantia Criminale, busta 99, fascicolo 47, fogli 6R–7V.
[89]   A.S.V., Quarantia Criminale, busta 99, fascicolo 47, fogli 26V–29R.
[90]   Bracewell, *Uskoks of Senj*, p. 211.

Personal motives apart, a Venetian galley captain would have had some incentive to allow such an attack to take place in that it damaged an Ottoman port at the mouth of the Neretva. Soon after the incident, Split became the principal center of Adriatic trade. Conceivably, the Venetians had a motivation to demonstrate that the mouth of the Neretva was an indefensible spot. Yet that said, it seems unlikely that Venetians would have allowed Calbo to get off the hook for a transgression that was clearly a breach of Ottoman/Venetian security agreements. In all probability, the Venetians were anxious to know which of their subjects, particularly which galley captains, might have been working with the Uskoks. The fact that no one came forward to claim that Calbo had any direct contact with the Uskoks, along with the confirmation from witnesses that Calbo had fired on the merchant ship after the Uskoks had commandeered it, must have convinced the Venetians of his innocence. In this regard, the Venetians were probably more interested in discovering a significant breach of loyalty than they were in determining whether the galley had provided maximum defense. Once these fears had been assuaged, they could then handle the problem of how to address the claims of the Muslim merchants.

One of the ways to address their claims was through direct testimonies. As with the arguments heard by the Cinque Savi, direct testimonies were a way to balance the problems that arose regarding trade. In this respect, Ottoman-Venetian trade represented a partnership, a partnership filled with difficulties, but a partnership nonetheless. While one might assume that Muslim merchants were only interested in gaining what they could from this partnership, the reverse was true. A number of merchants actually supported Calbo and defended his actions. Schender, a merchant from Sarajevo, stated that the Uskoks had gotten aboard the ship by claiming that they were fishermen and friends. After the crew of the galley had realized what happened, they fired three shots.[91] Agreeing with Schender, Mürüvvet Demirocciel, another merchant from Bosnia, reiterated that after realizing that the merchant ship was under attack, the galley had fired on the Uskoks. Mürüvvet contended that the galley had not tried to do more, because after commandeering the merchant ship, the Uskoks had turned their guns on the galley. Any further action by the galley would have put the merchants and their merchandise in danger.[92]

Some Muslim merchants, perhaps, were confident that the Venetians would honor their promise to return the merchants' goods. As in any good partnership, a high degree of trust seems to have existed. Mürüvvet commented that after he had escaped, he headed to Zadar to recover the goods that he had left on the ship.[93] Another one of the Muslims captured, Yusuf from Bosnia, testified that the Captain of Uskok affairs Pisani[94] went to Segne and negotiated his release from

---

[91]   A.S.V., Quarantia Criminale busta 99, fascicolo 47, fogli 76V–77R.

[92]   A.S.V., Quarantia Criminale busta 99, fascicolo 47, fogli 29R–30V.

[93]   A.S.V., Quarantia Criminale busta 99, fascicolo47, foglio 30V.

[94]   In the case Pisani is referred to as Captain Pisani.

prison.[95] These merchants seemed comfortable with the fact that the Venetians would act quickly to correct any wrongdoing. However, not all the merchants on the ship pursued this approach. Another group of Bosnians arrived in Venice with a messenger from the Porte demanding that they receive compensation for the goods that they had lost.[96] They undoubtedly understood that, since they had received the backing of the Porte, this type of pressure would be effective. Their strategy worked because in the end they received more than ten thousand ducats and dropped their complaints against Calbo.[97] This averted a larger crisis and in accepting the money the Ottomans declared:

> We the *silahdars* of the Noble Sultan have been sent to the leaders of Venice and we Murüvvet, Kāsim, Ibrahim, Hacı Şaman and Ali in regard to all our demands, declare that we have legally received the goods that have been recovered from the Uskoks by the Venetian leaders. We received from Vincenzo Alessandri, the value of the goods, 10,000 ducats each of which ducat is 6 lire.[98]

In this case the guaranteed protection and the accompanying cooperation between states had worked. The affected parties employed a Venetian legal system that was user friendly for Muslim merchants, while also applying political pressure through connections to powerful Ottomans officials. Both strategies could be effective, and though one might think of Ottoman/Venetian relations in more political terms, one must consider that the Venetians had constructed a legal system whereby Ottoman Muslims could voice their complaints effectively and expeditiously.

---

[95] A.S.V., Quarantia Criminale busta 99, fascicolo 47, foglio 69R.

[96] A.S.V., Deliberazioni Constantinopoli registro 7, foglio 165R, August 10, 1589.

[97] A.S.V., Deliberazioni Constantinopoli registro 7, foglio 187R, February 8, 1590.

[98] A.S.V., Documenti Turchi busta 8, fascicolo 998. "Biz bāli dergāh-I āli silahadarlarından, pādişāh hazretlerinin cānib-I şeriflerinden Venedik Beyleri hazaretlerine irsāl olunup ve biz Murüvvet ve Kāsım ve Ibrahim ve Hacı Şahman ve Ali bizim icün ve cümle metālib icün ikrār-I sahih iderüz kim itdügümüz îbrā mücebince Venedik beyleri hazretterlinin kordırgaların Uskok eliden kurtardiklar rızıkların cümle bahaları icün kendü talebimiz Vicenzo Alessandri 10,000 nakd dukat her dukat altı lidre."

Chapter 3
Moving Across Boundaries

In a case reviewed by the Cinque Savi in 1642, testimony revealed that a young woman named Lucia appeared one night at the home of the *podestà*, administrator, of Rovigno (Rovini),[1] pleading for help and stating that her relatives, a group of Muslims from Bosnia, had forced her onto a ship in Venice in order to return her to the family home in Sarajevo. The case was complicated. Lucia had arrived in Venice initially at the request of the podestà. No evidence explains his request, but it may have been connected with Lucia's assertion that she converted to Christianity. Yet problems developed, for this claim was disputed by her relatives who not only came to Venice to retrieve her, but also stated that they had received permission from the Cinque Savi to take her back home.

In the hearing, witnesses testified that after marrying a Muslim from Drniš,[2] Lucia left him and went to Šibenik (Sebenico)[3] where she stayed with a count. Accused of living licentiously, Lucia proceeded to Zadar where, because of the protestations of her family, she was put into a convent. Not happy with this living situation, she sought the assistance of a group of people who vowed to help her return to her husband. Yet she found herself in trouble again and turned to a man named Olidio Zaroffolo, who sent her to Piove di Sacco to serve his wife. Claiming that she was a Christian who had been baptized in Zadar, she left and took passage with a group of women who came to Venice. Not long after arriving there, she was tracked down by her relatives with the assistance of a woman named Lucietta and another local who held her in the *Fondaco dei Turchi* until her family could leave for Ottoman territories. Escaping in Rovigno, Lucia took refuge at the home of the podestà.[4]

This case provides a view of a woman who crossed state boundaries from Ottoman territories to Venice, who converted to Christianity and who left her family. It also provides a window on Venice's relationship with its periphery

---

[1]   Rovigno (Rovini) is a town on the Istrian coast. For a study of Venetian officials along the Dalmatian coast see Monique O'Connell, *Men of Empire: Power and Negotiation in Venice's Maritime State* (Baltimore: The Johns Hopkins University Press, 2009)

[2]   Drniš is located in Croatia.

[3]   Šibenik is a Croatian city on the Dalmatian coast.

[4]   A.S.V., Avogaria di Comun, Miscellanea Penale, busta 343, fascicolo 11, 1642. While the case is listed in the miscellaneous cases of the Avogaria di Comun, the heading states that it was tried by the Savi. No final verdict was included. Some of the material from this chapter was taken from Stephen Ortega, "Pleading for Help: Gender relations and Cross-Cultural logic in the Early Modern Mediterranean," *Gender & History,* vol. 20, no. 2 (2008), pp. 332–48.

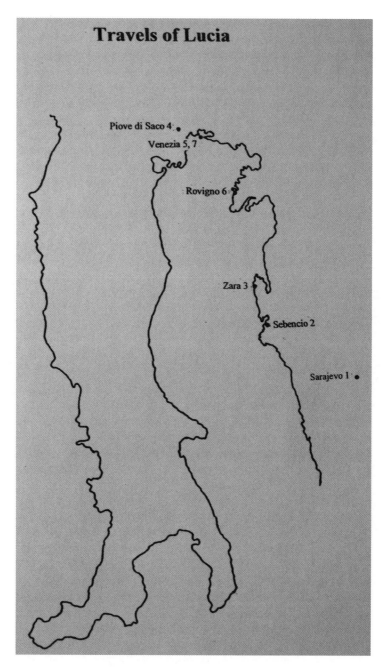

Fig. 3.1   Map of Lucia's travels. Drawn by author.

and with adjacent territories in the Ottoman Empire. Both the Venetians and the Ottomans tried to manage cross-cultural contact in areas in which boundaries between Christians and Muslims were more blurred. Different institutional bodies, including the Cinque Savi, also had to decide what type of social placement was appropriate for a person looking for sanctuary. In a complicated cases such as this one a generic solution did not exist, and issues such as the maintenance of borders, religious identity and the rights of male family members all had to be weighed carefully.

Contact Zones and Border Management

In contrast to others who claimed that her father was a Bosnian Muslim man named Braduvit, Lucia testified that he was a Christian named Catrade who had died in Jerusalem.[5] Soliciting this testimony, the Venetians, and in particular the Cinque Savi, were attempting to understand the legitimacy of the evidence each side was using to bolster its case. While the Venetians would have been interested in protecting someone who had been forcibly converted from Christianity to Islam, gaining a clear understanding of Lucia's background would have been important in deciding where she needed to be placed.

Given that she lived in Bosnia, conceivably a part of Lucia's family was Muslim and another part Christian.[6] The death of her father could have meant that his guardianship passed to another group of relatives who lived in the same household. She did make the distinction that the Braduvit family was her *casata*. This reference could have applied to either her extended or her nuclear family. Balkan families during this time were considered some of the largest in the world,[7] and a so-called Muslim 'uncle' was amongst the group of people who came to claim her in Venice. While we have no way of knowing her exact relationship to this man, having a Muslim uncle did not preclude her from having a Christian father and may explain why one of the ship's mates commented that she was confused as to whether she was a Muslim or a Christian.[8]

In considering this testimony, the Venetians would have been conscious of the fact that one of the defining characteristics of the western Balkans was that Muslims and Christians did not sense the same psychological, social or cultural separation that existed for people in Venice and even Istanbul. The traveler George Wheler, an English physician, commented that "the Christians here, for want of good instruction, and able and faithful pastors to teach them, run daily into apostasie, and renounce their religion for Turkish superstition, upon every small calamity and discontent that happens to them; and this not only among

---

[5]   A.S.V., Avogaria di Comun, Miscellenea Penale, busta 343, fascicolo 11.

[6]   Gábor Ágoston and Bruce Masters, eds., *Encyclopedia of the Ottoman Empire* (New York: Facts on File, 2009), p. 146.

[7]   Stoianovich. *Between East and West*, p. 140.

[8]   A.S.V., Avogaria di Comun, Miscellanea Penale, busta 343, fascicolo 11.

the common people, but even of the priests also."[9] The process of Islamization had not begun to gain a strong foothold in the Balkans until the early sixteenth century.[10] Here, contact was formed under different circumstances and boundaries were blurred by a greater sense of heterodoxy. Traveling on a Venetian diplomatic mission in 1550, Catarino Zeno noted that, in an Orthodox monastery in Milesevo, Muslims and Jews gave alms to the monastery and had prayers read to them by monks.[11] Similarly, Alexander Lopasic points out that "(a) Muslim could be witness to a Christian wedding or a godfather to his neighbor's children. The opposite, godfather-hood to a Muslim child at circumcision, would help towards establishing good neighborliness, so important to Muslim villagers."[12] In areas that were weakly supported by the Church the shift from popular Christianity to popular Islam was not very significant and people continued into the nineteenth century with many of the same practices that they had undertaken before.[13]

Contributing to the heterogeneity of the region and the difficulty of separating different communities was the fact that these territories were located at the crossroads of different civilizations. As local Christian forces fell during the fifteenth and sixteenth centuries, Ottoman conquests brought the Empire to the shores of the Adriatic. The Christian states of Venice and the Habsburgs bordered the westernmost territories of the Ottoman Empire, and Islam and western Christianity converged.

This political geography created a number of different connections which psychologically impacted local populations. Along the frontier, borders and

---

[9]   George Wheler, *A Journey into Greece* (London: Cademan, 1682), p. 441, cited in Noel Malcolm, *Bosnia: A Short History* (London: Macmillan London Limited, 1994), p. 58.

[10]   See Colin Heywood, "Bosnia Under Ottoman Rule," in *The Muslims of Bosnia-Herzogevina: Their Historic Development from the Middle Ages to the Dissolution of Yugoslavia*, ed. Mark Pinson (Cambridge, Ma.: Distributed for the Center for Middle Eastern Studies of Harvard University by Harvard University Press, 1996), pp. 22–53. Also see Malcolm, *Bosnia*, p.52. Malcom's information comes from N. Filipoviç, "Napomene o islamizaciju u Bosni i Hervegovini u 15. vijeku," Godišnjak akademije nauka umjetnosti Bosne i Hercegovene vol. 7, (1967), pp. 141–67. Malcolm notes that in the first few years after the conquest in the areas of east and central Bosnia 332 households were Muslim, while 37,125 households were Christian. This had changed significantly by the 1520s when the *defters* for the sanjack beyi of Bosnia counted 98, 095 Christians and 84, 675 Muslims. Evidence indicates that there was very little migration into the area, suggesting that the larger proportion of Muslims was because of conversions. Malcom also adds that by the late sixteenth and early seventeenth centuries that the Muslims had an absolute majority.

[11]   Alexander Lopasic, "Islamization of the Balkans," *Journal of Islamic Studies*, vol. 5, no. 2 (1994), p. 176.

[12]   Ibid., p. 175.

[13]   Abdusalem Balagija, *Les Musulmans yougoslaves* (Algiers: La Maison de livres, 1940), p. 31.

control of subject populations were constantly under dispute.[14] In a treaty agreed to in 1540 the Venetians and Ottomans reached an understanding that while certain towns were to be returned to Venetian control, Nauplia and Malvasia, two Venetian towns in the province of Morea, would now be considered Ottoman possessions. This understanding not only involved a cessation of hostilities but also a formal change in bureaucratic control.[15] Movement across the borders was commonplace. Christians used Ottoman mills to grind their wheat, Ottoman subjects worked on Christian lands and Muslim merchants traded in towns along the Dalmatian coast.[16] In this contact zone, Alexander Lopasic argues "groups developed eventually into a real frontier society with a thriving existence as intermediaries between the two opposing worlds, rather than becoming a center of further invasion and conquest."[17] An Ottoman judge could go to the Venetian port of Split to witness a document.[18] In a chronicle of events along the Dalmatian coast in 1575, Antonio Giustiniano commented that in regard to Cattaro[19] "every day many Turks congregate there and some of them also stay the night...."[20]

Each state looked to limit this type of non-sanctioned form of contact and developed different ways to intervene. In 1570 the Porte sent a correspondence to the bey of Dökakin telling him that Ali Bey had a close relationship with the Venetians and had to be watched.[21] In a case brought before the Quarantia in March of 1587, the counts of Possedaria[22] were accused of eating, drinking and interacting with Muslims who lived in the vicinity. Although the charges made by the provveditore and the *signori* of Novegradi (Novigrad), a coastal town in the vicinity of Possedaria, may have been fabricated as a vendetta,[23] the inquiry demonstrates the measures the Venetians took to control unwanted forms of exchange.

Part of the problem for the Venetian court was that constant interaction between the people of the two villages represented a cultural affinity. Some of the Venetian

---

[14] Peter Sahlins makes the point that "Political geographers, following conventional usage, generally distinguish 'boundaries' from 'frontiers'. The first evokes a precise, linear division, within a restrictive political context; the second connotes more zonal qualities and a broader, social context." Frontiers seems a more appropriate term for division between Ottoman and Venetian lands. Peter Sahlins, *Boundaries: The Making of France and Spain in the Pyrenees* (Berkeley: University of California Press, 1989), p. 4.

[15] Pedani, *I Documenti Turchi*, p. 139.

[16] Bracewell, *The Uskoks of Senj*, p. 33.

[17] Lopasic, "Islamization of the Balkans," p. 174.

[18] See chapter 5 introduction.

[19] Cattaro is a city in Albania.

[20] V. Solitro ed., *Documenti storici sull'Istria e La Dalmazia*, vol. 1 (Venezia: Coi tipi della ved. di G. Gattei, 1844), p. 82.

[21] Başbakanlik Arşivi, Mühimme Defteri, cilt 9, sira 199.

[22] Possedaria (Posedarje) was a Venetian possession along the Dalmatian coast.

[23] Preto, *I servizi segreti di Venezia*, p. 104.

subjects in the case spoke Turkish. Speaking Turkish would have made sense for people who lived on the Ottoman frontier. They not only have had relations with other Slavonic-speaking Muslims, but in all likelihood also had significant dealings with Turkish-speaking Ottoman officials. Venetian and Ottoman officials relied on one another for information and assistance. Zuane Babicul and Grayco, two Venetian subjects, were on their way to speak with a local potentate, Ahmed, when they found out about the actions of the people from Possedaria. These types of negotiations must have been fairly common and represented the high degree of cooperation that existed. Some of the charges against the Possedarians were founded on information that Mattio Memesich, a captain of one of the armed ships that had been sent to handle problems on the frontier, claimed had been imparted to him by a close friend, Yusuf, a Muslim from Ucitegl.[24]

Not all border relationships were amenable, and states attempted to use local officials and political proxies to maintain order and control over subjects who failed to acknowledge political frontiers.[25] In late 1582 Murad III wrote to the sanjack beyi of Kerka İdris[26] that due to complaints from the Venetian bailo the sanjack beyi should prevent incursions of Turkish subjects into Venetian territory.[27] The local governor was expected to control the activities of individuals who threatened to disrupt the peace. Preventing attacks was also the intention of the *beylerbey* of Bosnia, Murteza Pasha, when he agreed to prevent further wrongdoings against Venetian subjects, if the Venetians, in return, took action against a Venetian *provveditore*, administrator, who had made raids into Ottoman lands, kidnapped local subjects and erected a fort in the district of Ptrova Gora.[28]

Control over borders and surveillance of people were dependent on informants who passed on "suspicious activities" to the state. In 1576, Mazzarello who lived near Split, informed Giacomo Soranzo, the Venetian bailo, that Venetian subjects

---

[24]   Another case is also interesting in this regard. In Zadar in 1571 the marquis Rongonis discovered a case of treason. It was revealed that Comici of Istria, Giovanni of Este and two brothers from Zadar, Sime and Vidio Salavich had agreed to help the Turks take the city. For a lengthy period of time the aforementioned had been involved in secret talks at the home of the priest Rotta. Here, they decided that they would take control of the city's cannon and when chaos ensued, they would open the gates of the city to allow the Turks in. The plan might have worked if it weren't for the fact that the elderly serving woman of Rotta revealed the plot to Antonio from Ravenna who told the heads of the city, forcing the plotters to flee. See Solitro, *Documenti storici*, pp. 171–2.

[25]   Garrett Mattingly makes an important point in this regard. He comments that in fifteenth-century Europe because of the vast spaces in many places diplomacy was not conducted with the same vigilance that it is today; however, this was not true in Italy. Italian states were constantly aware of the machinations of their neighbors. This probably held true also for the Venetian and Ottomans at least on the Dalmatian coast. Garrett Mattingly, *Renaissance Diplomacy* (New York: Dover Publications, 1988), pp. 51–2.

[26]   An area along the Dalmatian coast.

[27]   Pedani, *I documenti turchi*, p. 229.

[28]   Pedani, *I documenti turchi*, p. 348.

had crossed the border and were cutting down trees that were now in Ottoman territory.[29] Given that the territories referred to lands over which the Ottoman government had very recently gained control, Venetian agents like Mazzarello had some incentive to monitor these developments. More importantly Mazzarello's understanding of the border included an acceptance of fixed boundaries. Artificial in certain ways, borders did differentiate territories in both the eyes of the state and the eyes of the local population.

Yet state intervention involved more than just maintaining control over borders. The state could also be compelled to play a role in personal and local disputes. These types of conflicts not only threatened trade, but also endangered very delicate relations along the border. Notably, this was the case when the Venetian government received word that the brother of the *voyvoda* of Popodoric had asked the Ottoman government to obtain blood money from the Venetians because a Venetian subject had killed his brother. The money was paid and the Venetian government made it clear that news of the payoff should be forwarded to the bailo so that he could tell the appropriate people at the Ottoman court.[30] Taking this action was a way of addressing local exigencies, while also advancing state interests.

People became involved in controversies that, although very local in nature, breached territorial jurisdiction and undermined the ability of states to protect their subjects from their neighbors on the other side of the border. Some of these disputes involved kidnappings. In February 1627 the Ottoman government sent a letter to the Venetians informing them that Ottoman officials believed that a Venetian subject had kidnapped the daughter of the *dizdar*[31] of the fort of Klis, Ahmed Ağa and taken her to Split.[32] The Ottomans contended that in Split she had been surrounded by thirty to forty priests and other men and women and forced to convert to Christianity. After her conversion, she was taken to Venice where, according to the testimonies of some Muslim merchants who were there at the time, she was now to be found in prison.[33] While further evidence revealed that she was not kidnapped but instead had chosen to leave her family to avoid being forced into an unwanted marriage, the case does reveal that governments wanted to make sure that when kidnappers crossed borders, they did not find safe havens. Kidnappings were common occurrences along the Dalmatian coast and constituted a significant source of revenue for people who participated in them. Many kidnapped Muslims ended up as either domestics, galley slaves on Christian ships, or laborers on estates. Women were particularly valuable resources as

---

[29]   Pedani, *I documenti turchi*, p. 218.

[30]   A.S.V., Senato Deliberazioni Constantinopoli, registro 4, foglio 50V, May 23, 1577.

[31]   Warden of a local castle.

[32]   For a more detailed account of this case see Eric Dursteler, *Renegade Women: Gender, Boundaries and Identity in the Early Modern Mediterranean* (Baltimore, Johns Hopkins Press, 2011) pp. 63–75

[33]   A.S.V., *I Documenti Turchi*, busta 12, fascicolo 1352.

domestics and many times merchants purchased them along the Dalmatian coast and then sold them to households in Italy.[34]

Strategies pursued by people whose relatives had run away willingly were similar to those of kidnapped families' victims. In 1579 the Porte sent a hüküm[35] to the bey of Klis[36] telling him that a certain Hamza was claiming that a Venetian had taken his daughter Fatma to Venice. The Porte ordered the bey to see if any of the Venetian border guards had seen or knew anything about these people.[37] Similarly, a declaration issued by an Ottoman judge in 1594 announced that a Christian who was married to a Muslim who lived in the European neighborhood of Galata had escaped to Venice with a Christian trader.[38] In trying to facilitate her return, Ahmed Ağa pursued his daughter all the way to Venice and gained an audience with the Collegio.[39] We see similarities in this case to that of Lucia: a change in religious identity, a trip to Venice and an attempt by the family to recover her.

People attempted to cross borders in order to gain political refuge, not in the modern sense, where a person is granted very specific political rights by a sovereign state, but instead for a promise of physical safety from one's enemies. After numerous abuses and the kidnapping of two of his children by the count of Trau (Trogir), Girolamo Fasaneo, a Venetian subject, escaped to Ragusa (Dubrovnik). Living in exile for six years, Fasaneo continued to send letters to Venice asking for the return of his children and the restitution of his property. In time, after converting to Islam and taking the name of Receb, he gained the support of Ottoman officials, including the beylerbey of Bosnia. This support, though, proved ineffective and the Venetians not only continued to ignore his requests, but also persisted in their attempts to kill him. Ultimately, after surviving numerous attempts on his life, Receb enlisted the support of the Porte by promising that if he could recover his lands, he would guarantee the sultan an extra 200,000 ducats in revenues a year.[40]

Receb's attempt to find refuge had many parallels with people who were forced into exile. Individuals who found themselves on the losing end of a dispute with a rival faction, rather than face imprisonment or death, chose to be sent away as a form of punishment. Gaining refuge for Receb necessitated gaining acceptance from another state and a supportive faction. Recognizing that this person or group of people had been on the losing side of a factional dispute, the granting state

---

[34]　Bracewell, *Uskoks of Senj*, p. 101–2.

[35]　An imperial decree.

[36]　Klis is in central Dalmatia.

[37]　Başbakanlik Arşivi, Mühimme Defteri, cilt 36, sira 362.

[38]　A.S.V., Documenti Turchi, busta 9, fascicolo 1052.

[39]　Dursteler, *Renegade Women*, p. 71.

[40]　Pedani, *I documenti turchi*, p. 376.

provided these refugees with the guarantee of safety and with a place in a new community.[41]

Yet granting refuge because of a factional dispute should be seen more as an ongoing negotiation than a permanent arrangement. Factional politics changed, and people changed alliances frequently. In a complicated affair noted in an anonymous diary that not only included an inheritance dispute between the families of Piero Baciccio and Simeon Alberti but also a love affair between Piero Baciccio and Elena Alberti, Piero Baciccio fled with his mother from Split and escaped to Klis, a town that was controlled by the Ottomans. Given the command of a number of men and promising great booty to those who would return with him to fight his enemies, Piero returned to the territories outside of Split to take his revenge. Yet developments did not work out the way that Piero expected. For upon his return, after killing a young man, Piero found out that the person he had killed was an Alberti and related to his beloved Elena. Weeping in the streets of Split, Piero was reluctant to return to Klis, but his traveling retinue threatened him, stating that if he did not return with them they would harm his mother. However, Piero was cunning and, not long after returning, decided that he would again try to return to Split. One night he and his mother obtained horses and attempted to leave. On the way, however, he encountered difficulties and was stopped by Yunus Bey and his men. Yunus called to Piero, stating that he was under orders from the sanjack beyi to prevent Piero from leaving Klis . Piero, though, was fortunate, for Yunus was willing to let him go, remembering that Piero had spared his life a year earlier. Aware of his good fortune and affectionately calling him 'my brother,' Piero embraced Yunus before departing.[42]

Containing a strange series of twists and turns, this case shows that, following his feud with the Albertis, the leaders of Klis quickly embraced Piero. The chronicler noted that when Piero arrived in Klis, "the Turks immediately made him secretary and senior dizdar and also gave him forty-two men that he could command...."[43] This example demonstrates the familiarity that existed on both sides of the frontier and shows that protection could be a very personal affair. Piero was not only able to cross borders and find support, he was also given status and a military rank. In all likelihood, he was considered a prominent person and a pivotal player in local politics.

Economic motives also contributed to attempts to find refuge in neighboring territories. In an Inquisition hearing in 1580, a group of Ragusan merchants wrote that in order to swindle another Ragusan, Giovanni di Lorenzo, out of some wool, Andrea di Giovanni had converted to Islam. Stating that Andrea di Giovanni had gone before an Ottoman judge, the merchants claimed that he had taken the name Mustafa Çelebi, changed into Muslim clothes, declared ownership of the

---

[41]   Christine Shaw, *The Politics of Exile in Renaissance Italy* (Cambridge, UK: Cambridge University Press, 2000), p. 7.

[42]   Solitro, *Documenti storici*, pp. 164–70.

[43]   Ibid., p. 165.

wool and placed it in storage with a local resident. Upon hearing this news, in the company of a group of the Ragusan merchants, Giovanni di Lorenzo traveled to Cruscenza[44] where he obtained a ruling from a judge there to have the wool released from the Ottoman subject. However, upon hearing the judge's verdict, Andrea di Giovanni enlisted the support of an Ottoman *emin*[45] who helped him recover the goods. Andrea di Giovanni used the power of a local official not only to avoid the protestations of his creditor, Giovanni di Lorenzo, but also to seek the backing that would help him overrule the local judge. While the border did not provide the cover he needed, the actual physical muscle of a local powerbroker served as sufficient protection. The border in this sense acted not as a line between two civilizations, but rather as a zone that divided the fiefdoms of local elites.[46]

Given the difficulty of preventing movement, the issue of finding refuge probably had a more immediate physical connotation which involved personal protection. Although Lucia's relatives received the permission of the Cinque Savi to return her to Bosnia, they still used their physical power to take her back. Receb's enemies, with the assistance of the bailo, pursued him and attempted to kill him on a number of occasions. The first time, while he was sleeping in a garden in Scutari, a group of people tried to kill him with an ax blow to the head. The second time, while he was traveling on a small boat to Galata, a Venetian ship fired on his vessel.[47] People's ability to cross borders and to insert themselves into other societies did not mean they were free from the threats of their family or other people from where they had originated. When Piero Baciccio crossed the border, he was provided with a group of men to allow him to settle his differences. This entourage guaranteed him a modicum of safety. Family members or sworn enemies were also capable of crossing borders in pursuit of people who had run away and taken up residence elsewhere.

Conversion and Social Placement

Fearing the wrath of her family after escaping, Lucia hoped that by pleading to the podestà of Rovigno that she was a Christian, she would be able to convince a so-called defender of Christianity to take her in and give her protection from her pursuers. Moving from place to place, people used religious conversion as a way of crossing borders and gaining entry into a new community. One's religious identity could be put forward as something that transcended family ties and other social arrangements. Claiming to be a member of a particular religious community

---

44 Cruscenza was near Belgrade.
45 An emin was a local Ottoman official.
46 A.S.V., Sant'Ufficio, busta 46, August 2, 1580.
47 Pedani, *I documenti turchi,* pp. 377–8.

provided entry and a certain degree of acceptance that might not be afforded to a member of another confessional group.[48]

People changed their religions and attempted to integrate themselves into new societies for variety of reasons. Andrea di Giovanni, the Ragusan merchant, changed his religious identity for business reasons and gained the favor of an Ottoman court and a local emin. Receb became a Muslim and received credibility with Ottoman officials. In changing religion, each sought sanctuary from his pursuers. The term sanctuary seems appropriate, not strictly in a legal sense, but more in terms of a sensibility that respected a person's right to seek refuge in a new religion. Legally, sanctuary dated back to classical times, when criminals and slaves sought protection at particular religious shrines. An individual looking to convert had to be accepted in a new place much in the way that a criminal sought sanctuary from another state or group.[49] This arrangement is particularly well illustrated in the cases of individuals who had already converted from their birth religions. To gain protection from the Church, a convert looking to return to Christianity had to come before the Inquisition and make what was termed a "spontaneous confession." An individual making a spontaneous confession was expected to admit his or her transgressions with a sincere heart. This action allowed the person to avoid stiff penalties such as life imprisonment or death.[50]

In order to gain the support of the tribunal in Venice, some individuals claimed that they had been forcibly converted to Islam and appealed for mercy from Inquisition authorities. Nicolo Givancia was born a Christian in the Turkish territories near Cattaro and when his family could not pay tribute, he was kidnapped and forcibly converted to Islam. On a trip to Mecca, he was freed by his patron, and within a month, he traveled to Venice where he ended up in front of the Inquisition, asking to return to Christianity.[51] Luis Hernandez stated in 1591 that he had been born in Portugal and taken by Moors during a war at the age of eight or nine. Forced into slavery he was taken to the Red Sea, where he was sold to a group of Muslims who brought him to Algiers and then to Goleta in Tunisia. Here, he was bought by another group of Muslims who took him to Istanbul where he remained a slave for ten years until being liberated. Claiming that he lived superficially as a

---

[48] On conversion stories see Mercedes Garcia Arenal, *Conversions islamiques: Identities religieuses en Islam méditerranéen* (Paris: Maisonneuve et Larose, 2001), Bartolomé Bennassar and Lucile Bennassar, *Les chrétiens d'Allah: L'histoire extraordinaire des renégats* (Paris: Berin, 1989), Pullan, *Jews of Europe*, Lucia Rostagno, *Mi faccio Turco: Esperienze ed immagini dell'Islam nell'Italia moderna* (Roma: Istituto per l'Oriente C.A. Nalino, 1983), and Lucetta Scaraffia, *Rinnegati: Per una storia dell'identità occidentale* (Roma: Laterza, 1993).

[49] Karl Shoemaker, *Sanctuary and Crime in the Middle Ages, 400–1500* (New York: Fordham University Press, 2010).

[50] Francisco Bethencourt, *The Inquisition: A Global History, 1478–1834* (Cambridge, UK: Cambridge University Press, 2009), p. 184.

[51] A.S.V., Sant'Ufficio, busta 98, June 12, 1642.

Muslim, he worked for his master for another five years, before coming to Venice on a merchant ship, whereupon he immediately came before inquisitors.[52]

Luis Hernandez's case reveals the long-term relationships that some converts had been involved in prior to making their decisions to seek a new life. The difficulty of separating from these ties was undoubtedly connected to the guarantees and security that a patron could provide. This reason probably explains why Hernandez waited five years after being liberated to leave his patron. Evidence exists that the Venetians helped people in this type of situation even when patrons requested their slaves returned. In 1604 when Zulficar Ağa, an Ottoman Muslim, asked the Venetians to return a person that he said was his slave, the Venetians replied they could not return anyone who stated that he or she wanted to live as a Christian. Instead they offered sufficient money.[53]

Fellow Christians provided connections that converts needed to cross the Mediterranean to potential safe havens. Michael de Orlandis stated that he became a Muslim because he felt that he could more easily assist Christians who had been forcibly converted to Islam return to their lands. When he finally decided that he wanted to return to Christian lands he was assisted by the Venetian bailo in Istanbul.[54] Born a Christian to French parents, Herman de Rourve was captured by Tatars at the age of 15 after he had been sent with a French regiment to fight in Hungary. Fifteen years later, he claimed that he had been forced to convert. Subsequently, he married, had four children and moved to Istanbul. All his children were baptized Christians, one while he was in Tatar lands and the other three at the church of San Pietro in Galata. While living outwardly as Muslims, he claimed that he and his family remained spiritually Christians, even at times visiting some of the Christian churches in Istanbul. Deciding that he wanted to receive confession, he went to the French embassy in Istanbul, where he was told by a priest that he would have to go before the Inquisition in order to be accepted back into the Catholic Church.[55]

The recommendation from the priest illustrates that the Inquisition in Venice represented a point of entry and that conversion provided a means for establishing a new life. The influence of the Inquisition is noteworthy in that the board had the institutional power to facilitate this type of cross-cultural transfer. This type of assistance would have been essential for someone who had broken free from former ties and wanted to be accepted into new patronage relationships.[56] Marino Zed said that he had lived in the village of Banjaluka[57] as a Christian until the age of 19, after which he had an altercation with a Turkish soldier and his men who

---

[52]   A.S.V., Sant'Ufficio, busta 68, July 4, 1591.

[53]   A.S.V., Senato Deliberazioni Constantinopoli, registro 10, fogli 29 RV, May 4, 1604.

[54]   A.S.V., Sant'Ufficio, busta 88, October 5, 1632.

[55]   A.S.V., Sant'Ufficio, busta 98, January 16, 1642.

[56]   Rothman, *Brokering Empire,* pp. 122–36.

[57]   Banjaluka is a town in northern Bosnia north of Sarajevo.

allegedly forced him to convert to Islam. Living as a Muslim for four or five years, he first served a local pasha and then was sent to war. Subsequently, while his patron was away in Istanbul, he left Banjaluka and traveled first to Buda and then to Zadar, whence he embarked for Venice to regain his Christianity. Interestingly, he commented that in making the trip to Zadar he had traveled with his father. His father's encouragement could have been one of the reasons that he decided to escape. Regardless of his reason, he understood that coming to a center of Christianity like Venice would allow him to break free of his patron to join a new community.[58]

Breaking free from one's patron and appearing before the Inquisition served as a transitional moment in fitting in to a new place. Christian converts not only had to escape patrons, they also in some cases had to distance themselves from well-established Muslim lives. In 1642, Giulio Ceasero, the son of a Neapolitan, came before the Holy Office and testified that at the age of seven he had been captured by corsairs with a group of other Neapolitans traveling on a ship between Naples and Salerno. Claiming that people had forced him to become a Muslim, he said that a number of a slaves told him that conversion was the best option and he took the name of Mustafa, married a woman named Rasina, and proceeded to have two children, both of whom died. After a number of years of living as a Muslim, and asserting that he wanted to regain his Catholic faith, he departed from the place he was living, leaving his wife behind, and passing through Šibenik before he finally reached Venice. Here he was instructed to go to the Holy Office to tell his story, and there claimed that he had spent 23 Easters in the lands of the Turks.[59] Once again, the Inquisition provided an entry point, a way to build new ties and a means to gain a sanctuary.

The Importance of Gender

Looking for a sanctuary was also a major concern for Elena, a Bosnian woman, who came before the tribunal of the Inquisition asking for forgiveness because she had been forced to convert to Islam. Arguing that the only reason that she had converted was that she had been beaten regularly by the wife of the family she was living with, she stated that when forced to perform Muslim rites she had never done so from the heart. Alleging that she had escaped at the first possible opportunity, she claimed that she was hidden by a Christian and came to Venice not only to regain her Christian faith but also to put distance between herself and the Bosnian world that she had lived in.[60]

Elena's case raises two important questions: did women converts find different types of sanctuary than men, and if they did, why was Elena treated differently

---

[58] A.S.V., Sant'Ufficio, busta 98.
[59] A.S.V., Sant'Ufficio, busta 98, January 21, 1642.
[60] A.S.V., Sant'Ufficio, busta 77.

than Lucia? Both were women who not only decided to leave their family/patrons, but also took to the road. When women crossed borders and solicited the help of the Venetian government, they became involved in affairs that had not only significant social consequences but potentially political ones as well. Apart from the issue of conversion, their actions and their consequences were closely tied to questions as to how states, in this case the Venetian state, treated women who had broken free from their primary relationships and who had now decided to seek out a new social placement.

Gender has become an important criterion for understanding not only how individuals interact, but also how societies are ordered. According to Joan Scott, "gender is a constitutive element of social relationships based on perceived differences between the sexes, and gender is a primary way of signifying relationships of power."[61] It allows us to examine relations more closely between men and women and helps us redirect the focus of our inquiry. Instead of accepting the notion that the sexes are governed by a biological determinism, the study of gender assumes that relations between men and women are shaped by a series of historical, social and cultural factors.[62]

Thinking in terms of how gender impacted early modern conversion, we need to consider how women looking to convert were received by the authorities. For instance, Jewish and Christian narratives in early modern Istanbul demonstrate that in many cases women became Muslims because they realized that conversion might allow them to gain freedom from slavery, to escape bad marriages or to gain custody of their children. These women used Muslim courts to achieve this end, because they realized that the courts would consider a woman's desire to convert to Islam as the central issue in the case.[63] Along similar lines, in Venice, Christian women understood that converting to Islam did not give them the hope of a gaining a title or achieving power, but rather provided them with an opportunity to find an alternative to a depressing life and gave them the chance to fit in in a new place.[64] While we have no empirical data on the types of Muslim women who converted to Christianity in Venice, evidence of new Muslims who submitted conversion petitions to the sultan in the late seventeenth and early eighteenth centuries reveals that the majority of women who converted were either widows or single.[65]

---

[61]   Joan Wallach Scott, *Gender and the Politics of History* (New York: Columbia University Press, 1999), p. 42.

[62]   Ibid., p. 32.

[63]   Marc Baer, "Islamic Conversion Narratives of Women: Social Change and Gendered Hierarchy in Early Modern Istanbul," *Gender & History*, vol. 16, no. 2 (2004), pp. 425–58.

[64]   Anna Vanzan, "In Search of Another Identity: Female Muslim-Christian Conversions in the Mediterranean World," *Islam and Christian-Muslim Relations*, vol. 7, no. 3 (1996), pp. 327–33 and Dursteler, *Renegade Women*.

[65]   Anton Minkov, *Conversion to Islam in the Balkans: Kisve Bahasi Petitions and Ottoman Social Life, 1670–1730* (Leiden: E.J. Brill, 2004), pp. 170–71.

While Lucia was technically married, she had been separated from her family which put her in the same demographic category as the women who approached the Ottoman government and looked to free themselves from former commitments.[66] The controversy over her religious identity had to do with a dispute between Lucia and her male relatives. They pursued her, and through means such as physical coercion and legal maneuvering, attempted to bring her back.

Basing their case on social norms that stretched across the Mediterranean, their arguments, exhortations and demands shaped perceptions of her during the trial. As mentioned, Lucia had married a Muslim from Drniŝ. According to cultural norms of the time, a marriage arrangement had been worked out between her family and her husband's: hence her own family's anxiety to return her to him. Their belief was explicitly stated when they mentioned that Lucia had escaped from her husband. This notion echoed the types of references that were made to slaves.[67]

Men and women during the early modern period did not base most marriages on the concept of romantic love and mutual consent. Islamic concepts of marriage in the Ottoman Empire were based on the idea that "the ultimate logic of the laws of marriage and the closely related laws of slavery is to create, not a family around the persons of husband and wife, but a patriarchal household."[68] In seventeenth-century Kayseri, while marriage was theoretically the choice of the bride and groom, the discretion of the family and societal pressures ultimately determined the decision.[69] Similar conditions existed in Italy. During the Renaissance, Guido Ruggiero comments that "marriage was a significant form of social and economic placement...."[70] Sandra Cavallo and Simona Cerutti in their study of marital relations in Piedmont add that "the marital relationship, by legitimating female sexuality, represented the situation of the greatest security and was recognized as fully honorable. Outside of this form of stable bond with a man, the female figure

---

[66] Ibid., p. 189.

[67] This is not a commentary on Islamic society or Muslim men of the time. This point is only made to demonstrate that the witness testifying as recorded by the scribe in the Avogaria di Comun used the word "escape." This is as much a commentary on Venetian attitudes as it is on relatives of Lucia.

[68] Colin Imber, "Women, Marriage and Property: Mahr in the Behcetü'l-Fetava of Yenişehirli. Abdullah" in *Women in the Ottoman Empire: Middle Eastern Women in the Early Modern Era*, ed. Madeline Zilfi (Leiden: E.J. Brill, 1997), p. 82.

[69] Ronald C. Jennings, "Women in Early Seventeenth Century Ottoman Judicial Records: The Sharia Court of Anatolian Kayseri," *Journal of the Social and Economic History of the Orient*, vol. 18, Part I (January 1975), p.76. Jennings believes that a family would exercise great caution in arranging a marriage for fear of ending up in court and also the risk of having shame brought upon them.

[70] Guido Ruggiero, *Binding Passions: Tales of Magic, Marriage and Power at the End of the Renaissance* (New York: Oxford University Press, 1993), p. 14.

was, in fact, regarded with suspicion and distrust...."[71] These social expectations reinforced the notion that a woman had to accept male dominance.

By leaving her husband Lucia rejected these norms and undermined the arrangements that her family had made for her. Lucia had pleaded to the Venetians that she did not want to return to her family because of the likelihood that they would kill her. While women were subjected to the power of families and masters, we must not assume that they were always willing to live with the consequences of their relationships.

Overcoming an intolerable situation must also have involved understanding what options were available. Women in the Ottoman Empire did have some power in dealing with husbands and male relatives. In Kayseri the few times that women did resist an arranged marriage, their rights were upheld.[72] According to Hanafi law,[73] a woman could not be married against her will and had some choice in the matter even if defying the will of her father.[74] In eighteenth-century Istanbul a woman could offer her husband what was called a "*khul* exchange" as means for withdrawing from a marriage. If the kadi court agreed, a wife was permitted to break nuptial ties by returning any property or monies that her husband had given her prior to the wedding.[75] Along similar lines, women had a certain amount of latitude in going to the court. In the eighteenth-century Rumelia in order to be granted a khul separation, a woman could claim, amongst other things, that her husband was in ill health, that she had been physically abused or that the two parties could not agree. In certain circumstances which arose less frequently a woman was allowed to maintain full financial rights if she had been mistreated very badly or her husband had been blasphemous.[76]

Without knowledge of or access to these options, a woman might decide upon flight but be deterred by the social stigma attached to long distance travel.[77] Women traveled to the market and to church on Sundays, but very rarely across national boundaries. The only women who traveled long distances in great numbers were

---

[71]   Cavallo and Cerutti, "Female Honor," p. 78.

[72]   Jennings, "Women in Ottoman Judicial Records," p. 77.

[73]   One of the schools of Islamic law.

[74]   Jennings, "Women in Ottoman Judicial Records," p. 79.

[75]   Madeline Zilfi, "'We Don't Get Along': Women and Hul Divorce in the Eighteenth Century" in *Women in the Ottoman Empire: Middle Eastern Women in the Early Modern Era*, ed. Madeline Zilfi (Leiden: E.J. Brill, 1997), pp. 275–81.

[76]   Svetlana Ivanova, "The Divorce Between Zubaida Hatun and Esseid Osman Ağa: Women in the Eighteenth Century Shari'a Court of Rumelia" in *Women, the Family and Divorce Laws in Islamic History,* ed. Amira El Azhary Sonbol (Syracuse: Syracuse University Press, 1996), pp.118–19.

[77]   Two works on women travelers that refer to the conditions under which women traveled are: Linda Colley, *The Ordeal of Elizabeth Marsh: A Woman in World History* (New York: First Anchor Books, 2007), Mary De Filippis et al., *Dutch New York between East and West: The World of Margrieta van Varick* (Bard Graduate Studies for Studies in the Decorative Arts) (New Haven: Yale University Press, 2009).

those in gypsy bands and prostitutes. Travel was not only considered too dangerous, but also, given the responsibilities of home and children, impractical.[78] As a woman on the move, Lucia had broken away from the role and the responsibilities that shaped most women's lives. Possibly this set of circumstances was why her family claimed, justifiably or not, that while in Zadar she had fallen in with the wrong people and had lived as a prostitute.

Believing Lucia's family's side of the story involves accepting that women were most secure by staying at home. Obviously this line of thinking creates certain problems. For one, why should we assume that the family and sedentary existence represented the nexus of all security? For Lucia, the family acted not as the basis for stability but as a source of danger. Given that she seemed to lack power even in the home itself,[79] flight must have been one of the most effective ways of overcoming an oppressive personal situation. Women were certainly capable of enduring the hazards of the road. Elena, the Bosnian woman who appeared before the Inquisition, stated that when she ran away, she had hidden in the mountains for a while, before making her way to Venice.[80]

Given the twists and turns of her travels, we would be hard pressed to believe that Lucia had put together a coherent strategy to come to Venice. Instead she responded to events as they unfolded and altered her plans in a fairly haphazard manner in order to obtain shelter and protection. Her travels involved relying on a variety of different people. While we do not know precisely why the count in Šibenik allowed her to stay with him, she may well have acted as his servant or his mistress or both. After leaving Zadar she worked as a servant for Olidio Zaroffolo's wife in Piove. Taking this position was obviously a way of gaining a temporary roof over her head.

Finding a place undoubtedly took precedence over all other concerns for a person who had broken free from the traditional bonds and whose family members challenged that decision. In 1586 correspondences from the Venetian government indicate that, by working through an Ottoman official in Bosnia and the grand vizir, the second most powerful person in the Ottoman court, Hettor Salem, a former Christian turned Muslim, tried to convince the Venetians to return his wife Dorothea to him on the grounds that she was a Muslim.[81] While in the Balkan town of Alessio, a man named Ahmed had killed Dorothea's father, the Venetian Ottavio Barbarigo, and then married her mother. Subsequently, both mother and daughter converted to Islam. Unhappy with this arrangement, Dorothea's mother attempted to murder her new husband so that the family could return to Christianity. Forced

---

[78]   Hale, *Civilization of Europe*, p. 148.

[79]   The case of Lucia raises the question of what type of power women had when they took to the road.

[80]   A.S.V., Sant'Ufficio, Busta 77.

[81]   A.S.V., Senato, Deliberazioni Constantinopoli, filza 6, March 28,1586 and A.S.V., Senato Deliberazioni Constantinopoli, registro 7, fogli 33R–36R. See also Vanzan, "In Search of Another Identity," p. 331.

to escape, the family traveled to Venice and then on to Rome where Dorothea was re-baptized and married to Hettor from Puglia. [82]

Subsequently, though, the family's fortunes took a strange twist. Hettor injured another man in a dispute, and he and Dorothea decided to flee, finally arriving in the Venetian possession of Budva.[83] From here, Dorothea's husband and brother went to another town to trade, and there they converted to Islam. Shocked by the news, Dorothea went to the governor of Budva and asked for passage to Venice. Still sought after by Hettor, who claimed that she was a Turk, Dorothea returned to Italy hoping to find Hettor's brother and father. This development created problems for the Venetians, and they contemplated whether to turn Dorothea over to the custody of the closest Ottoman judge or to help her search for Hettor's brother, a person they referred to as a man of honor.[84]

Given the hazards, a woman moving between the two civilizations had to be involved in constant role-playing and strategizing. After failing to kill her husband, Dorothea's mother and her daughter escaped to Venice with an Alessian merchant by the name of Paolo Mariani.

Mariani may have protected them, but he may also have taken one or both of them as his concubines. The idea that a woman such as Lucia or Dorothea would collude with a person such as Mariani or the count of Šibenik must have been very threatening to the families of each woman. This possibility would have been seen as a severe transgression of what would have been considered to be "acceptable" conduct. Local societies had means and customs in place for dealing with these types of issues, but the fact that each woman had crossed a border created a new type of power dynamics and a different set of potential resolutions.

Similar Cultural Attitudes

The travels of Lucia and Dorothea indicate that civilizational boundaries were not mutually exclusive domains in which one set of rules applied on one side of the border and another set on the other. People passed from one world to another with a surprising familiarity and understanding. Yet crossing a boundary for reasons of protection necessitated some type of support on the other side of the frontier.

---

[82]   A.S.V., Senato, Deliberazioni Constantinopoli, filza 6, March 28, 1586, A.S.V., Senato Deliberazioni Constantinopoli, registro 7, fogli 33R–36R. Dorothea went to the Pia Casa di Catecumeni in Rome as opposed to Venice because of connections that her family had in Rome. Going to Rome also allowed her to gain an audience with the pope to absolve her of the sin of apostasy for previously having converted to Islam. On cases involving this question see Filippo Tamburini, *Santi e peccatori: Confessioni e suppliche dai Registri della Penitenzeria dell'Archivio Segreto Vaticano (1451–1586)* (Milano: Istituto di Propoganda Libraria, 1995), pp. 17–18.

[83]   Budva is a town on the coast of Montenegro.

[84]   A.S.V., Senato, Deliberazioni Constantinopoli, filza 6, March 28, 1586 and A.S.V., Senato Deliberazioni Constantinopoli, registro 7, fogli 33R–36R.

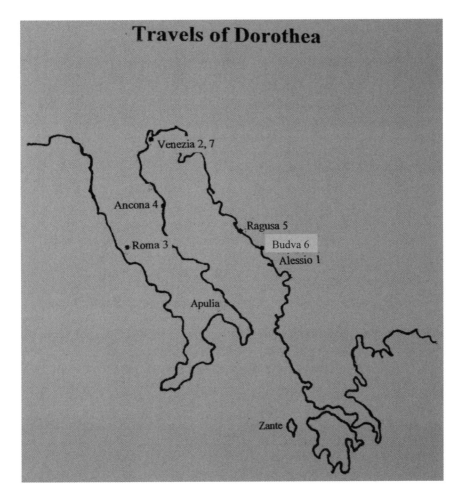

Fig. 3.2   Map of Dorothea's travels. Drawn by the author.

Borders were "fluid" only for those who could establish connections and who could appeal to other people in a cultural manner that achieved favorable results. While the meeting between Yunus Bey and Piero Baciccio near Klis might not have represented what we in modern terms call a friendship, it certainly embodied a high degree of mutual respect and a certain affinity. Preserving Piero's life was not the only option available to Yunus. Since he came with an armed following, he could easily have killed Piero and his mother or brought them back to Klis. He had been ordered to do so, and both acts would have been justified. Yet Yunus chose another option and allowed the two to continue on their journey.

Yunus's action and his connection to Piero had to do with a personal sense of honor. Given that Piero had saved his life the first time, Yunus felt a need to reciprocate. The powers to take and to give life were important to personal reputation. While, in the first instance Piero was in a position of weakness, in the second case he was in a position of strength. Each party understood and was prepared to disobey orders from superiors for the sake of personal honor.

Preserving one's honor has been at the center of different debates as to what has unified the Mediterranean over time. Existing as one of the two pillars of the honor/shame paradigm, many have argued that honor represents a trans-Mediterranean sensibility.[85] While honor has had and continues to have a variety of different connotations, one of the central ways that families have sought to maintain their honor was by controlling women. Jane Schneider argues that in Mediterranean society,

> the repository of family and lineage honor, the focus of the common interest among the men of the family or lineage, is its women. A woman's status defines the status of all men who are related to her in indeterminate ways. These men share the consequences of what happens to her...." [86]

While Schneider's comment does not take into account female agency, or the ways in which women were able to resist male domination, it does allow us to think about how men perceived their relationship to women and how they would have defended this relationship in public. Invoking honor implied that an individual in question had something to gain and also something to lose.[87] A person's reputation was at stake and citing honor meant negotiations were necessary to restore the status quo.

Given these negotiations, honor is best thought of as a rhetorical strategy, rather than an immutable code.[88] Although Hettor Salem argued that Dorothea should be returned to him on the grounds of their marriage, the Venetians had to decide whether he possessed the requisite power to defend his honor. In Lucia's case, the official in Rovigno commented that her family stated that in order to protect the family honor, they either wanted her put in a convent or returned to her home.[89] This claim represented the family's testimony as articulated by the

---

[85]   See Anton Blok, "Rams and Billy Goats: A Key to the Mediterranean Code of Honour," *Man*, New Series, vol. 16, no. 3 (1981), pp. 427–40, David Gilmore, ed., *Honor and Shame and the Unity of the Mediterranean*, American Anthropological Association 22, special publication (Washington DC: American Anthropological Association, 1987), Jean Persitany, *Honour and Shame: The Values of Mediterranean Society* (London: Weidenfield and Nicolson, 1965) and Jane Schneider, "Of Vigilance and Virgins: Honor, Shame and Access to Resources in Mediterranean Societies," *Ethnology*, no. 3 (July 1971), pp. 1–23.

[86]   Schneider, "Of Vigilance and Virgins," p. 18.

[87]   Thomas Cohen, "Three Forms of Jeopardy: Honor, Pain and Truth-Telling in a Sixteenth-Century Italian Courtroom," *The Sixteenth Century Journal*, vol. 29, no. 4 (1998), p. 987.

[88]   Ibid., p. 987.

[89]   A.S.V., Avogaria di Comun, Miscellanea Penale, busta 343.

Venetian official and served as one form of evidence in deliberations on how to rule on this question. Officials would rule in the favor of a male relative's honor even in the most extreme of cases. In a case brought before the Vatican in 1497, the authorities ruled that a man from the Portuguese archipelago of Madeira had argued persuasively that to restore his honor, he was justified in killing his wife, because she had committed adultery with a merchant from Florence.[90]

Families believed that their status and virtue could be maintained by protecting their female relatives' virtue.[91] In a case in eighteenth-century Kayseri,[92] in which a woman and her two children were killed, the husband wanted to restore the family's honor by insuring that the woman's honor, which might have been compromised during the attack, remained untarnished.[93] In a romance in the northern Italian town of Feltre between the son of a noble family, the Facenos, and the daughter of a non-noble family, the Cumanos, the Faceno family had grave doubts about the wisdom of their son marrying a woman from a lower rank, while the Cumano family was concerned that Gian Battista Faceno had impregnated their daughter and also promised to marry her. If the good name of the Cumano clan was to be vindicated, their daughter's reputation had to be restored.[94]

Part of maintaining the reputation and the honor of the family meant ensuring that female members were confined to certain spaces. In the sixteenth-century Islamic world, even in cases where women did have power, men felt a need to keep females off the streets. This type of control was embodied in marriage contracts where women were expected to give up their independence in return for the support of a man.[95] Restoring a woman's "reputation" could also be achieved, as Lucia's family argued, by putting her in a convent. In Renaissance Italy, the convent was a place that a woman could be placed, "…to salvage family honor when a dowry could not be raised or a suitable marriage could not be arranged."[96] After traveling to Venice to retrieve his daughter, Ahmed Ağa was convinced by the Venetians that allowing her to stay in the convent was a suitable way for her to remain in Venice.[97] Convents allowed the Venetian noble class to keep women out of public spaces.[98] While Lucia's situation was very different, her family's

---

[90]   Tamburini, *Santi e peccatori*, p. 49.

[91]   Schneider, "Vigilance and Virgins," p. 18.

[92]   Kayseri is a town in central Anatolia.

[93]   Suraiya Faroqhi, "Women and Wealth in the Eighteenth Century Anatolian Countryside," in *Women in the Ottoman Empire: Middle Eastern Women in the Early Modern Era*, ed. Madeline C. Zilfi (Leiden: E.J. Brill, 1997), p. 21.

[94]   Ruggiero, *Binding Passions*, pp. 57–87.

[95]   Pierce, *Morality Tales*, 153–6.

[96]   Ruggiero, *Binding Passions*, p. 25.

[97]   A.S.V., Senato, Deliberazioni Costantinopoli, registro 18, fogli 38R–47V.

[98]   Jutta Gisela Sperling, *Convents and the Body Politic in Late Renaissance Venice* (Chicago: University of Chicago Press, 1999), p. 13.

principal concern was to alter her behavior, return her to a more moral life and find her a more acceptable place within the social order.

While families may have felt that private spaces such as convents kept these issues secret, restoring one's reputation at times was pursued in a public setting such as a court. In a case that eventually came before the Ali bin İsa's kadi court in Galata in 1594, Mehmed bin Abdullah who lived in the quarter of Sinan Pasha in the district of Beşiktaş stated that he was dropping his accusation against the Venetian Gianni Veledi. Mehmed had accused Veledi of seducing his wife Marina and helping her escape to Venice. Mehmed now stated that Gianni was innocent of the earlier charges and had played no part in the episode. Most importantly, he declared that he wanted to clear Gianni's name and abandon any further claims that might arise from the case.

The connection between a man's honor and a woman had a bearing on many aspects of this affair. Mehmed's honor had been damaged by the fact that someone had seduced his wife and then taken her to Venice. Mehmed's decision to take the case to court indicates that he believed legal recourse was a better option than personal revenge. The best way that his honor could be restored was by making the guilty party pay for his transgressions. Gianni Veledi's name had also been besmirched by the fact that Mehmed had implicated him. By paying Mehmed, Gianni restored his good name and avoided further consequences.[99]

Lucia's case also involved a complicated politics between her family and her husband. Disgraced by her actions and anxious to restore her virtue, her family, rather than her husband, traveled to Venice.[100] These actions were taken to establish credibility with the Venetian government and with the magistrate. In his work on crime and honor in sixteenth-century Rome, Thomas Cohen argues that a "pre-scientific empiricism" defined the testimonies in a case in which the accused were charged with thievery. When questioned, a person had to "descend from the highlands of reputation to the piedmont of pure accuracy." Once presented, the details of the narrative needed to be accurate because the story was open to refutation.[101] The same set of circumstances existed in Lucia's hearing. A series of witnesses were called to testify and all of them were expected to contribute to the accuracy of the claim. The line of questioning attempted to separate "fact from fiction." Yet what type of truth were the Venetians looking to uncover, or counter-narrative to suppress? If it was Lucia's religious identity, one could surmise that her claim of being a Christian would have been sufficient. No other criteria were necessary to establish this point. Lacking this intention though, a more useful way of thinking about the gathering of evidence might be that the outcome of the hearing had already been established and that witnesses had been selected to confirm the decision. Evidence was more likely based on the reputation of Lucia's

---

[99]   A.S.V., I Documenti Turchi, busta 9, fasc. 1052.

[100]   On the question of a husband's control over his wife, see Imber, "Women, Marriage and Property," pp. 83–4.

[101]   Cohen, "Three Forms of Jeopardy," p. 993.

family rather Lucia's wishes. In essence, their influence and their honor shaped the nature of the inquiry.

Without this type of intervention, the state felt more comfortable intervening on its own. In 1682 the Cinque Savi arrested a woman named Aisé who maintained that she was a Muslim, though she had been seen near the *Fondaco dei Turchi* with a rosary in her hand. Aisé contended that she had been born a Christian in Livorno, enslaved by an Ottoman pasha at the age of seven and brought to Istanbul where she lived for a period of twenty years. After the death of the pasha, she was sold to an Armenian merchant who abandoned her in Venice. Claiming that she was Muslim, she found her way to live with Muslim merchants in the fondaco where she was arrested and sent to the Catecumeni for religious instruction. While ultimately we don't know what happened to Aisé, another Armenian charged her with constantly changing her religious identity, and she was to be brought before the Inquisition.[102]

In many ways Aisé's situation paralleled that of Lucia's. Her pleas failed to convince those in charge of the legitimacy of her claims. As a woman alone, Aisé did not have corporate protection. While she did find refuge in the *Fondaco dei Turchi,* none of the merchants defended her against her accusers. Lacking connections, she did not have the ability to tap into a network in which as Anna Vanzan notes she "could navigate across polities,"[103] nor could she call on people to defend her religious identity or present a logical argument to explain her predicament. In this regard, she lacked social credibility and the knowledge needed to justify her claims.

While Lucia's family's social credibility put them in a more advantageous position to deal with Venetian authorities, they may also have been forced to go to Venice to allay any misgivings her husband had about their goodwill. In Islamic marriages the practice of a man giving his wife *mahr*[104] in return for her hand in marriage was a legal requirement.[105] In particular, in Hanafi law the payment of mahr was due after sexual intercourse, and theoretically, it gave the man control over his wife's sexual organs.[106] Should the marriage fail, the man's family would have satisfaction only if all monies were returned. In the absence of this arrangement Lucia's departure would have produced significant enmity between the two families. While this sentiment still does not tell us why her family was willing to put Lucia in a convent, it does raise questions as to what may have arisen concerning prior payment. Going to great lengths to have their sons

---

[102] Anna Vanzan, "La pia casa dei Catecumeni in Venezia, Un tentativo di devshirme Christiana? " in *Donne microcosmi culturali*, a cura di Adriana Destro (Bologna: Pàtron, 1997), pp. 243–4.

[103] Lauren Benton, *Law and Colonial Cultures: Legal Regimes in World History 1400–1900* (Cambridge, UK: Cambridge University Press, 2002), p. 25.

[104] A form of payment.

[105] Imber, "Women, Marriage and Property," pp. 87–8.

[106] Ibid., p. 87.

and daughters returned may not have been unusual for families. In Lucia's case, her family clearly received word that she had gone to Venice, and they went to considerable lengths to pursue her, which must have been a costly undertaking. Undeterred by the hazards of travel, they not only paid one visit but also pursued her after she had escaped from them.

Families strategized in a variety of ways to have relatives returned. In 1592, Fiorenza Podocataro, the daughter of Lodovico Podacataro and a relative of the family of the Venetian dragoman Giacomo Nores, came before the Inquisition board in Venice and stated that the Turks had made her a slave when they captured the city of Nicosia on Cyprus, during the war of the early 1570s. After being taken to the Bulgarian city of Sizigar, she decided that it was far too dangerous to remain a Christian and she converted to Islam, took the name Tuttia, lived as a Muslim for 22 years, married her master and had three children. Everything changed after her husband died, for relatives claiming to be her father and her mother arrived and told the people of the town that they had arranged a marriage in another place. From Sizigar, Fiorenza and her family went to Istanbul and from there on to Venice.[107]

Fiorenza's story points to the resourcefulness of a family in their attempt to reclaim their daughter. Given the years that had passed, remarkably, they knew how to find her, stake claim to her and announce that they planned to marry her to someone else. Similar logic also held true in regard to Lucia. A group of men, well-respected from the Venetians' point of view, had arrived in Venice and demanded that Lucia, who had in their words dishonored her husband and her family, be returned to their care so that the correct social order could be restored. Like Fiorenza's family, their claim was based on that fact that they had the right to arrange her marriage.

Marrying a person from a similar religious background clearly played a major role in how families viewed these arrangements. In 1574, a letter was sent from the governor of Split to the Venetian Senate, telling the story of a young Muslim named Adel who a year earlier had come on a number of occasions to one of the villages surrounding Split. He was a trader and not only admired, but also loved by those in this region because of his honesty and his discretion. On one occasion when he came to trade he was passing by the house of the Vorniches, a rich and important family in the town, and caught the eye of their youngest daughter, Maria. His interest was more than just a passing fancy and the two took to one another immediately, with Adel returning on numerous occasions to pass by the house to see her. While she spoke in confidence to her sister of her affection for him, she also expressed great fear because Adel was a Muslim. The situation reached a climax when after completing his business affairs for the day and seeing Maria and her sister in the street, Adel began to sing an old Slavonic love poem,

---

[107] A.S.V., Sant'Ufficio, busta 69, October 22, 1592.

The Turk is in love with our dove. I am the Turk. Her face is whiter than my wax and is more beautiful than the roses that I care for. The Turk is in love with our dove. I have surely heard her speak, but her words are far sweeter than honey. And your dove is nobler than my horse.[108]

Maria's family, fearful of the scandal that might ensue, rushed her home and considered what action to take. They decided that the only reasonable way to prevent her from seeing Adel was to send her to a convent, but before this action could be taken, she became ill and died, undoubtedly leaving her admirer heartbroken.[109] Although Adel was obviously well-known and even liked, any romantic involvement was out of the question.

Adel's inability to develop a relationship with his beloved, though, does not indicate that an impenetrable barrier existed between the two cultures. An awareness both parties could understand shaped the encounter between Adel and Maria's family. Adel was very careful in the family's presence. The deference he showed not only conveyed a certain amount of respect, but also recognition of certain social parameters and cultural norms. The family was able to discern Adel's intentions from the song he sang in Maria's presence. The song obviously held meaning on both sides of the Muslim/Christian divide and represented one aspect of shared culture. Adversarial positions did not necessarily have to do with cultural distance or lack of familiarity. In fact, familiarity and proximity probably bred greater recognition and better understanding of how to deal with one's so-called enemies.

Within a world of similar cultural mores, the interests of the individual had to be subordinated to the interests of the clan and the religious community. Much discussion has been generated about the early modern period as a time when the existence of an individual consciousness free of corporate identity began to surface.[110] As we see here, an individual's desires could be separate from those of his or her family. Lucia attempted to assert her own wishes when she ran away from her family and so did Dorothea when she left Hettor Salem. Yet any attempt to deviate from accepted social norms had to be presented in a way that conformed to certain conventions. The individual could not put forward an argument based on his or her free will to act independently of certain structures and institutions. Ronald Weissman points this out in regard to the question of Renaissance identity:

---

[108] Solitro, *Documenti storici*, pp. 216–19. The words of the poem are as follows "Il Turco s'innamorò della nostra colomba---Io sono Turco. Il suo volto è piu bianco della mia cera ed è più delle rose che ho stillato. Il Turco s'innamorò della nostra columba---Io sono turco. La pur sentita a parlar, ma con quelle parole, questo miele è amaro. E la vostra colomba è più nobile del mio cavallo."

[109] Ibid.

[110] This is a thesis that was first put forward by Jacob Burckhardt in his classic study of the Renaissance, *The Civilization of the Renaissance in Italy* (London: The Phaidon Press, 1944).

> While I do not deny the heuristic utility of categories such as class, corporation, or Renaissance individualism, I suggest that a more appropriate unit of analysis for studying Renaissance society is neither the individual nor the group, but rather the social relationship that links individuals to each other and to groups.[111]

Lucia's family invoked the importance of this linkage when they contended that what was at stake was not Lucia's personal belief but instead her social bonds to her family. This bond also applied to Fiorenza Podocataro. Although she had been away from her family for over twenty years, had married another man, was a mother to three children and had changed her religion, everybody understood why she subordinated her needs to her family. This logic not only made sense, it also worked.

Commenting on sixteenth-century France, Natalie Zemon Davis notes "in a century in which the boundary around the conceptual self and the bodily self was not always firm and closed, men and women nonetheless could work out strategies for self-expression and autonomy; and the greatest obstacle to self-definition was not embeddedness but powerlessness and poverty." She adds that "embeddedness rather than precluding self-discovery prompted it."[112] Lucia acted in direct relation to constituent social circumstances and out of a need to break free from the ties to her family. She could have made an independent decision and still been a part of her family. Movement was her form of self-expression and her answer to powerlessness. Yet looking for a new place to fit in, the legitimacy of one's self-expression was weighed in relation to the power of the concerned parties. In Lucia's case the Cinque Savi were cognizant of the fact that her family had either some status or connections to powerful people in Bosnia.[113] They had to weigh the consequences if they decided not to return her to her family. This thinking also applied to the case of Dorothea. To refute Hettor Salem's claim that Dorothea should be returned to him, the Venetians gathered Muslims in Venice to witness her claim that she was a Christian. This measure diminished Hettor's ability to

---

[111] Ronald F.E. Weissman, "Reconstructing Renaissance Sociology: The 'Chicago School' and the Study of Renaissance Society," in *Persons in Groups: Social Behavior as Identity Formation in Medieval and Renaissance Europe*, ed. Richard C. Trexler (Binghamton: Center for Medieval and Early Renaissance Studies, 1985), p. 40.

[112] Natalie Zemon Davis, "Boundaries and the Sense of Self in Sixteenth Century France," in *Reconstructing Individualism: Autonomy, Individuality, and the Self in Western Thought*, ed. Thomas C. Heller et al. (Stanford: Stanford University Press, 1986), pp. 53, 63.

[113] While there is no hard evidence that Lucia was from a powerful family, certain facts seem to point to the Venetians' willingness to reject Lucia's claim that she was a Christian and believe the family's argument instead. First, there was the Cinque Savi's decision. This not only indicates that the board honored the family's request, but also demonstrates that the family knew who to turn to have their needs addressed. Even after Lucia had escaped, the podestà turned to one of her relatives to hear his side of the story.

solicit the support of powerful people to invoke the sanctity of the family in these types of matters.[114]

Another case also demonstrates the complex issues tied to religious identity and the importance of family and gaining acceptance in Venice. In 1584 Francesca Michiel arrived in Venice with a letter from her son, Ganzafer, the head gatekeeper of the Ottoman palace. As a boy Ganzafer had been kidnapped from an Italian family and taken to Istanbul where he had been enlisted as a *devshirme*.[115] Twenty-five years later, after re-establishing contact with his mother, he asked the Venetians to give her and her family a small stipend. Not surprisingly, in view of his status, they agreed to this request.[116]

The ability of an Ottoman official to extract such a concession also demonstrated a family's ability to win recognition across territorial boundaries. Why else would the Venetians give in to the demands of someone who for all intents and purposes was a renegade Christian? In another situation this would not have happened. Hettor Salem did not have as much luck, for the Venetians not only tried to protect Dorothea, they also did everything in their power to prevent him from coming to Venice. Did the Venetian authorities fear that, if he came before the Inquisition, the authorities would attempt to grab him and bring him up on charges that he had rejected his Christian faith, or was their concern that he would find some way to take Dorothea back with him? These were complex issues not only in regard to an individual's faith but also in terms of one's identity. Thus, even though Lucia may have considered herself to be a Christian, her religious identity and her position in the world were tied to the will of her family and her husband. She broke free of their authority not by going to a local Ottoman judge, but instead by leaving the Ottoman Empire and going to Venetian territories. At least initially there was no indication that she made any claims that she was a Christian as a way of enlisting support, either to the count in Šibenik, or to anyone else she encountered on her journey. Along the Dalmatian coast, it may not have mattered that a wayward Muslim woman was staying with a Christian man.[117]

However, at the time that she decided to go Venice, Lucia's claims to be a Christian became not only an important part of her strategy, but also the basis of her separation from her family. She obviously hoped that by stating that she was a Christian she would find a place for herself in this new world. Yet finding a place in this new world proved trickier for Lucia, for her family pursued her to Venice,

---

[114] A.S.V., Senato Deliberazioni Constantinopoli, registro 7, foglio 33R, March 27, 1586.

[115] A devshirme was a young Christian taken to Istanbul to be converted to Islam and to learn the Turkish language and the culture of the place. Ultimately, these individuals worked for the state in a variety of different capacities, some rising to positions as high as the grand vezir.

[116] A.S.V., Senato, Deliberazioni Constantinopoli, filza 6, December 29, 1584. For a longer discussion of this case see Dursteler, *Renegade Women*, pp. 1–33.

[117] Clearly, this question needs further study.

forcibly took her and then obtained permission from the Cinque Savi to return her to Bosnia. The decision reveals the importance that the family placed on having their actions sanctioned by the Venetian state. While measuring the enforceability of the decree is difficult, the fact that Lucia's relatives felt that they needed to obtain this ruling indicates that it held some weight and some credibility with people they would encounter in their return trip to Bosnia.

Part of their strategy was trying to ensure that the case was mediated in the right jurisdiction. If Lucia had been able to receive the protection of powerful Church authorities, like that of Dorothea, she would have been likely able to fend off her family's pursuit. Obtaining refuge and/or sanctuary involved more than just escaping to another place. A person in her situation needed to find people who were willing to fight the local political battles that might develop over this type of situation. Lacking this support, the border was not as impenetrable as Lucia may have thought. Other forces were also at work, including the power of male dominance, the integrity of the family and the role of honor. These forces not only characterized personal relations, but also played an important role in shaping identities. Even stating that one was a Christian had its limitations and when the distillation of factors involved powerful forces and incontrovertible arguments, cross-cultural logic overcame local and civilizational concerns. While the text of the final decision of the Cinque Savi is unavailable, the Venetians' earlier decision indicates that they clearly favored the side of her family. The logic that they presented, the cultural capital they possessed and the power they commanded held up across borders.

Chapter 4
Projecting Ottoman Power

Lucia's case suggests the importance of thinking about the role of movement in cross-cultural relations. Her decision to cross from Ottoman to Venetian territories and then to Venice represents what could happen when a woman attempted to place herself in a new political setting. But cases like Lucia's need to be explored not only in terms of the face-to-face contact but also in regard to connections that developed between individuals and the Ottoman state and to ties that existed between travelers and other powerful people in the Ottoman Empire who could influence events beyond imperial boundaries.

Rather than thinking solely in terms of state diplomacy, Ottoman influence must be thought of in a very broad sense. Ottoman power in Venice was projected through envoys, treaties, institutions and personal influence. In many respects this expression of power reflected a microcosm of Ottoman social and political networks. Letters, political edicts, court rulings and recommendations were all presented as evidence in claims and disputes that not only reflected relationships between states but also represented symbols of power and means for interpreting how different matters should be handled.

Ottoman Diplomacy

In thinking about the projection of Ottoman power, one must first consider that the Ottoman state was a very different entity than its modern counterpart. Palmira Brummett notes that "the sultan measured his domains in terms of lands, seas, reputation, and submission." The empire had two major parts, Rumeli and Anatolia, other provinces such as Egypt and Syria and affiliated territories like Algiers. Frontiers were delineated by fortresses and by control of the sea, and administration of overseas territories was related to the reach of imperial power.[1] A person who lived within the boundaries of the Empire was theoretically a subject, but not necessarily an Ottoman. Those people who considered themselves Ottomans had an attachment to a person or groups of people within the Ottoman court rather an internalized sense of loyalty to the state. In this regard, "Ottomanness" was more narrowly defined than modern nationality and encompassed only a select part of the population. Şerif Mardin points out that

---

[1]   Palmira Brummett, "Imagining the Early Modern Ottoman Space," in *The Early Modern Ottomans*, eds. Virginian Aksan and Daniel Goffman (Cambridge, UK: Cambridge University Press, 2007) pp. 47–8.

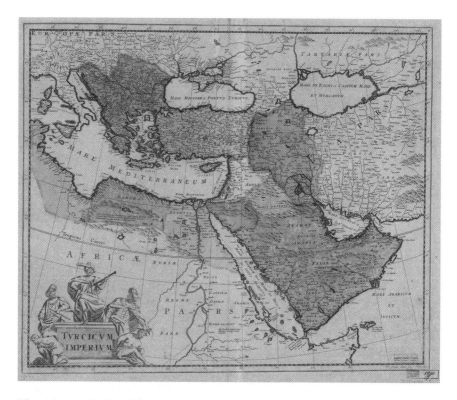

Fig. 4.1   F. De Wit, *Turcicum Imperium*, plate 19 (1670s). Harvard Map
Collection.

the Ottoman Empire nourished within its social frame two ways of life. Associated
with the 'great' culture were such features as war and administration as life-time
occupations, freedom from taxation, the use of language highly permeated with
Persian and Arabic words, and orthodox Islam. The rural masses and particularly
the Turkish tribesmen, on the other hand, used Turkish vernacular, engaged in
buying and selling in agriculture, were taxed to the gills, had access only to
primitive technology and were suffused by heterodox currents.[2]

---

[2]   Şerif Mardin, "Civil Society and Culture in the Ottoman Empire," *Comparative
Studies in Society and History* 2 (1969), p. 270. Mardin goes onto to add that "Indeed, the
concept of medeniyet (city dwelling, or civilization) was the core of the self-image of the
Ottoman ruling class and of its pretensions. By contrast the term 'Turk' was used in the
pejorative sense because it meant being tribal." p. 271. This view is certainly subject to
criticism in that it tends to homogenize high and low culture. Peter Burke comments that
in Europe popular culture varied greatly from place to place. See Peter Burke, *Popular
Culture in Early Modern Europe* (New York: New York University Press, 1978), p. 29. For
our purposes Mardin's comment illustrates how many people in the Ottoman Empire were
not connected to court culture.

Court administrators and functionaries felt close ties to the Ottoman state principally because they worked within the confines of the palace. Proximity and connections to powerful patrons and officials created loyalty. On the one hand, while local governors in many instances had been trained within the culture of the Ottoman court, on the other hand their presence acted as a thin overlay rather than a firmly entrenched state presence.[3]

Rather than exercising direct control, the Porte enlisted people's loyalties through a series of reciprocal political and economic arrangements. Karen Barkey points out that, "(s)tate control was exerted through ties from the periphery to the center, segmenting elites and common people, all of whom were responsive to the center but not to each other."[4] People who were given *timars*, the agreement of land for military service, were tied to state through a mutual understanding. They were allowed to collect revenues from the land they were allotted by the state and in return were expected when necessary to raise a local force to fight for the sultan. But even this arrangement was conditional and reflected the ability of the central government to impose its will on local groups. In the more remote parts of the empire such as Yemen, eastern Anatolia and Iraq, local land arrangements were maintained.[5] Kadis, the imperial judges mentioned in earlier chapters, could also be found in cities and villages throughout the territories of the empire. Semi-autonomous yet under the jurisdiction of the sultan and the *Şeyh-ül-islam*,[6] they fulfilled an important role both in local and in state life by making judgments related to both secular (*kanun*) and religious (*şeriat*) law.[7]

Given the tremendous political diversity of the empire, one might assume that scholarship on Ottoman diplomacy towards the Europeans would reflect the diversity of Ottoman political relationships. But the traditional view has been that as an Islamic state, the Ottoman Empire conducted little diplomacy outside of its own borders. Nuri Yurdusev notes that scholars have assumed that "with a belief in permanent war with, the inferiority of and contempt for the emerging European nation-states, the Ottomans cannot of course have been expected to have a positive attitude toward diplomacy, described as the principal institution of

---

[3]   On the question of provincial governors see I.M. Kunt, *The Sultan's Servants: The Transformation of Ottoman Provincial Government, 1550–1650* (New York: Columbia University Press, 1983). Kunt argues that in the early part of the seventeenth century most provincial governors were men who had been appointed from central administration posts. Kunt also points out that the term for provincial administration, *dirlik*, literally means livelihood or revenues that state officials were able to earn from the localities that were allocated to them. p. 9.

[4]   Karen Barkey, *Bandits and Bureaucrats: The Ottoman Route to State Centralization* (Ithaca: Cornell University Press, 1994), p. 26.

[5]   Şevket Pamuk, "Institutional Change and the Longevity of the Ottoman Empire," *Journey of Institutional History*, vol. 35, no. 2 (2004), p. 230.

[6]   Chief jurisprudent.

[7]   Barkey, *Bandits and Bureaucrats*, p. 38.

those very nation-states of Europe."[8] Along similar lines, Bernard Lewis contends that Ottoman military strength and their belief in the superiority of Islam over Christianity gave them little interest in the affairs of the Europeans.[9]

The fifteenth and sixteenth centuries were a time in which Europe increasingly looked to place a resident ambassador in foreign capitals. Creating what has been associated with the birth of modern diplomacy, European states believed that having an informed individual on the "inside" gave them an upper hand in matters of state.[10] One noteworthy appointment that the Venetians made was placing an ambassador in Istanbul. This individual (referred earlier as the bailo) was the eyes and ears of the Venetian government. He was not only granted access to the Ottoman court but was also able to establish close relations with some important Ottoman officials. For the Venetians, his presence in Ottoman lands ultimately translated into the opportunity to gain better information, to establish more favorable trading rights and to exploit local political problems.[11]

While the bailo's role and his importance in managing Venetian/Ottoman relations should not be minimized, other forms of diplomacy illustrated different expressions of power. Daniel Goffman notes that Italian and in particular Venetian diplomacy was developed in relation to the presence of the Ottoman Empire in European affairs. Even the concessions granted to Europeans living in Ottoman territories reflected intra-Ottoman communal politics rather than European initiatives. From the Italian wars onward in 1494, the Ottoman Empire played an important role in European politics. The Pope and the Neapolitans sought out the Porte's help in their struggle with the French, and the Ottomans represented the one state with the power to keep the Habsburg emperor Charles V from expanding his reign.[12]

Ottoman Envoys

If power was less about a permanent physical presence in a particular place, one way in which Ottoman demands could be communicated to foreign states was

---

[8]   A. Nuri Yurdusev, "The Ottoman Attitude toward Diplomacy," in *Ottoman Diplomacy: Conventional or Unconventional* (New York: Palgrave MacMillan, 2004), p. 7.

[9]   See Lewis, *Muslim Discovery of Europe*, pp. 17–57.

[10]   N.S. Anderson, *The Rise of Modern Diplomacy, 1450–1919* (London: Longman, 1993).

[11]   Eric Dursteler, "The Bailo in Constantinople: Crisis and Career in Venice's Early Modern Diplomatic Corps," *Mediterranean Historical Review* 16 (2001), pp. 1–25. Also see Dursteler, *Venetians in Constantinople*, pp. 28–32. Christiane Villian-Gandossi, "Les attributions du Baile de Constantinople dans le fonctionement des Èchelles du Levant au XVI siècle," *Recueils de la Societè Jean Bodin* 33, part 2 (1972), pp. 227–42.

[12]   Daniel Goffman, "Negotiating with the Renaissance State: the Ottoman Empire and the new diplomacy," in the *Early Modern Ottomans: Remapping the Empire* (Cambridge, UK: Cambridge University Press, 2007), pp. 61–2.

through their envoys' missions. The envoy was an important political figure in the pre-modern world. As representatives of a particular authority in the late classical world, envoys delivered different types of both internal communications and foreign correspondences and served to establish formal contact between different groups on public matters. Envoys were also important conduits between senders and receivers of information and acted as purveyors of mediation and negotiation.[13] While Ottoman envoys' lack of a formal or more permanent position in Venice makes them seem less visible than the Venetian bailo, their role in early modern politics should not be discounted. The individuals selected to deliver information and to negotiate diplomatic matters were important members of the Ottoman bureaucracy. They were individuals who were considered to be very loyal to the sultan, and the Ottomans took a significant amount of time preparing an envoy for a mission. Delegations that accompanied envoys were usually quite large, encompassing as many as six or seven hundred people. The envoy was provided with sufficient funds to meet his expenses and with the necessary attire for the occasion, which could include robes and weapons. Gifts were also selected that were appropriate for the mission. A ceremony was arranged before departure and firmans (edicts) were sent to officials in Ottoman provinces telling them to ensure safe passage through their territories. After crossing a border, festivities were held in cities along the route and in many cases local nobles came out to greet the envoy and his entourage.[14]

Many times messages of state were delivered by a çavuş, a palace official who fulfilled a number of functions. Besides acting as a representative of the Ottoman imperial guard, a çavuş was an individual who played a very important role in the palace by maintaining contacts and delivering messages in the Ottoman periphery and in foreign lands. In his journey in Ottoman lands in the early eighteenth century, French traveler Joseph Pitton de Tournefort noted that

> The Chiaus's (çavuş) are employd in more honorable Commissions: they carry the Emperor's orders over his whole dominions and are charged with the Letters he writes to Sovereign Princes: they are, as it were, Exempts of the guard to the Grand Signor. Their number is about 500 Men, commanded by a Chief who is called a Chiaus Bacchi.[15]

These were quite powerful individuals. For example, Hamza Chiaus, a figure at the Ottoman court at the end of the sixteenth century, owned two ships and was

---

[13]   Britani Curry and Gittanjali Shahani, *Emissaries in Early Modern Literature and Culture: Mediation, Transmission, Traffic, 1550–1700* (Farnham England: Ashgate Press, 2009), pp.4, 6.

[14]   Bülent Arı, "Early Ottoman Diplomacy: Ad Hoc Period," in *Ottoman Diplomacy*, ed. A Nuri Yurdisev (New York: Columbia University Press, 2004) pp. 48–52.

[15]   Joseph Pitton de Tournefort, *A Voyage into the Levant: Performed by the Command of the Late French King, vol. 2* (London: n.p.,1741), p. 251, http://books.google.com/books?id=qQt_L-BSe8sC/.

actively engaged in trade with Venice. While he never traveled to the city, he was involved with a merchant Pasqualino Leoni, who shipped him silk.[16]

The presences of a çavuş and other palace officials in foreign cities was very important for Ottomans because the regime was dependent on these individuals for gathering information, making important announcements and cutting political deals outside of the palace. In 1384 an Ottoman çavuş arrived in Venice with a message of friendship and a proposal to form an alliance against Genoa. The çavuş Ilyas came to the city in 1487 looking to collect tribute and to discuss Christian slaves who were held by the Ottomans and in 1525 the çavuş Hüseyn came to announce the circumcision of the four sons of the sultan.[17] In 1567 Ibrahim, a dragoman, arrived in Venice to announce the Ottoman conquest of parts of Hungary. Yunus, another dragoman, came to Venice on six different missions and from the early sixteenth century until the war of Cyprus, dragomans were considered to be official ambassadors.[18]

The arrival of a specific type of Ottoman envoy could also be related to a particular set of circumstances. For instance, a guarantee of safe conduct for the new bailo in 1645 was delivered to the Venetians by Murad, a janissary, and Hasan, a gatekeeper and bodyguard. Janissaries were chosen to protect Venetian officials traveling through Ottoman territories, and protection constituted an important part of the exchange. Also related to his palace function, in 1589 Mustafa, the treasurer of the court, came to Venice to buy gold cloth for the Ottoman court.[19]

The Venetians had to consider the prestige of the individual with whom they were dealing, and some visits led to complicated politics. In 1547 the çavuş Mehmed was accused of taking a young Christian boy as a slave. In coming before the Collegio, Mehmed denied the charges, stating the boy had been born a Muslim instead. The senators were quick to accept his story and did not pursue the case any further, indicating the sensitive nature of confronting a palace official.[20] In 1609 Mustafa, a *müteferrika*, member of the cavalry, came to Venice with a group of people and stayed in a house in San Luca with a woman named Chiozotta. The Venetians found it odd that Mustafa was not carrying a letter from either the grand vizir or the bailo and noted that his entrance did not follow the correct protocol. They also noted that according to a Bosnian official, while traveling through Split, Mustafa had extorted money and goods from Muslim merchants who were headed to Venice. To these charges, Mustafa replied that he had been given orders by the sultan to come to Venice without having to consult others and denied that he had

---

[16]   Eric Dursteler, "Veneto-Ottoman Trade in the Early Modern Era," *Turcica*, vol. 34 (2002), p. 117.

[17]   On Ottoman delegations to Venice see Walter Zele, "Aspetti delle legazioni ottomane nei *Diarii* di Marin Sanudo," *Studi veneziani* 18 (1989), pp. 241–84.

[18]   Pedani, *In nome del Gran Signore*, pp. 203–7.

[19]   Ibid., pp. 208–9.

[20]   Ibid., p. 57. One of the reasons that the Venetians responded in the way they did was because Mehmed was the son of the Sanjack of Herzegovina.

Fig. 4.2   Jean-Baptiste Vanmour, *Head çavuş of the Ottoman Porte* (1700-1737). Rijksmuseum.

stirred up trouble when traveling through Split. While the Venetians could have sent Mustafa away with a reprimand, instead they chose to give him goods and pay for his transit home. Cleary, they had to be careful when dealing with someone who could cause problems with Ottoman officials.[21]

---

[21]   A.S.V. Collegio, Esposizioni Principi, registro 21, fogli 59R–63V.

According privilege to those in power whom the Venetians were looking to help manifested itself in different ways. Not only did a spokesperson coming from the sultan in 1504 have his expenses paid, but he also stayed as a guest in the home of Vettor Morosini. It is interesting to note that another spokesperson sent from the sanjack beyi of Valona, who was in Venice at the same time, did not stay in the same place, but rather on the Giudecca.[22] Prestigious accommodation must have been somewhat commonplace for important diplomatic guests, for another spokesperson, Khalil, who came from the sultan in 1524 was housed on the Grand Canal in the house of Andrea Corner at San Samuel.[23] Khalil not only spoke excellent Latin, but also asked to see Ser Lunardo, the podestà of Mestre, whom he considered to be a very good friend.[24]

The treatment and the presentation of Ottoman subjects in Venice conformed to certain accepted ways of treating an important visitor and to ascribed forms of public presentation. In 1514 an Ottoman emissary, Ali Bey, traveled to Venice with a retinue of 80 people, 25 of whom were *spahi*.[25] Housed on the Giudecca at the Ca Malipiero, he arrived in the Piazza San Marco on his way to the Collegio in grand style.[26] The Venetian diarist Marino Sanudo commented that in anticipation of his arrival in the great square,

> The Venetians sent forty gentlemen of every age all dressed in scarlet and three cavaliers Alvise Mozenigo, Gabriel Moro, and the doctor Piero Pasqualigo to escort (the Ottoman guest).... The messenger from the sultan and others came in splendid fashion about an hour and a half later. First came Turks wearing fezes, one behind the other, with presents in hand. There were ten pieces, made up of cloth of gold, crimson, Turkish blue, and other colors of cloths of silk, numbering ten that each one brought. Then three who brought two pieces of camlet, the ends for one were blackish-blue and one brought a red *fazuol* with Turkish gold and another a small carpet. Then came another Turk who wore a helmet of gold and following was the messenger of the sultan wearing a suit of gold Turkish cloth and a large fez.[27]

---

[22]   Marino Sanudo, *I Diarii di Marino Sanudo*, vol. 6, eds. Rinaldo Fulin et al. (Venezia: F. Visentini, 1879–1903), cols. 29, 38.

[23]   Ibid., vol. 33, col. 259.

[24]   Ibid., cols. 266, 267, 278.

[25]   Spahi were cavalrymen who obtained a grant of land in return for military service.

[26]   Sanudo, *I diarii*, vol. 17, col. 504.

[27]   Ibid., vol. 17, col. 521. "Et fo mandato a levar dicto orator con li piatti per zerca 40 zentilhomeni do ogni età vestiti di scarlato, et questi tre cavalieri di seda: sier Alvise Mozenigo, sier Gabriel Moro, e sier Piero Pasqualigo doctor......prima alcuni do soi turchi con fesse in cao l'uno drio l'uno drio l'altro con li presenti in mano, quali fono 10 peze tra panno d'oro, cremesin, turchesco paonazo, et altri colori di panni di seda, numero peze 10 che cadaun portava la sua; poi tre, quali portavano do peze di zambeloto fine per uno, paoneze e negre, e uno portava uno fazuol rosso con oro turchesco, e uno altro uno tappeto picolo, poi un turco era col zacolar d'oro in testa, et demum l'orator con un casaca di panno d'oro turchesco e una gran fessa in testa."

Subsequent trips by Ali Bey to Venice from the Giudecca were also characterized by his public presence. Not only was he visible on the Piazza San Marco, but he also traveled up the Grand Canal to the *Fondaco dei Tedeschi* and dined with four other Turks at the house of the Venetian noble Piero Zustignian.[28]

Edward Muir notes that "in Renaissance Europe ceremonies were in broadest terms an expression of the world order and more narrowly a formulation of political rules that usually appeared in written word much later."[29] In receiving foreign visitors, the Venetians carefully tried to make the ritual correspond to the office and position of the foreign guest. Each diplomatic visitor represented an ambiguous political relationship, and ceremonies looked to make these encounters predictable and standardized.[30] Place, participants and gestures all played a role in how a particular individual was received.[31] Yet ritual involved both complicated politics and messages. In his study of Renaissance Florence, Richard Trexler notes that "the network of domestic and foreign antagonisms, the fears of the Florentines at the successes of allies all mitigated against straightforward ritual expression."[32] In this regard, diplomatic events were purposefully vague and designed to appease a variety of different political interests.

Ottoman rituals also were designed to communicate complex messages. Religious festivals, charitable acts, the accession of a new sultan and preparation for battle were all ways that the Ottoman government projected its power via rituals. When power was transferred to a new sultan, the opportunity existed to receive oaths of allegiance and guarantees of service. Like European ceremonies, Ottoman festivals involved many different groups of people and conveyed different social and political messages. The Ottomans were particularly interested in impressing foreign envoys with the scale and pageantry of their festivals. Careful attention was placed on where people were seated and with whom they were placed.[33]

Part of the reason that rituals involving foreign dignitaries had to be so carefully thought out was that the treatment of an envoy, a person of status, represented a form of communication between regimes. The symbolic nature of a ceremony was a way in which the importance of a person and an alliance could be expressed. While involving a bureaucratic component, envoys and the ceremonies surrounding their presence were ways in which the heads of governments reached

---

[28] Ibid., vol. 17 col. 551. Also see Zele, "Aspetti delle legazioni."

[29] Edward Muir, *Civic Ritual in Renaissance Venice* (Princeton: Princeton University Press, 1981), p. 187.

[30] On ceremonial diplomacy see Deborah Howard, "Cultural Transfer between Venice and the Ottomans in the Fifteenth and Sixteenth Centuries," in *Forging European Identities, 1400–1700* (Cultural Exchange in Early Modern Europe) vol. 4, ed. Herman Roodenburg (Cambridge, UK: Cambridge University Press, 2007), pp. 142–52.

[31] Muir, *Civic Ritual*, pp. 234–5.

[32] Richard Trexler, *Public Life in Renaissance Florence* (Ithaca: Cornell University Press, 1980), p. 285.

[33] Pedani, *In nome del Gran Signore*, pp. 25–6.

an understanding with one another and also a means in which regimes articulated support and shared interests. This scenario took place in 1480 when an envoy from the sultan arrived in Venice with the news that the Ottomans did not want to agree to peace with Naples without the consent of the Venetians and was also the case in 1484 when an Ottoman emissary asked that the Ottoman navy be granted access to Venetian ports.[34]

Some of the envoys came with requests directly related to personal matters concerning the grand vizir and the sultan. For instance, Hassan and Mustafa, the two Ottoman subjects who brought their claims before the Avogaria di Comun in 1574, were envoys from the grand vizir,[35] and in 1605 Nathan Ashkenazi was sent to acquire goods for the sultan. Ashkenazi presents an interesting case in thinking about how individuals created connections with the highest levels of the Ottoman government and used these connections to conduct business elsewhere. Born a Venetian subject in Udine, Nathan Ashkenazi's father Saloman left for Istanbul in 1556 at a time when Jews were forced to leave his native city. Establishing connections in the Ottoman capital, Ashkenazi established a relationship with the powerful Grand Vizir Mehmed Sokollu and acted as an intermediary with the Venetians during the War of Cyprus. Nathan, the son and servant of the sultan, arrived in Venice late in the winter of 1605 looking to buy gold, silk and wool cloths that were in short stock. Ashkenazi remained in Venice until August to collect his goods and return to Istanbul.[36]

The case raises the issue as to whether Ashkenazi was operating under strict orders from the sultan or had the ability to act on his own. Given the amount of time he spent in Venice and the close relationship his family had with the Venetian government one would assume that he had latitude to do what was necessary to ensure the transaction took place. As noted, intermediaries and other cultural brokers were able to cross religious and social boundaries with relative ease. This trust also demonstrates the importance of an envoy in articulating the reliance that the Ottoman and Venetian regimes had on one another. Riccardo Fubini notes that in the late fifteenth century, Florence embassies "served as political bonds among regimes which provided each other with mutual support in potential situations of crisis."[37] When thinking about Venetian/Ottoman cases we might extend the idea of mutual support through diplomatic exchange even further. In Ashkenazi's case, the sultan needed specific goods and though the Venetians were lacking the cloth, they were anxious to fulfill his wishes.

---

[34]   Pedani, *In nome del Gran Signore*, pp. 204.

[35]   A.S.V., Avogaria di Comun, Miscellenea Civile, busta 278, March 19, 1574.

[36]   Pedani, *In nome del Gran Signore*, pp. 25–6. On Saloman Askenzi, see Arbel, *Trading Nations*, pp. 77-86.

[37]   Ricardo Fubini, "Diplomacy and Government in the Italian City States of the Fifthteenth Century, (Florence and Venice)," in *Politics and Practice in Early Modern Italy: The Structure of Diplomatic Practice*, ed. Daniela Frigo (Cambridge, UK: Cambridge Univeristy Press, 2000), p. 26.

Political Agreements and Communication

Much of what the sultan and his government expected was expressed through *ahdnâmes*. Ahdnâmes were promise letters or guarantees of safety to non-Muslim communities. They were also used as peace treaties with foreign states and as agreements with non-Muslim subjects of other lands living in the Ottoman Empire. The ahdnâmes were the means through which Europeans were able to administer their own communities by adjudicating their own legal matters, establishing their own churches and enjoying a certain amount of autonomy. But the ahdnâmes also had the effect of allowing the Ottomans to make their diplomatic and legal power felt in matters deliberated on and judged by other states.[38]

In theory, while ahdnâmes reflected the Ottomans' belief that their relations with other states were unilateral, they also involved areas of mutual interests.[39] The Ottomans believed that by granting foreigners freedom of trade and residence in the Ottoman empire, they would receive a guarantee of peace, and if the peace was violated the agreement would be null and void. In 1403, Süleyman Çelebi, the son of the sultan Bayezid, concluded a pact with Venice, Byzantium, Genoa, and the Hospitallers of Rhodes that included a sworn oath that each of the parties and their children would live in peace.[40] In an ahdnâme made with Venice in 1521, the stipulation was made: "Accepting the friendship with them according to this pact which has been mentioned, I am swearing with strong oaths... that as long as they shall observe the pact and the friendship and do nothing contrary to the pact, from my side I will do nothing contrary to the pact."[41] Halil Inalcik contends that the Ottomans put significant stock in these agreements because they were tied to the tenets of Islamic law. [42] Along these lines, different European sources referenced the ahdnâmes as sacred capitulations and believed that because of the religious sanctions, these agreements represented the gold standard. Yet Ottoman writings at the time provide a different interpretation by using the terms *ahdnâme-i hümayun*, imperial capitulations.[43] Part of the issue in interpreting the cultural reasoning behind the capitulations may be our desire to draw a rigid distinction

---

[38] Hans Theunissen, "Ottoman-Venetian Diplomatics: The *'Ahd-Names*. The Historical Background and the Development of a Category of Political-Commercial Instruments together with an Annotated Edition of a Corpus of Relevant Documents," (PhD thesis, Utrecht University, 1960), p. 306–9.

[39] For a discussion on ahdnâmes as treaties see Goffman, "Negotiating with the Renaissance State," pp. 64–8.

[40] Theunissen, "Ottoman-Venetian Diplomatics," p. 192.

[41] Viorel Panaite, *The Ottoman Law of War and Peace*, Eastern European Monographs, no. 571 (New York: Columbia University Press, 2000), p. 288.

[42] Halil Inalcık, "Ottoman-Venetian Relations," *Venezia centro di mediazione tra Oriente e Occidente, secoli XV-XVI: aspetti e problem*, a cura di Hans Georg-Beck et. al, vol. 1 (Firenze: Olschki, 1977), p. 89.

[43] Maurits H. Van Den Boogert, *The Capitulations and the Ottoman Legal System* (Leiden: E.J. Brill, 2005), p. 20.

between sacred and secular interpretations without recognizing the variety of issues at hand.

A number of Ottoman and Venetian ahdnâmes were drawn up over an extended period of time. As early as 1361 the Venetians looked to gain trading privileges from the sultan. In 1384 the Venetians wanted to make an agreement to obtain grain from Ottoman lands and in the treaty of 1403 the Venetians had obtained important concessions regarding trade. These agreements were extended in 1446 and 1454[44], and in 1478, the Ottomans issued another ahdnâme to the Venetian envoy Giovanni Dario at the conclusion of the Ottoman/Venetian war. Rather than directly naming the Doge, the document was addressed to the Signoria, the upper echelons of the Venetian government. This type of salutation may indicate that the relationship between Mehmet and Giovanni Mocenigo had not been well established. Mocenigo had replaced Andrea Vendramin earlier that year. In contrast, in the Venetian/Ottoman ahdnâme of 1482, Mocenigo was addressed directly.[45]

Before the 1478 ahdnâme arrived in Venice, Venetian officials in the Balkans were told to adhere to its provisions. An Ottoman official accompanied Dario to Venice to ensure the Venetians agreed to the terms. The ahdnâme closely followed earlier agreements that had been drawn up in 1446 and 1454. The content part of the document treated the parties as equals in which each side was expected to guarantee security of transport and safety from attacks against pirates, while the second part asked the Venetians to pay tribute for trading privileges, to give 100,000 ducats for past debts, and to turn over the Greek areas of Limnos and Scutari to the Ottomans. The document concluded with the understanding that each side would restore territories that were taken during the war.[46]

In referencing the 1478 ahdnâme, Diana Galliand Wright and Pierre MacKay contend that the Ottomans' military power was so formidable that the Venetians' ability to maintain any Greek possessions had to do with the goodwill of the Ottoman sultan Mehmed rather than a negotiated settlement. Thus while the aforementioned Lemnos and Scudar were to be returned to the Ottomans, territories that had been taken prior to the war were not a part of the treaty and did not need any mention.[47]

The management and control of territory and of people was an important component of inter-state relations. In 1595, Hüseyin ağa came to Venice to reaffirm the peace between the two regimes and to announce the succession of Mehmed III to the throne.[48] The Ottoman/Venetian peace had to be reconfirmed each time a new sultan came into power. In theory, each leader guaranteed the

---

[44]   Inalcık, "Ottoman-Venetian Relations," pp. 89–90.

[45]   Theunissen, "Ottoman-Venetian Diplomatics," p. 371.

[46]   Diana Galliand Wright and Pierre MacKay, "When the Serenissima and the Grand Turco Made Love: The Peace Treaty of 1478," *Studi Veneziani* 53 (2007), pp. 262–4.

[47]   Ibid., p. 264.

[48]   Pedani, *In nome del Gran Signore*, p. 173.

peace, but in practice it also had to do with the long standing relationship between the Venetian and the Ottoman regimes. Part of the reason for re-establishing this guarantee had to do with the fact that peace was always challenged and regimes had to respond to a variety of situations. In 1579, the Venetian senate sent out dispatches to its governor in Zadar and the heads of the cavalry that Ottoman subjects had attacked the village of Berdo in retaliation for three Morlachs[49] who had been killed by Venetian subjects from this village. The Venetians not only wanted to find out who had killed the Morlachs but also to make sure that the people who moved into these border areas would protect their interests. Attempts to guarantee mutual cooperation and peace were maintained by the Venetians' understanding of protocol. On the same day that the Venetians notified their local governors of the problem, they also sent a message to the bailo telling him that guarantees should be passed on to the sultan that these transgressions would not continue to take place.[50]

The 1595 ahdnâme addressed the Doge Marin Grimani directly, requiring that the friendship and peace between the two peoples be re-established along the lines of the earlier ahdnâmes. This approach was taken to accentuate the amount of cooperation that had taken place over the years. The language was careful to praise the Doge for his status and his position as a Christian leader and to recognize the importance of the bailo. That the Doge was addressed personally represented another level of respect. The ahdnâme then listed a variety of different issues, including freedom of movement, protection of merchants including those from North Africa in Venice, taxes and access to legal protection. What is notable about the way in which these areas were addressed is the recognition of shared interests. Ottoman subjects needed to move freely through Venetian territories so Venetian subjects needed to be granted the same privilege. Merchants had to be protected against fraudulent transactions and be guaranteed restitution. Ships needed to be able to dock at foreign ports and required safe havens from pirates. Though the Ottomans dictated the terms of the agreement, the language of the treaty also involved reciprocity and negotiation. Integrity of borders, protection of subjects and the security of trade could only be fulfilled if both sides were willing to cooperate.[51]

The issue of fixed frontiers is particularly important, because the Ottomans' recognition of accepted borders challenges the idea that the Ottomans were only interested in expansion as opposed to stability. In this regard, treaties emphasize the importance of safeguarding certain spaces, one of which was frontiers. In 1597, the Ottomans sent an ahdnâme to the Polish king Sigismund III stating "The beys of the sanjacks of Silistra and Akkerman, the harbor masters and the tax collectors, should not let anybody go to Poland across the river Dniester except

---

[49] The Morlachs were rural people who lived along the Dalmatian coast.

[50] A.S.V., Deliberazioni Costantinopoli, registro 5, fogli 116V–118R

[51] Belin, "Relations diplomatiques," Ottoman version pp. 396–408, French translation pp. 408–24.

the servants of my felicitous threshold and the merchants of the two sides."[52] The stipulation in the ahdnâme demonstrates the importance that Ottomans gave to maintaining control of their subjects. Borders were complicated, because as we have seen in the previous chapter, people crossed boundaries to flee from certain situations at home. Item 20 in the Venetian/Ottoman ahdnâme of 1595 stated that fugitives, both Ottoman and Venetian, who crossed boundaries into neighboring territories must be returned. Protection of ships was emphasized because the seas, like borders, were considered to be contested spaces. Here corsairs and other independent parties threatened both Ottoman and Venetian imperial interests.[53]

One way in which we can measure the degree of importance the Ottomans attached to the ahdnâmes is by correlating them to *hüküms* and firmans the government issued in regard to similar concerns. A hüküm was an edict or an imperial order. It was sent from the *Divan-i Hümâyun* of the Ottoman chancery. The Divan consisted of the offices of the grand vizir, the nişancı, the court secretary, the baş defterdar, the treasurer, and the kadiaskers, the chief judges of Anatolia and Rumelia, all of whom were subordinate to the sultan and were part of the organ of government responsible for communicating with people in the provinces.[54] Beyond these individuals, different officials at the level of vizir were also involved in the drafting of communications. Within the council, executive and judicial and legislative matters were deliberated, and responses in the forms of edicts were issued to the relevant parties.[55]

In creating a system of communication, a hüküm served as a means for legitimating the power of the sultan and the supremacy of the sultanate. Baki Tezcan argues that the Ottoman sultan evolved from a warlord to a great lord to an emperor in the sixteenth century. The tension that existed between different lords was resolved by the creation of a patrimonial political system. In creating this type of state, Tezcan believes that the system changed from a feudal system to one based on fictive ties of kinship tied to "political slavery." In contrast to slave owners in the American south, the term "political slavery" refers to Ottoman sultans' major obligations to the people under them. People who had high positions derived much of their power from their relationship to the sultan, and they passed down orders through a chain of command that stretched from the capital to the provinces.[56]

---

[52]   Dariusz Kolodziejczyk, *Ottoman-Polish Diplomatic Relations (15ᵗʰ–18ᵗʰ Century): An Annotated Edition of 'Ahdnames and Other Documents* (Leiden: E.J. Brill, 2000), p. 311. (The ahdname sent by Mehmet III to King Sigismund III.)

[53]   Belin, "Relations diplomatiques," p. 403.

[54]   Selçuk Akşin Somel, *Historical Dictionary of the Ottoman Empire* (Lanham, MD.: Scarecrow Press, 2003), p. 130.

[55]   Bruce McGowan, "Ottoman Political Communication," in *Propaganda and Communication in World History: The Symbolic Instrument in Early Times*, vol. 1, eds. Harold D. Lasswell et al. (Honolulu: University of Hawaii Press, 1979–80), p. 462.

[56]   Baki Tezcan, *The Second Ottoman Empire: Political and Social Transformation in the Early Modern World* (Cambridge, UK: Cambridge University Press, 2010), pp. 82–93.

In issuing a hüküm, the Divan reinforced the authority of the sultan as the arbiter of disputes between his own and foreign subjects. For instance in 1573, an edict sent to a local bey stated that the Venetian navy had informed the Ottoman state that three slaves had run away and the bey was to be on the lookout for these people and not provide them with this assistance.[57] This edict was issued at the time of the peace after the War of Cyprus and undoubtedly reflected an Ottoman desire to make good on their agreements.

The fact that the Venetian navy had contacted the Ottoman central government illustrates that a hüküm was connected to a complaint or concern that had been brought to the attention of the Porte. This type of petitioning process allowed individuals to inform the Ottoman central authority of a variety of different transgressions against the government's rule. In 1578 an edict was sent to Karli Bey, in which the Porte noted that the Venetians complained that Ottoman subjects were taking slaves in Venetian lands, and this practice should cease.[58] Their complaint to the Porte indicates that these Venetian subjects felt that they would have better success by going directly to the central government than by dealing directly with a provincial official who in this case appears to have been either an adversary or someone who needed coaxing from the top to settle the problem.

On other occasions, on receipt of information from the Venetians, edicts were sent to local Ottoman officials ensuring that Venetian subjects traveling across Ottoman lands received protection and the necessary funds. This type of protection would have corresponded to the protection discussed earlier in regard to the Venetians' security concerns for Ottoman subjects. In 1570 in an edict issued to a local bey, the Porte commanded that he release Venetian subjects who were bringing letters to the Venetian bailo.[59] This demand reflected a punishment/reward system in which Ottoman subjects who assisted Venetian guests of the Ottoman government were provided good compensation. In an edict issued in 1556, the Porte offered four janissaries a timar for escorting the Venetian bailo across Ottoman lands.[60] In another case the Ottomans told a man living in Cyprus that he would be given land and 15 akçe for going to Algeria to escort the Venetian bailo.[61]

Many times an order was sent to a kadi to uphold a legal obligation. For instance, in 1585 an edict was sent to kadis of Avloyna (Vlorë) and Drac Nova in Albania stating that an Ottoman captain Murad was attacking Venetian islands and taking goods and slaves and that he should be stopped in order not to break the peace.[62] Clearly, the order was given to ensure that the terms of an ahdnâme were not breached. But why rely principally on kadis as opposed to other local

---

[57]   Başbakanlik arşivi, Mühimme Defteri, cilt 23, sira 709.

[58]   Başbakanlik arşivi, Mühimme Defteri, cilt 9, sira 549.

[59]   Başbakanlik arşivi, Mühimme Defteri, cilt 9, sira 97.

[60]   Başbakanlik arşivi, Mühimme Defteri, cilt 2, sira 1738.

[61]   Başbakanlik arşivi, Mühimme Defteri, cilt 25, sira 660.

[62]   Başbakanlik arşivi, Mühimme Defteri, cilt 58, sira 195.

officials in this case? One reason may have been that kadis were more reliable in handling these matters. In a study on hüküms issued on Palestine, Uriel Heyd states that very few of the edicts were directed at kadi abuses. Kadis also had power that extended beyond just juridical matters.[63] In his study on two Anatolian towns Çankırı and Kastamonou, Ergene Boğac argues that kadis were responsible for representing the local to the center. The government could depend on kadis to make accurate reports and act as credible witnesses. In many cases the government was not interested in hearing a claim if a kadi did not support that individual's or that group's petition.[64] Given that Murad's actions can also be thought of as a rebellion, the court acted as a place where not only locals could go to seek justice but also foreign subjects as well. While the Porte was asking the kadis of Avloyna and Drac Nova to take action, the courts also presented a local point of contact for those who had filed the complaint.

Issuing these types of edicts was important to the Ottomans in maintaining their territorial sovereignty. The notion of sovereignty in the early modern world has been interpreted in different ways. One definition is that supreme authority was able to gain control within a particular expanded territory. This type of rule differed from the Middle Ages in that sovereigns did not have to compete with others for political authority and central control and territorial integrity were more constant.[65] In contrast, Lauren Benton states that "….territory plays tricks. Mere patches of regulated land may appear to signify claims to vast holdings, while integral sovereign space may fracture into many odd-shaped pieces." She adds that "subjecthood was defined by a set of political and legal relationships shaped by strategic maneuvering and interpretation and subject to challenge."[66] These ideas warrant consideration in regards to the Ottoman Empire. Palmira Brummett notes that the Ottoman mapmaker Matrakçi Nasuh used fortresses as "markers of space" and located tombs as places protected by the sultan. Sovereignty was dependent on locals' willingness to respect this type of hegemony.[67] In 1572 a hüküm was sent to local bey stating that during the war of Cyprus, a Venetian subject had taken a tower in the Bosnian city of Mostar and had tried to make it into castle. The Porte told the bey to prevent it from happening.[68] In 1576 a hüküm was sent asking if the people of the town of Karucadaga really paid taxes to the Venetians, and might in

---

[63]   Uriel Heyd, *Ottoman Documents on Palestine, 1552–1615: A Study of The Firman according to the Mühimme Defteri* (Oxford: Clarendon Press, 1960), p. 20.

[64]   Ergene Boğac, *Local Court, Provincial Society and Justice in the Ottoman Empire* (Leiden: E.J. Brill, 2003), pp. 44–5.

[65]   Dan Philpott, "Sovereignty," in *The Stanford Encyclopedia of Philosophy,* ed. Edward N. Zalta, Summer 2010), http://plato.stanford.edu/archives/sum2010/entries/sovereignty/.

[66]   Benton, *A Search for Sovereignty*, pp. 30–31.

[67]   Brummett, "Imagining the Early Modern Space," p. 52.

[68]   Başbakanlik arşivi, Mühimme Defteri, cilt 21, sira 108.

fact be Ottoman subjects.[69] And in 1575 an edict sent to Ferhat Bey ordered him to make sure that people who were selling cows to the Venetians pay taxes.[70]

In 1628 an edict from the Porte was sent to the sanjack beyi of Alcahisar and the kadi of Ürgüb, both in Serbia, explaining that in former times in the sultan's lands in towns, villages and trading centers merchants from Dubrovnik, while traveling and stopping at rest stops, carried weapons and dressed like Muslims in order to protect themselves against robbers and brigands. The mention of towns, villages and trading centers indicates that the Ottomans defined their sovereignty in terms of established centers. Even though locals were opposed to Christians dressing like Muslims, the Porte noted that given that the subjects of Dubrovnik continued to be loyal, they should be afforded these privileges. The order also indicates the difficulty of guaranteeing the safety of foreign guests and establishing sovereign control in outlying territories.[71]

Sovereignty was particularly difficult to maintain in places where the Ottomans had more limited control. In 1571, a hüküm was sent to the kadi of Uskub, warning him that the son of a man named Bugdan Bey was always sending his men to Venice and possibly selling corn to the Venetians. The kadi was asked to ensure that these activities were stopped.[72] In 1572 the Ottomans told Mora Bey that he should send Ottoman Christians and others who were having social relations with the Venetians to jail;[73] And in 1584, an order was sent to a bey telling him 50 to 60 Christians living in Ottoman territories near Karadag had joined Venetian soldiers and must be identified and then imprisoned.[74] All these communications represented attempts to protect the government's perceived sovereignty.

Ottoman sovereignty and the government's political and legal power were expressed in many different ways in dealing with Venice and other foreign states. For one, kadis were asked to render decisions on cases involving conflicting claims between either the two states or subjects of the two states. This was the case in 1575 when the Venetians, in hopes of placating the demands of a group of Turkish and Jewish merchants whose goods had allegedly been taken by a group of Venetian subjects from a ship that was returning from Ancona, wrote to the governor in Zadar that

> ......because it is possible the *sanjack beyi* may not be content with your information and may take evidence from another quarter, because of the appeal of the interested parties, we think it would be helpful to show some courtesy both to the *kadi* who will examine the case and to those who will be examined in connection with it. We wish you to make use in this matter of our most loyal subject Vicenzo of Alessandria, who is at present in that part of the world, or

---

[69] Başbakanlik arşivi, Mühimme Defteri, cilt 28, sira 873.

[70] Başbakanlik arşivi, Mühimme Defteri, cilt 26, sira 228.

[71] Başbakanlik arşivi, Mühimme Defteri, cilt 84, sira 37.

[72] Başbakanlik arşivi, Mühimme Defteri, cilt 18, sira 20.

[73] Başbakanlik arşivi, Mühimme Defteri, cilt 18, sira 20.

[74] Başbakanlik arşivi, Mühimme Defteri, cilt 55, sira 94.

failing him, of our good doctor Almissa (to whom we will convey our gratitude for the service rendered by him) or by anyone else you judge more appropriate. You must authorize him to present the *kadi* and the witnesses who are to be examined with goods to the value of 50 ducats, as you will see from the enclosed document. You shall divide the goods among them according to the status of the individual, so that, on account of the favorable testimony that will be given by these and other responsible officials, the *sanjack beyi* will be inclined to make a favorable report to Constantinople.[75]

The Venetians realized that a payment at this level could provide a legal rendering, an official decision that the Venetians could point to as a piece of evidence.

Kadis could also have a tremendous amount of influence with a specific faction or in a particular territory. The Habsburg ambassador, de Busbeq, commented that when two of his servants ended up in a fight with a local kadi over a dispute over who would have access to a boat crossing from Pera to Istanbul, "a cry was raised and the Turks rushed together from the whole of Pera with shouts that Christians had laid violent hands upon the judge."[76] A kadi's influence spread over great distances in some lands. In his travels through Albania, Eviliya Celebi noted that the kadi of Durrës "has authority over 73 villages."[77] A kadi's decree might be important if proof became necessary later, and the Venetians wanted to make clear to Ottoman authorities their desire to distance themselves from the actions of their subjects who had attacked the ship with Jewish and Muslim merchants. Gaining the support of the local kadi not only exempted them from responsibility but also reaffirmed their commitment to work with the Ottoman government in regard to issues of mutual importance. Here, personal contacts and connections to powerful provincial figures not only brought the two societies together but also constituted crucial aspects of sensitive diplomatic contact.

Part of the reason that the Venetian government was willing to recognize the decisions made by kadi courts is that the movement of money and goods across

---

[75]   A.S.V., Senato, Deliberazioni Constantinopoli, registro 4, fogli 117R–118R, May 13,1575. "et perche essi sanzacco non contento forse della informatione vostra ad instanzia delli interessati prederne un'altra d'altra parte guidicando noi, che possa giovar molto a questa l'usare cortesia al kadi, che esaminera et a quelli ancora che saranno esaminati volemo sevendo vi in cio del fidellissimo nostro Vicenzo di Alessandria, che la presente si ritrova in quelli parte non overo egli, del detto nostro dottore Almissa al quale faremo comoccasione conoscere esserci grata la servitu dal lui per overo di qualche altro, che giudicarete piu a proposito, debbiate dargli libertà di presentare il kadi, et testimonii, che si esaminassero di roba fra tutti per valor di ducati cinquanta. Siccome parimente dalla inclusa copia vedrete compartendoli fra loro secondo la qualita delle persone, a finé, che dalla buona depositione, che dall'loro esser fatta per causa de simili, et altri officiali, che haverá il carico, possa il Sanzacco trarne l'informatione che si desiderá et piu facilmente disponersi a far buona relatione a Costantinopoli."

[76]   de Busbeq, *The Turkish Letters*, p. 211.

[77]   Robert Dankoff and Robert Elsie, *Evliya Çelebi in Albania and Adjacent Regions* (Leiden: E.J. Brill, 2000), p. 151.

Fig. 4.3   Sünbül Ali, Kadi, *The Habits of the Grand Signor's Court*, folio 9b (circa 1620). British Museum.

boundaries necessitated a certain standardization of practices and recognition of institutional procedures. In April of 1577 a letter was received through the bailo concerning a legal ruling by the kadi of Galata, Ali bin Huseyn, that stated that Haci Hizir should be given a sum of 128,000 *aspri* left to him by his son, who had been murdered in Venice.[78] The ruling of the local judge in Istanbul was not only taken seriously by Venetian officials but also represented the interdependence of two legal systems. Inheritance issues were handled with some regularity by both governments. In a letter sent to the bailo in January of 1587 concerning a Turk who had appeared in Venice to collect the inheritance of the Derviş from Begbazar, who had died in Venice three years earlier, the Venetian Senate asked that in order

[78]   A.S.V., I Documenti Turchi, busta 7, fascicolo 873, Italian translation fascicolo 874, April 14, 1577.

to resolve this situation the bailo should "arrange with the pasha that, just as the goods of his subjects who die in our state are handed over upon certification by the agents of the Sultan, the same shall be done for the goods of our subjects who die in their country, on certification by our ambassadors."[79] The reciprocity expressed in the Senate's communication indicates the degree of collaboration that existed between the two governments.

Many levels of cooperation existed between Ottoman and Venetian officials. In 1584, Cafer Pasha, an official in Istanbul, sent a letter to the Doge asking for the restitution of the goods and prisoners taken when the ship on which the bey of Jerba, son of Ramazan Pasha, was traveling with his family and was attacked by a Venetian captain.[80] While the bey of Jerba's status undoubtedly added weight to Cafer Pasha's request, since powerful people received attention that other people did not, the case demonstrates that assisting a subject when dealing with legal or other disputed matters was not something that was foreign to powerful people with connections to the Ottomans. Clearly, this type of intervention was a major factor in attempting to settle a dispute. Pressure from other officials was applied as well. In 1640 the *defterdar* (treasurer) of Bosnia, Mustafa, sent a letter to the Venetian government asking that 20 Spanish reals taken from his servant by Venetian representatives in Split be restored to a certain Haci Eyüp.[81] While we have no way of knowing what type of connection Haci Eyüp had to Mustafa, the defterdar, it is clear that this type of intervention could prove to be very helpful. In this regard, these ties were important because they underscored a level of social connections that were important in establishing one's status.

Status was an important factor in the conduct of negotiations. In the minds of the Venetians, people with powerful backers represented more than just the anonymous Ottoman subject. If only in an abstract manner, they connected the bearer to an individual tied to the power structure. To conduct business negotiations with a man in Venice named Felippo Emanuel, "Usnif"[82] and two other individuals appeared as representatives of the "emir of the camlets."[83] Given that the two parties could not reach an agreement on how to conclude the negotiations, and undoubtedly out of respect for the emir, the Venetians allowed each side to voice

---

[79]   A.S.V., Senato, Deliberazioni Constantinopoli, registro 7, foglio 58R, January 8, 1587. On the exsitence of this practice in the fifteenth century see Deborah Howard and Francesco Bianchi, "Life and Death in Damascus: The Material Culture of the Venetians in the Fifteenth century," *Studi Veneziani*, N.S., 46 (2003), p. 234.

[80]   A.S.V., I Documenti Turchi, busta 8, fascicolo 941.

[81]   A.S.V., I Documenti Turchi, busta 13, fascicolo 1467.

[82]   Usnif is the Venetian rendering of an Islamic name. It is difficult to determine the Islamic equivalent.

[83]   The emir of the camlets was probably a name that was given to this individual by the Venetian. Emir was an Arabic name assigned to someone who was a chief or a leader. Camlets were high quality woolen cloths made from camel's or goat's hair that were imported principally from Ankara. See Kafadar, "A Death in Venice," p.205.

his complaints to the Senate.[84] Other connections involved revealing ties to powerful officials in the periphery. In 1546 the beylerbey of Rumelia, Ali, sent a letter to the Venetian government asking for tax relief for his emissary, Hurrem, who had been sent to Venice to sell silk.[85] As head of a province, the beylerbey of Rumelia was a powerful figure within the Ottoman administration. A beylerbey had control over a number of districts and district governors within the province of Rumelia. A man such as Ali was trained at the Porte and rose within the ranks of the Ottoman system through a series of geographical and career moves. In order to ensure an individual's utmost loyalty to the sultan and to the Ottoman state, the Ottomans prevented their provincial officials from settling in any one place. In fact, in the 1580s it was exceptional for a sanjack beyi, a district governor, to be in one place for more than three years. During this period the majority of beylerbeys served no more than two years.[86] Thus, while Ali's connection to Hurrem was probably based on a personal tie, other people had to work through a series of connections to have someone as powerful as a beylerbey intervene.

On occasion, relations were triangulated between Venice, Istanbul and the Ottoman and Venetian peripheries. In October of 1579, bearing letters from Sultan Murad III and the grand vizir, a Muslim named Ahmed had come to the governor of Cattaro asking about the whereabouts of a relative of his who had been taken captive by a group of Venetian subjects from the village of Perat.[87] Anxious to please Ahmed's powerful backers the Venetian government wrote the governor of Cattaro and told him to tell any other people who inquired into the situation that the Venetians were very interested "in pleasing the sultan and the grand vizir who had written their recommendations" and so would do what they could to ensure that the captives were released and the goods restored.[88] Yet the pledge to intervene on behalf of these did not only correspond to the wishes of the sultan and the vizir, but also referred to an agreement that had been made following the War of Cyprus. Both parties agreed that neither side would blame the other, but instead hold only the guilty parties responsible. In fact, the Venetians were anxious to inform the sanjack beyi of Castelnuovo that the attack was solely the responsibility of the Perastini and not that of the governor of Cattaro.[89] Ahmed's ability to get these powerful figures to intervene on his behalf thus not only reflected his connections on a local level but also demonstrated his ability to transform a local incident into an

---

[84] A.S.V., Senato, Deliberazioni Constantinopoli, registro 8, fogli 160RV, September 24, 1594.

[85] A.S.V., I Documenti Turchi, busta 5, fascicolo 60.

[86] Kunt, *The Sultan's Servants*, p. 75.

[87] Perat is located along the coast in what is now Montenegro.

[88] A.S.V., Senato Deliberazioni Constantinopoli registro 7, foglio 138R, October 3, 1579.

[89] A.S.V., Senato, Deliberazioni Constantinopol, registro 7, fogli 140 R–V, October 24, 1579. "ma solamente a finé di gratificar il Smo Sor Turco & il Maco Bassá che ne ha scritto á loro raccomandatione."

important diplomatic matter that forced the Venetians to honor their commitments to the Ottoman sultan. The Venetians were so cognizant of this commitment that they informed the governor of Cattaro to use his personal contacts and go directly to Ahmed's residence to explain what had happened and offer a resolution.

Ahmed's letter from the sultan was also obviously an important component in resolving his case and reflected how relations between the center, the periphery and foreign states worked. Along similar lines, in June of 1564, a letter in the name of Süleyman the Magnificent was sent to the Doge Girolamo Priuli listing the names of a group of Muslim merchants who claimed they had been captured and robbed of their goods in the waters surrounding Valona. The Venetians were quick to avoid any potential problems and called for the bailo, Daniele Barbarigo, to turn over 25,000 ducats of gold as an indemnity against any further complaints from the aggrieved parties.[90]

Many Ottoman subjects came bearing letters that were probably more of a bureaucratic nature rather than a request or a demand from someone at the center of power.[91] Karen Barkey points out that "...it was during the reign of Süleyman that the concept of the state gained larger significance, becoming more than the sultan himself or even the individuals who staffed the bureaucracy."[92] Undoubtedly, many letters were produced at the Ottoman chancery and given to the sultan for his approval.[93] In November of 1583 a letter bearing the seal of Murad III was sent to the Doge asking that the Signoria give the merchant Hacı Ahmed 5,500 piastres that were seized when the man that he had been traveling with, a Persian by the name of Ali, had decided to convert to Christianity.[94] Even this type of correspondence must also have made a significant impression because soon after arriving with the letter from the sultan, Hacı Ahmed was able to go before the Collegio and obtain a decree whereby he was reimbursed the money that he had lost.[95] Given the number of requests that the Collegio received on

---

[90]   A.S.V., I Documenti Turchi, busta 6, fascicolo 786.

[91]   Max Weber points out that "The patriarch is the natural leader of the daily routine. And in this respect, the bureaucratic structure is only the counter-image of patriarchalism transposed to rationality. As a permanent structure with a system of rational rules, bureaucracy is fashioned to meet calculable and recurrent needs by means of a normal routine." Max Weber, *Charisma and Institution Building: Selected Papers* (Chicago: The University of Chicago Press, 1968), p. 18.

[92]   Barkey, *Bandits and Bureaucrats,* p. 29.

[93]   Jan Reychman and Ananiasz Zajączkowski point out that the principal complex of offices from which letters or documents were dispatched was called the Sublime Porte or the Babiali. It was headed by the grand vizir. This institution was finally abolished in 1730. See Jan Reychman and Ananiasz Zajączkowski, *Handbook of Ottoman Diplomatics* (The Hague: Mouton, 1968), p. 159. The other possibility is that the document was drawn up in the offices of the Imperial Divan.

[94]   A.S.V., I Documenti Turchi, busta 7, fascicolo 929, Italian translation, fascicolo 930. That is not to say that Haci did not have close contacts with the Porte. It is merely to point out that there were bureaucratic procedures for dealing with issues like this one.

[95]   A.S.V., I Documenti Turchi, busta 7, fascicolo 927, Italian translation fascicolo 928.

a regular basis, Ahmed's backing from the Porte undoubtedly distinguished him from others who petitioned the government. In all likelihood the Venetians were accustomed to receiving letters sent from the Porte related to financial matters. Four years earlier, a letter from Murad III had been sent, asking that the 10,000 ducats that Venice was holding in its treasury for the deceased merchant Hasan bin Inayetullah should be turned over to the correct inheritor, his cousin Hüseyn bin Haci Murad.[96] These types of letters not only facilitated people's requests, but also established a procedure for pursuing these matters to the point of resolution.

Attachments to the state and to other powerful figures in the Empire were not limited to Muslims. Other connections crossed sectarian lines and reflected different forms of patronage and partnerships. Ibrahim Pasha, an Ottoman government official in Cairo, sent a letter to the Venetians asking that two Jewish merchants, Abramo and David Querido, be allowed to settle as traders in Venice.[97] The case is particularly interesting because four years later Daniel Rodriga, a Jewish merchant of Iberian origins, put forward a proposal whereby Jewish Levantine merchants would be allowed to live in Venice permanently. While the Venetians were reluctant to make this concession, they did make an agreement whereby certain Levantine Jews were allowed to live and trade in Venice for a period of ten years.[98] Part of the Venetian thinking was related to the fact that some Jewish merchants had connections to powerful Ottoman figures. In fact, in 1563 Venetian officials confiscated the contraband of a Jewish Levantine merchant and suffered the consternation of Ottoman officials because it was discovered that at least some of the goods belonged to the grand vizir, Mehmed Sokollu.[99] The merchant's ties to such a powerful figure in the Porte undoubtedly influenced the Venetians' handling of the case, for in a message sent to the bailo the Venetian government told the bailo to compensate the grand vizir for whatever losses he had incurred.[100] The world of commerce and the world of politics were not as separate in the early modern world as they are today. An official's bureaucratic position did not preclude him from engaging in other activities. While Sokollu's relationship to the Jewish trader might be considered a conflict of interest in a modern setting,

---

[96]   A.S.V., I Documenti Turchi, busta 7, fascicolo 888. Given the amount involved here, this letter may indicate that the person had a close personal relationship with someone at the Porte.

[97]   A.S.V., Senato, Deliberazioni Constantinopoli, filza 6, August 1583.

[98]   For further information on Rodriga and the condotta granted to Levantine and Ponentine Jews see Renzo Paci, *La scala di Spalato e il commercio veneziano nei Balcani fra cinque e seicento* (Venezia: Deputazione di storia patria per le Venezie, 1971) and Ravid, "Legal Status of the Jewish Merchants."

[99]   Arbel, *Trading Nations*, p. 20. Arbel also comments on pp. 103–4 that Saruq was the actual owner of the confiscated merchandise and only after the goods were sequestered did Saruq donate a portion to the vizir in order to help him out of his predicament. For information on Mehmed Sokollu see Radavan Samarčić, *Sokollu Mehmed Pasha* (Istanbul: Sabah Kitapları, 1996).

[100]   Arbel, *Trading Nations*, p. 103.

in the early modern world these types of situations were not considered to be improper. In fact, a government position probably put a person in a better place to exploit commercial opportunities.[101] It also benefited a trader who ran into problems, for when the time came to settle the dispute the connection to Sokollu was certainly an advantage.

Individuals with connections to the Porte undoubtedly carried similar recommendations to the one that Ahmed presented to the governor of Cattaro. They were a way of establishing the person's credentials and the purpose of his or her visit. Documents were also a necessity if one was to pass from one land to another and foreigners could be subject to arrest if they were not carrying the correct papers.[102] Brunehilde Imhaus points out that a foreigner coming to Venice had to be in possession of various types of documents. First, foreign subjects had to present a letter of recommendation from the state to which they were attached. Second, they also had to carry a letter of safe conduct from the Venetians while traveling through Venetian territories.[103] It must have been obligatory for Ottoman subjects traveling to Venice to receive this letter of safe conduct from the bailo or another Venetian consul in one of the provincial Ottoman cities. In a number of different instances Ottoman subjects arrived in Venice with the requisite approval from a Venetian official.[104] This procedure also probably applied to many Venetian subjects traveling across Ottoman lands.[105] In 1624, Murad IV sent a letter to the beylerbeys, sanjack beyis, and kadis along the road from Venice to Istanbul, informing them that the Venetian ambassador should be granted free passage to Istanbul to attend the ceremonies of the new sultan's accession to the throne.[106]

Clearly, not everyone had the ability to receive a recommendation from people in positions of power. Many arrived in Venice as slaves or as transients, hoping to establish ties rather than actually having them. For instance, Ali, a Turk from Gallipoli, found himself at the mercy of the Venetian authorities because he did not

---

[101] An interesting example of this involves an outstanding debt between two Ottoman vizirs and Venetian merchants. The sultan sent a letter to the Doge asking him to intervene and settle a debt of 487,000 akçe owed to Ayas Pascià and Mustafa Pascià who had always sold large orders of wheat on credit. Tayyib Gökbilgin, "Le relazioni veneto-turchi nell'eta di Soliman il Magnifico," *Il Veltro*, Marzo-Agosto 1979, pp. 277–90.

[102] E. John B. Allen, *Post and Courier Service in the Diplomacy of Early Modern Europe* (The Hague: Martinus Nijhoff, 1973), p. 69.

[103] Imhaus, *Le minoranze orientali*, p. 249.

[104] I do not make this point from any specific reference regarding the necessity of this document. Rather, I state this because of the number of times people went to the bailo to receive a recommendation (see Pedani, *In nome del Gran Signore*) and also from E. John B. Allen's contention that these types of documents were mandatory in Europe.

[105] Tayyib Gökbilgin points out that Venetian subjects and merchants who wanted to go to Bursa first had to receive permission from the Venetian bailo. Undoubtedly, this must have been done in cooperation with an Ottoman ministry. Gökbilgin, "*Le relazioni veneto-turchi*," p. 79.

[106] A.S.V., Documenti Turchi, busta 12, fascicolo 1306.

have the backing of a powerful person. Locked in a Venetian prison, Ali was given the opportunity to choose baptism as a way out of his predicament.[107] While little evidence remains of the conditions that he was forced to live under during his stay in confinement, clearly his status as a foreigner, and more importantly as a Muslim, must have made him feel more secluded and helpless. In all likelihood many of these people must have been lost in the crowd shuffling across imperial borders.[108]

Not all recommendations by Ottoman officials or connections to Ottoman officials met with a positive response from the Venetians. In fact, Ahmed Bey sent a letter to the Doge expressing his disappointment that the Jews he recommended had not been received favorably by the Venetian government.[109] We must remember that each society had its point of entry and rules of conduct that had to be adhered to. Not all people were welcome, nor were they accorded certain advantages. In 1571, during wartime, the Porte sent an edict to Sinan Pasha telling him that while a man by the name of Signore Pauli had claimed that was he a relative of Venetian nobles, the only reason that he had done this was to get out of paying taxes. The Porte concluded that because of his treachery his goods should be confiscated and that he and his men should be sent to jail.[110] Letters from their respective governments helped to avoid some of these problems and also set up a procedure for establishing an individual's place within the social order. Status not only dictated where a person would stay and the type of gifts he or she would receive, it also contributed significantly to the types of benefits that he or she might enjoy.

The Language of Letters and other Diplomatic Material

If letters and the status of the people who sent them reveal a lot about how relations worked across borders, the language of correspondence also tells us a lot about how power functioned.[111] In early pre-modern Arab Islamic societies, style, as

---

[107] Istituzioni di Recovero e di Educazione , Catecumeni, busta 4, March 1594.

[108] While it is difficult to have any idea as to the number of people who traveled from East to West or from West to East without a recommendation, we do have a sense that these types of people were numerous in Italy. See Braudel, *The Mediterranean*, vol. 1, pp. 334–8. Braudel points out that in Venice while immigrants from Friuli were considered industrious, those from the Romagna and the Marches were thought of as criminals. To this he adds that "Undesirable and usually clandestine visitors, they would enter the city at night by regular passages, using the services of some barruol who could not refuse his boat to men often armed with firelocks, *de roda*, and who forced him gently or otherwise to carry them to the Giudecca, Murano, or some other island. To forbid entry to these visitors would have kept down crime, but it would have required constant vigilance and local spies." (pp.335–6)

[109] A.S.V., I Documenti Turchi, busta 8, fascicolo 1021, Italian translation.

[110] Başbakanlik Arşivi, Mühimme Defteri, cilt 18, sira 93.

[111] Cipher was a coded language that governments also used to communicate with one another. It can be seen as a form of cooperation and shared understanding. On the use of language and cipher in diplomacy see Robyn Adams and Rosanna Cox, eds., *Diplomacy in Early Modern Culture* (New York: Palgrave Macmillan, 2011).

opposed to persuasion, was the central characteristic in letter writing. One aspect of style that was considered important was textual unity, and many letters were restricted to just one theme. Issues that necessitated a more formal guarantee than a verbal response were communicated through writing, and two types of letters existed that served this function, the more formal or administrative and the less formal, or more personal.[112]

In his work on letter writing in the middle Islamic period, Adrian Gully comments that "It is no coincidence that the main focus of 'official' letter writing in pre-modern Islamic society was the social relationship between the writer— the initiator of the letter—and the recipient." Much of the understanding of this relationship required knowledge of how to craft a letter that correctly articulated the social hierarchy. Words were not the only way of making distinctions, and layouts were scrutinized to meet social and political requirements. Salutations reflected the ability of the writer to combine linguistic skills with contextual understanding.[113]

In the Ottoman context, letters represented an increasing Ottoman presence in networks of communication with different social actors throughout Eurasia.[114] Given the different points of contact the empire had with different states and social groups, communications were diverse and coded in very different ways. The more elaborate the *intitulatio*, or the opening, the more formal the relations. Correspondences with Charles V and other monarchs opened with elaborate descriptions of the power and the expanse of the sultanate. The intitulatio of a standard letter from Süleyman stated that "I who am Süleyman Şah han..., the sultan of sultans, the proof of the emperors, the shadow of the God on the lands, the sultan and padişah of the White Sea, the Black Sea, Rumelia, Anatolia, Karamania, of Rum...."[115] The emphasis on the expanse of the Ottoman realms indicates the importance of invoking conquest as a basis for relations and as a mechanism for articulating power. Yet, we must be careful not to place too much emphasis on the purely ceremonial as opposed to the material.[116] The description of the sultan's territories also delineated the lands, peoples and resources that he controlled.

Other correspondences were framed in the language of exchange. In 1561 the inspector of finances for Bosnia Herzegovina, Mehmed, in the name of the

---

[112] Adrian Gully, *The Culture of Letter Writing in Pre-Modern Islamic Society* (Edinburgh: Edinburgh University Press, 2008), pp. 1–23.

[113] Ibid., p. 84.

[114] Kaya Şahin, *Empire and Power in the Reign of Süleyman: Narrating the Sixteenth Century* (Cambridge, UK: Cambridge University Press, 2013), p. 225.

[115] Daniel Clarke Waugh, *The Great Turkes Defiance* (Columbus: Slavica Press, 1978), p. 17.

[116] See Mehmet Sinan Birdal, *The Holy Roman Empire and the Ottomans: From Global Imperial Power to Absolutist State* (New York: I.B. Tauris, 2011), pp. 4–5. Birdal argues that patrimonial societies rely on ceremony and office for the creation of wealth, while bourgeois capitalist societies innovate to grow their economies.

sanjack beyi Haydar Pasha, asked for 1,000 kilos of rice from the Venetians. In the letter, Mehmed offered high praise for the Doge and the other Venetians, without mentioning the Doge's name specifically. The omission undoubtedly had to do with the fact that the finance minister was not at the level of the Doge. The finance minister used the term *muhibbi*, or devotion, to describe his relationship to the Doge. Respect was conveyed by the use of terms such as excellency, felicitous, noble, glorified and exalted. Reference was also made to the fact that the Venetians were the commanders of the Christian nation and members of the greatest Christian sect. While these salutations were representative of the finance minister's recognition of the correct letter-writing protocol, the language of the letter makes it clear that the exchange could take place only if the sanjack beyi and his representative understood the constituent power relations and could correctly articulate the social standing of the involved parties. [117]

In another letter involving a request to the Venetian Doge for salt from the same Mehmed on behalf of Haydar Pasha, the relationship between the two parties was articulated in a different way. In this letter Mehmed noted that the mutual devotion and friendship between the sultan and the Doge was the foundation of the relationship between the Venetians and the Ottomans.[118] In effect, Mehmed used mutual devotion as a form of persuasion to have the Doge grant him his request. Praise and persuasion were two of the ways parties could make themselves heard diplomatically. But these two forms of presentation were not mutually exclusive. In making the request for the salt, Mehmed used the same opening that he had in his letter requesting the rice. While mutual devotion may have existed, the Doge needed to be addressed with the appropriate salutation. In his request for the rice, Mehmed also used persuasion as well as praise to gain a positive response. While no attempt was made to reference the Doge's relations to the sultan, Mehmed tried to persuade the Doge by mentioning that a Venetian servant known to the Ottomans, Aloiso Narancer, would broker the deal.[119]

Emphasis of personal connections was an important form of persuasion. In 1590, the *kapudan pasha*, the admiral of the navy, Hasan, recommended his brother-in-law, Marcantonio Vedova, for a position as secretary of the Senate and asked that Marcantoni's wife, Camilla, be given the baker's shop that she had requested at Sant' Aponal.[120] Hasan was born Andretta to a family in Venice and at young age went to work on a ship. During his travels, he was captured and finally sold to 'Ulug 'Ali, a corsair. In time, Andretta converted to Islam and became a favorite of his owner, who gave him the name Hasan. Under 'Ulug 'Ali's tutelage,

---

[117] M. Tayyib Gökbilgin, ed, "Venedik Devlet Arşivindeki Türkçe Belgeler Kolleksiyonu İslerine İlgili Dilgi Belgeler," *Belgeler*, cilt 5–8, sayi 9-12 (Ankara: Turk Kurumu Basimevi, 1971), p. 34.

[118] Ibid.

[119] Ibid.

[120] A.S.V. I Documenti Turchi, busta 8, fascicolo 1013, Italian translation fascicolo 1014.

Hasan Pasha became a prominent corsair, finally rising to the position of paşa of Algiers in 1577 and 1582, and by 1588 he had become kapudan pasha.[121]

In the letter, Hasan acknowledged the Doge as the leader of the Christian world, similar to ahdnâmes and other bureaucratic letters. The reference undoubtedly had something to do with Hasan's close connection to the Venetians and his understanding of decorum and protocol. Terms in both Turkish and Arabic were used to point to the different ways in which the idea of friendship could be expressed. The relationship between the Ottomans was based on durable long-lasting ties, respect, honor and reverence for each other. Each side was dependent on the other to maintain cooperation and to share respect.[122]

While Hasan's praise of the Venetians can be interpreted as a sign of his appreciation, Virginia Mason Vaughn comments that "such formalities were not simply a matter of custom and decorum; the stylized language cloaked and contained tensions, and in some cases, dangerous intrigues."[123] In Hasan's case, the obvious problem was his conversion to Islam. His conversion made him a renegade and at least in theory an enemy of Christianity. Yet Hasan addressed this problem by discussing the shared histories between Venice and Ottomans. He spoke of the arrival of the Venetian bailo at the Ottoman court to receive a letter related to the aforementioned request and how his presence reinforced the strength of the relationship between the Ottomans and the Venetians. In having an audience with the sultan Hasan noted that the bailo bowed his head in order to give the sultan the respect he deserved. This point reinforced the power of the sultan and the Ottoman state. Note was made of the perfect etiquette and dignity that accompanied the presentation of the letter to the bailo. Again emphasis was placed on the depth of the friendship and how its endurance eclipsed all other issues, including seemingly Hasan's conversion and his acceptance of a position in the Ottoman government. Hasan referred to Marcantonio as an *intisab* or someone with whom he had very close relations and who the Venetians had treated with *riayet*, respectful consideration and grand honor, though he was a stranger.

Hasan also spoke about how appreciative he was of the way that the Venetians had handled his request, and he promised that he would do what he could to protect Venetian interests. Expressing this point further reiterated the notion of reciprocity. If using praise was a way of maintaining respect and protocol, it also articulated cooperation. Cooperation was not based merely on presentation but also on the ability to deliver. From his position in the Venetian court, Hasan was not looking for just ceremonial recognition; he also wanted tangible, material results, an office in Venice for a close relation, and a sense of security for his family. In referencing the relationship between the two states, given that the Venetians had delivered, the

---

[121] Dursteler, *Venetians in Constannople*, pp. 123–4

[122] A.S.V. I Documenti Turchi, busta 8, fascicolo 1013

[123] Virginia Mason Vaughn, "Representing the King of Morocco," in *Emissaries in Early Modern Literature and Culture: Mediation, Transmission, Traffic, 1550-1700*, eds. Brinda Charry and Gitanjali Shahan(Farnham, UK: Ashgate Press, 2009), p. 80.

Ottomans could be expected to do the same. Further documentation reveals that Hasan wrote back to the Venetian Senate reiterating that if he could be of any help to the Venetians at the Porte he would be more than happy to receive Venetian requests. Not only is the request interesting because of the fact that an Ottoman official was asking for a position in the Venetian government for a close relation by marriage, it is also noteworthy because Hasan portrayed himself as an insider at the Porte for the Venetians.[124]

The letter from the Ottoman dragoman Ibrahim to the Venetian dragoman Michele Membre reveals how personal connections could be used to curry favor. In 1567, Ibrahim sent a letter to Membre from Dubrovnik after he had left Venice to return to the Ottoman Empire. In the letter, written in Turkish with Latin characters, Ibrahim thanked Membre for helping him and a Jewish merchant, Aronue Nahmiez, sell goods for their patron Mustafa Çelebi during their stay in Venice and avoid paying taxes. Ibrahim noted that if Membre needed help with trade in the future, Ibrahim would be more than happy to comply. After praising Membre, Ibrahim then stated that Mustafa Çelebi wanted another of his representatives, Giuseppe Hudara, to be granted the same privileges and protection.

After asking for this favor, Ibrahim proceeded to discuss business more related to the affairs of the empire. Here, he explained that the goods of Hüseyn, referred to as *dostlûgumuz*, or our friend, were being held in a ship that had been attacked by the Uskoks. Note was made that the goods should be returned to Hüseyn's representative, Baruk, who received an endorsement from Hüseyn and Mustafa as well as the Venetian bailo. In the letter's final section, Ibrahim asked for better protection from Venetian ships for Ottoman subjects against Uskok attacks, noting that the Venetians paid a lot for unreliable security. In concluding Ibrahim wished the Doge and other important Venetians officials well.

The letter reveals the close connection between personal relationships, trade and cross-cultural diplomacy. Ibrahim opened the letter by referring to Membre as his close friend or brother. By putting this reference at the opening, Ibrahim demonstrated that his personal connection to Membre had helped facilitate commercial and diplomatic matters with the Venetian government. But this personal relationship was only as important as the person who acted as Ibrahim's backer, Mustafa Çelebi. Mustafa Çelebi was such an important individual that it was contingent on the Venetians to accept another of his representatives, Giuseppe Hudara. This request was framed by Ibrahim's statement that Mustafa Çelebi served as a much better ally than an enemy. In his Italian translation of the letter, Membre referred to Mustafa as the head of the merchants of the sultan. This position meant that Mustafa had a significant amount of influence independent of Ibrahim's relationship to Michele Membre.[125]

---

[124] A.S.V., I Documenti Turchi, busta 8, fascicolo 1011, Italian translation, fascicolo 1012, follow-up fascicolo 1014.

[125] Bombaci, "Una lettera turca in caratteri latini...", Turkish pp. 138–40, Italian translation, pp. 140–44.

This influence was evident both in the language of letters and in other forms of written and verbal communication. As we have seen in the case of Lucia, the Bosnian woman, the type of power that could be projected across boundaries contained a gendered language. This type of language was supported by people behind the scenes, individuals and groups who held the power necessary to make agreements enforceable and had the power to craft diplomatic correspondences. Ottoman envoys who arrived in Venice were powerful members of the Ottoman court whose power was expressed through ceremonial display. Decisions that had been rendered by local kadis and letters from local governors reflected both legal and political influence. Yet ties to the Ottoman state went beyond connections to the local officials, for at times individuals bore letters that came directly from the Porte. While many of these were probably of a more bureaucratic than personal nature, they did serve as important letters of introduction for people looking for political cover. The Venetian government was more apt to act on the request of a person bearing a letter of recommendation or other correspondence from a powerful Ottoman official. This type of documentation was essential to anyone traveling any great distance. It not only helped guarantee a modicum of protection, but also distinguished the bearer from the masses of people who passed from East to West and West to East. More than just a passport, written connections to the sultan and his officials designated a certain status and prestige in a world in which connections to powerful people served as important markers of how an Ottoman presented either himself or herself to the authorities when visiting Venice. Letters prepared by the Ottoman state were not only important, but also in many ways defined the individual. One without powerful patrons and protectors had very little leverage during a time when specific types of power dictated the terms of negotiations and agreements.

Chapter 5
A Mediterranean Conflict:
Alliances, Factions and Networks

In March 1618, the Venetian government received a letter in the name of Sultan Mustafa I.[1] The letter noted that a group of Muslim merchants from Bosnia, Herzegovina, Klis and other Ottoman districts had wanted to travel from Split to Venice in order to trade. At the time, the merchants had received a warning that a Spanish fleet was operating in the Adriatic and that they should therefore exercise caution before boarding the Venetian ships. Aware of the threat and anxious to alleviate the merchants' fears, the Venetian consul in Bosnia told the merchants in front of the tribunal of Nurulla, the chief judge of Sarajevo, that the Spanish were not interested in attacking Venetian ships and if an incident did take place the Venetians would compensate the merchants for any of their losses. This promise was to be reiterated, for upon their arrival in Split, the merchants, hearing the threat again, went to the governor of Split, Velutello, who, like his colleague in Bosnia, signed a similar agreement in front of Ismail, a kadi from Klis who had come as a witness. Thus, secure in the knowledge of these promises, the merchants set off for Venice confident that they would not be attacked. Their worst fears, though, were to be realized, for during the journey the Spanish fleet approached the merchant ships, causing the escorting Venetian galleys to turn back. Unprotected, the merchant ships headed for shore, where the merchants were forced to flee and leave their goods on the ships, whereupon the Spanish then boarded the vessels and took everything that had been left. The letter of March 1618 concluded that given the promises that had been made and considering the circumstances, the Venetians should honor their commitments and compensate the merchants for their losses.[2]

This letter from the Ottoman sultan referred to an attack that Pedro Téllez-Girón, the Duke of Osuna who had been appointed the Spanish viceroy of Naples, had launched against the Venetian fleet in July of 1617. The letter raises a variety of different questions regarding the nature of the case and the logic the parties to the dispute used in stating their positions. For one, the sultan's letter indicates that the Venetian galleys' failure to protect the merchant ships rendered them responsible.

---

[1]   Sultan Mustafa I was in power for only three months before being deposed. While conventional wisdom has it that the reason for his removal was his mental incapacity, Baki Tezcan states that intra-Ottoman politics and a lack of education and exposure to the world in all likelihood is a better explanation. See Tezcan, *Second Ottoman Empire*, p.109.

[2]   A.S.V., Senato, Deliberazioni Constantinopoli , registro 12, fogli 48V–49V, March 4, 1618.

From the perspective of the Ottoman government, the Venetians' promise through their officials in Sarajevo and Split that they would provide restitution in the event of an attack represented a guarantee, a contractual arrangement. But the Venetians, at least initially, did not agree with this demand and disputed the Ottoman claim. Instead, the Venetians believed that the Duke of Osuna should be responsible for returning the goods, in that he had launched the attack and acted as the provocateur. By laying blame on the Duke of Osuna, however, the Venetians were only telling part of the story for the incident itself did not stand alone and represented part of an ongoing war that pitted different parties in the Mediterranean, in Europe and in Asia against one another. Diplomatic agreements, treaties, influence-peddling and the right of force were all a part of struggle that saw different factions use the incident as a means for gaining the upper hand in battles over influence, power and territory.

Control of the Sea

The ongoing war involved a very complex geography. While the years between 1573 and 1645 have been thought of as the long Venetian/Ottoman peace, each party was involved in a variety of different conflicts. Christian ships attacked Ottoman convoys in the Eastern Mediterranean. The Venetians struggled with the Habsburgs in Austria and in Spain. The Ottomans were engaged in a twelve-year war with the Safavids between 1578 and 1590 and were involved in a long-term battle with the Habsburgs that involved constant territorial gains and losses. A lack of a monopoly on violence made it impossible for one power to gain political hegemony, and different groups such as militias, local armies, mercenaries and regional factions all participated in different types of warfare.[3]

In the Mediterranean, corsairs, buccaneers and privateers undertook military operations, which on many occasions were sponsored by different states.[4] Molly Greene notes that "Crossing the sea meant crossing an endless series of frontiers, ill-defined but nevertheless very real, as one moved in and out of the shadows of state authority." Different types of conflict defined these boundaries, and when military borders did exist, they were established by how far Christian and Muslim galley ships were willing to venture from their home bases.[5]

---

[3]   For Venetian and Ottoman/Habsburg relations see Setton, *Venice, Austria and the Turks*. For the Ottomans and the Safavids see Adel Allouche, *The Origins of the Ottoman-Safavid Conflict (906–962/ 1500–1550)* (Berlin: Klaus Schwarz, 1983) and Ernest Tucker, "From the Rhetoric of War to the Realities of Peace: The Evolution of Ottoman-Iranian Diplomacy through the Safavid Era," in *Iran and the World in the Safavid Age*, eds. Willem Fleur and Edmund Herzig (New York: I.B. Tauris, 2012), pp. 81–90.

[4]   Greene, *Catholic Pirates and Greek Merchants*.

[5]   Molly Greene, "The Ottomans in the Mediterranean," in *The Early Modern Ottomans: Remapping the Empire*, eds. Virginia Aksan and Daniel Goffman (Cambridge, UK: Cambridge University Press, 2007), p. 112.

Like the Spanish attack against the Venetian ships and Uskok raids against maritime shipping, many confrontations took place in territorial waters and coastal areas near ports. These and other attacks at sea raised questions as to what constituted legal and what constituted illegal activities. One view is that no political entity had sovereignty over the sea. The sea was a place where everyone had the right to navigate and to transport goods. This idea was tied to natural law and to a universal belief that the sea was a special place that could be used by everyone. The Dutch writer Hugo Grotius was particularly supportive of this position in his 1609 work *Mare Liberum*. In arguing for the freedom of navigation in the Indian Ocean, Grotius supported the rights of Dutch merchants to transport their goods free of interference from the Portuguese. Yet even Grotius, one of the early proponents of a form of international law, had a bias that favored the interests of Dutch commerce and that undermined the idea of seas free from attacks on merchant shipping.[6]

Some of the contradictions found in Grotius's writings can also be seen in the work of Alberico Gentili, an Italian who for three years worked as an advocate for the Spanish crown in England. Like Grotius, Gentili believed that while the sea should be a free trading zone, individual cases warranted different considerations. Gentili noted that while a Sardinian and Maltese attack against an English ship carrying munitions to the Ottomans should be condoned because "…canon law forbids furnishing Saracens with munitions of war, and the Turks are Saracens," in this case the attack seems unwarranted because the owners may have been unaware of the goods on board.[7]

Gentili's reasoning reflected a variety of concerns. As a Spanish advocate, he believed that, as allies of the Spanish, the Sardinians and the Maltese were enemies of the Ottomans, and thus justified in their attempt to interrupt military supplies headed to the Ottoman empire. But he also noted that Spain's treaty with England was based on a defensive war and the Habsburg emperor, a relative of the king of Spain, was fighting an offensive war against the Ottomans. Gentili noted that "Kinship and private interests do not determine public policy, and the naming of the Emperor among the supporters of Spain is empty form."[8] Legality was a complex question in which jurisdiction, guilt and innocence were framed by different political concerns and interpretations of what constituted accepted logic. While Gentili could not ignore Christianity's clash with the Ottomans, or the right of Christians to attack their "enemies," he also reasoned that the state of war between the Ottomans and Spain was more complicated than just a Christian/Muslim fight. The Ottomans were at war with "heathens" (the Persians) and in all likelihood their power would not be used against Christians.[9]

---

[6]   Benton, *A Search for Sovereignty,* pp.131–4

[7]   Alberico Gentili, *Hispanicae Advocationis*, vol. 1 (New York: Oxford University Press, 1921), pp. 32a, 33a.

[8]   Ibid., p. 34a

[9]   Ibid.

Gentili added that "in fact it was lawful to take these things to the Turks under the Orders in the Council of Queen Elizabeth. The Englishman follows the law of his native land, not the canon or civil law."[10] Given that England had its own system of governance, then it was under English law that English merchants should be judged in their dealings with Ottomans.

> The King of England is a sovereign prince and the head of ecclesiastical affairs in his own domain and he cannot permit his people to be made subject to the laws of either of the Emperor or the Pontiff. Under the Law of Nations only a completed act calls for punishment. Under it the Maltese may interfere with those who are on their way to sell contraband to an enemy but may not punish them.[11]

Gentili's assessment points to the numbers of ways in which jurisdiction could be interpreted. As a sovereign state, the English were not subject to either imperial or religious authorities. Yet a form of international law did exist in which a completed exchange of illegal goods could be adjudicated but not goods that were still in transit. Under these terms the Maltese could interfere, but they could not punish the alleged perpetrators. Gentili's ambiguity provided all the concerned parties with a means of justifying their claims.

Lauren Benton comments that "the imagined legal structure was one of layered sovereignty, in which rights to patrol and control sea space did not diminish the rights of either overarching powers or of all of Christendom."[12] For instance, the Venetians believed that their control of the Adriatic, in what came to be known as the Gulf of Venice, began in the north and extended to a line that stretched from Otranto in the southern part of Puglia to Vlorë in Albania. Venetian control was not based on their own right to navigate, but instead on their ability to prevent others from using the Adriatic. Benton notes that "this amounted to a property right that was nominally different from dominion."[13] This idea was derived from the medieval notion that a state could not claim territorial domain to the sea, but it could gain jurisdictio or use rights over bodies of water. Jurisdictio was the equivalent of a property right that was acquired by donation or prescription from the emperor, and it justified Venetian control over the city and its territories and gave them the right to collect taxes and to hold court over these areas.[14]

The justification of Venice's domination of the Adriatic also preoccupied early modern Venetian writers, and Paolo Sarpi, the noted Venetian reformer

---

[10]   Ibid.

[11]   Ibid.

[12]   Benton, *A Search for Sovereignty*, p. 123.

[13]   Ibid.

[14]   Richard Perruso, "The Development of the Doctrine of *Res Communes* in Medieval and Early Modern Europe," *Tijdschrift voor Rechtsgeschiedenis* 70 (2002), p. 81.

and intellectual,[15] believed that the birth of the Venice's existence was tied to its control over the sea. In the same way that states controlled land based territories, the Venetians had established sovereignty in the Adriatic at the time when the sea was not under any other power's control. Venice's preeminence in the sea was not based on rights granted to it by the Pope or the Emperor; the Venetians had independently developed a deep understanding of the different ports, inlets, shores, and they were the ones in a position to make laws and guarantee the security of maritime commerce which served the public utility and helped in the resolution of disputes.[16]

Part of Sarpi's argument also involved the guarantee of security to other ports along the coast between Ravenna and Aquielia, which had been without patrons until the Byzantine emperor Justinian had gained control of the region in the sixth century. Sarpi used historical examples to justify the idea that the Venetians were the heirs to this tradition. In 1393, the Senate sent a letter to the Captain of the Navy in the Adriatic, in which the Captain was asked to use his galleys to protect the sea against pirates and thieves. Emphasis was placed on the expenditures that had been made and the blood that had been sacrificed in order to protect the sea. Further mention was made that other states were not to have armed vessels in these waters. [17] The Archduke of Austria married the sister of the King of Naples in 1399 and asked for safe conduct from the Venetians from Puglia to the Dalmatian coast. In 1486, the Pope approached the Venetians, in response to Ottoman incursions into the sea, asking that the Venetian navy ensure that the Adriatic was free from corsair attacks. Philip II confirmed that as others had control over land territories, the Venetians held dominion over the Adriatic Sea. Looking for protection, the Pope asked the Venetians in 1577 to intervene against the galley of the Marchese of Vico and to provide protection to vulnerable ships. The acknowledgement of Venice's dominance of the Adriatic was so well understood that in addressing the Venetians the King of Portugal called them "masters of the Adriatic Sea."[18]

Sarpi's treatise reflects the different considerations the Venetians had in justifying their domination of the Adriatic. As discussed earlier, the Venetians had to find a way to prevent Uskok attacks. The Uskoks were aligned with the Austrian Habsburgs, and in 1615 the war of Gradisca broke out between the Venetians and the Archduke Ferdinand of Styria,[19] with fighting taking place in and around

---

[15] On Sarpi see Gaetano Cozzi, *Paolo Sarpi tra Venezia e l'Europa* (Torino: G. Einaudi, 1978).

[16] Paolo Sarpi, *Domino del Mar Adriatico della Serenissima Republica di Venezia* (Venezia: Roberto Mietti, 1685), p.16, http://books.google.com/books?id=Fn45AAAAcAAJ&printsec.

[17] Ibid.

[18] Ibid., pp. 32, 28, 30, 29, 37.

[19] Styria is a region in southeast Austria.

Fig. 5.1   V.M. Coronelli, *Map of the Gulf of Venice* (1690). Antiquariaat
Sanderus Map Collection.

the Uskoks' home base in Senj and also in Venetian border areas.[20] Ultimately,
the Venetians were willing to give territories in the Friuli in exchange for the
cessation of Habsburg support of the Uskoks. Other conflicts and rivalries also
challenged Venetian supremacy in the Adriatic. Corsair attacks were common, and
the Venetians were constantly involved in preventing raids against their merchant
ships. As Venetian power waned in the sixteenth and seventeenth centuries,
Ancona, the principal port for the papacy, became an important center of Adriatic
trade.[21] Ragusa or Dubrovnik competed with Venetian trade and received backing
from both the Ottomans and the Spanish. In direct competition with the Venetian
traders, Ragusan merchants did a steady business along the Adriatic coastline.[22]

Spain also represented one of the biggest threats to Venetian rule. With the
union of Castile and Aragon in 1479, Spanish kings ruled over Sicily, and in 1504

[20]   John Marino, "The Venetian Territorial State: Constructing Boundaries in the
Shadow of Spain," in *Spain in Italy: Politics, Society and Religion, 1500–1700*, eds.
Thomas James Dandelet and John Marino (Leiden: E.J. Brill, 2007), p. 245.

[21]   On Ancona see Peter Earle, "The Commercial Development of Ancona," *The
Economic History Review*, New Series, vol. 22, no. 1 (1969), pp. 28–44.

[22]   Peter Sugar, *Southeastern Europe under Ottoman Rule, 1354–1804* (Seattle:
University of Washington Press, 1996), p. 168.

they gained control of Naples. Within the Spanish imperial system, the outermost provinces were expected to protect the inner ones, and the Spanish territories in southern Italy were thought of as a barrier against incursions from the Ottomans and groups in North Africa.[23] Looking to expand its shipping and gain further protection from its enemies, in the seventeenth century, the Spanish looked on the Adriatic as an area in which to increase their territorial influence. Part of implementation of this strategy involved the arrival of Pedro Téllez-Girón as the viceroy of Sicily in 1611. Téllez-Girón was concerned that Sicily did not have enough force, in particular galleys, to defend against attacks from the Ottomans. To address this problem, Téllez-Girón increased the galleys in Sicily to nine in 1612, and over the next two years, his fleet delivered severe blows to the North African fortresses of La Goleta and Cherchell, while also successfully attacking the Ottomans in the Aegean.[24]

The Spanish View of the Conflict in the Adriatic

To reward his successes, Pedro Téllez-Girón arrived in Naples to serve as its viceroy in 1616. At the time, with a population of approximately 270,000, Naples was the second largest city in Europe next to Paris and thus the position of viceroy carried a significant amount of prestige. Much of the importance of the Neapolitan viceroy within the Spanish system was connected to the viceroy's ability to fit within the framework of Spain's imperial designs. Referring to the reign of Philip II, Aurelio Musi notes that "The Spanish sovereign offered a dual constitutional personality: he was the nexus of a vast complex of states with local powers, but he was the only person holding title to sovereignty and the right to make decisions in the domestic politics of each of the states and to set foreign policy for the entire monarchy."[25]

Part of the projection of empire was related to the ability to convert "local allies into projectors of power."[26] Téllez-Girón had been very successful in both defending and expanding the Spanish frontier. As viceroy of Sicily, he had been expected to put down rebellions and to defend Spanish interests against attacks from the Ottomans, corsairs and other enemies of the Spanish state. This undertaking proved challenging, because on many occasions he fought both

---

[23] Aurelio Musi, "The Kingdom of Naples in the Spanish Imperial System," in *Spain in Italy: Politics, Society and Religion 1500–1700*, eds. Thomas James Dandelet and John Marino (Leiden: E.J. Brill, 2007), p. 83.

[24] Luis Linde, *Don Pedro Girón, duque de Osuna: La hegemonia española en Europa a comienzos del siglo XVII* (Madrid: Ediciones Encuentro, 2005), pp. 101–2.

[25] Musi, "Kingdom of Naples," p. 85.

[26] Wayne Lee, "Projecting Power in the Early Modern World," in *Empires and Indigenes: Intercultural Alliance, Imperial Expansion, and Warfare in the Early Modern World*, ed. Wayne Lee (New York: New York University Press, 2011), p. 11.

internal and external opponents.[27] He accomplished this task by building alliances with other naval squadrons such as Genoa and Malta. These connections were important in expanding superiority at sea and in gaining the upper hand against the Ottomans. Attempts were also made to provide munitions and soldiers to Greek Christians who were enemies of the sultan.[28] These relationships advanced the cause of Christianity and also provided Téllez-Girón with influence in Ottoman territories.

In building up his forces and in establishing alliances, Téllez-Girón understood that his power should be used to confront states, like the Ottomans and Venice, who were antagonistic to Spanish interests. His antipathy towards Venice was formed in concert with the Marquis of Bedmar, the Spanish ambassador to Venice. The two of them were charged by Venice in 1618 of conspiring to overthrow the Venetian government. While a debate exists as to whether or not the Venetians manufactured the story, the close relationship between Don Pedro and the Marquis indicates that they cooperated on many matters.[29] One of these matters was a concern that Venetian control over the Adriatic would have a significant influence over Italian politics. They shared this fear with Don Pedro de Toledo who became the governor of Milan in 1615. The struggle for control of the duchy of Milan pitted the Spanish state, including the Duke of Osuna and other Spanish officials, against the Duke of Savoy who was backed by the French and the Venetians, both of whom opposed the Pax Hispanica in Italy.[30]

These alliances demonstrate that the politics of contested areas should not be seen as separate from one another, but should be seen as part of interconnected spaces that brought different Spanish and other actors together. Individuals such as Pedro Téllez-Girón and Don Pedro de Toledo were part of a larger struggle that was taking place across the Mediterranean in which local and trans-regional politics were intertwined. In January of 1617, Téllez-Girón sent a letter to Don Pedro de Toledo stating that he had been ordered by Madrid to prevent troops from Holland from coming to Italy to help the Venetians. As viceroy of Naples,

---

[27]   For an overview of the Duke's time as viceroy of Sicily see Linde, *Don Pedro Girón*, ch. 3, pp. 99–124.

[28]   Cesáreo Fernandez Duro, *Duque de Osuna e su marina: Jornadas contra Turcos e Venecianos* (Madrid: Sucesores de Rivadenyera, 1885), pp. 28, 34–5. Google books, pdf.

[29]   On the plot see Richard Mackenny, "Myth, Legend and the 'Spanish' Conspiracy against Venice in 1618," in *Venice Reconsidered: The History and Civilization of the Italian City State*, John Jeffries Martin and Dennis Romano (Baltimore: John Hopkins Press, 2000), pp. 185–216. Mackenny states that while the Spanish were looking to challenge Venetian interests, the Venetians also used the idea of an external conspiracy to strengthen their own state. No direct proof exists from non-Venetians sources that the conspiracy ever took place, and Téllez-Girón stated emphatically to the Spanish government that he was not involved in trying to overthrow the Venetian government.

[30]   To understand the complexity of these relationships and the end of the Pax Hispanica see John Elliot, *The Count Duke of Olivares: The Statesmen in the Age of Decline* (New Haven: Yale University Press, 1986), pp. 52–5, 55–65.

the Duke worked in coordination with Don Pedro de Toledo and sent both infantry and cavalrymen to assist the governor of Milan in his struggle. Other material needs were also important and Téllez-Girón noted that Don Pedro de Toledo lacked shields, thus Naples would provide Milan with 3,000 of them. The transfer of men and military equipment represented a type of trans-imperial exchange in which regional actors not only advanced their own interests but also supported the ambitions of the Spanish Crown.[31]

Yet rather than seeing the interests of these individuals as purely the administrative interests of the Spanish bureaucracy, we also need to consider what personal interests were at stake. Gen Liang argues that the Spanish government was made up of many personal networks, some of which were familial and maintained generational control over different areas.[32] Pedro Téllez-Girón came from one of the wealthiest families in Castille. His life was characterized by a significant amount of movement and by a variety of connections to different patrons. For instance, in 1603, Téllez-Girón arrived in Paris to meet with his uncle, Don Juan Fernández de Velasco who became his mentor after his father died.[33] This connection allowed him to become part of a family network. In 1606, in recognition of the fighting he had done in Flanders on behalf of the Crown, he became the head notary of Castille, a position both his father and his grandfather had held.[34]

Téllez-Girón's portrayal of his experience on the frontier in Flanders also must have contributed to his appointments in both Sicily and Naples. We have seen the importance of people who could negotiate different border situations, but we must also consider how border narratives and contact zone encounters were constructed by individuals who were looking to enhance their personal power. In 1616 a report was issued that described an encounter between the Ottoman fleet of a famous Ottoman renegade corsair by the name of Arzan and that of the Duke of Osuna, Pedro Téllez-Girón. The report noted that Arzan's fleet had attacked coastal areas, had taken prisoners and had captured Genovese ships. While both sides suffered casualties, the Christian forces were able to gain the upper hand, largely due to the efforts of one Spanish soldier named Francisco Roel who jumped on one of Arzan's vessels and attacked the crew and thereby lost his life. Other Spanish soldiers followed suit, and in time, Arzan was forced to flee to a fortified castle.[35]

The report clearly emphasized that, while many Spanish soldiers had died, in the end the valor of Téllez-Girón's forces had won out. Spanish honor had

---

[31] Duro, *Duque de Osuna*, Carta del Duque de Osuna para D. Pedro de Toledo, gobernador de Milan, refiriendo las *contrariedados* que sufre de la Córte, pp. 321–3.

[32] Gen Liang, *Family and Empire: The Férnandez de Córdoba and the Spanish Realm* (Philadelphia: University of Pennsylvania Press, 2011), pp. 21–3.

[33] Linde, *Don Pedro Girón*, p. 52.

[34] Ibid., p. 54.

[35] Duro, *Duque de Osuna*, Relacion de la verdadera que 10 galeras del Duque de Osuna, pp. 312–16

Fig. 5.2   Bartolomé González y Serrano, *Portrait of the Duke of Osuna* (circa
             1615). Last accessed at http://spanishbaroqueart.tumblr.com/
             post/21232770399/bartolome-gonzalez-y-serrano-portrait-of-the-
             duke.

been restored because of the brave actions of the Téllez-Girón's fleet. The report
confirmed that the Duke and his forces had the capability to confront Spain's
enemies and reinforced the idea that Spain had the military power to gain
sovereignty in Mediterranean waters.

   Success against the Ottomans was a constant theme in descriptions of the
exploits of the Duke's fleet. In July and August of 1613, while he was the viceroy
of Sicily, a report noted that a squadron of the Duke's ships confronted the
Ottoman armada. In the battle, the Ottoman captain, Sinan Baja, was wounded
and later died. According to the report, 1,200 Christians were liberated and 600

Turks were taken captive, some of who were high officials.[36] In May of 1617, a triumphant account was given of the Duke's forces' confrontation with two galleys and three other Ottoman ships. After attacking the ships, the Duke's forces boarded and found a number of expensive goods that were owned by Muslim and Jewish merchants. The ship also contained a number of enslaved Christians who were subsequently liberated.[37]

These attacks raise questions as how to classify these types of confrontations and how to understand their justification. The seventeenth century represented the highpoint of Mediterranean pirate activities. With the arrival of Spanish wealth from the Americas, the reduction of the Ottoman navy in the eastern Mediterranean and the decline of traditional trading states such as Venice, Genoa and Barcelona, Muslim and Christian corsairs filled in the vacuum.[38] Many of the attacks in the Mediterranean were committed by northern powers such as the English and French against established powers like the Venetians and the Spanish who were exclusionist and protectionist in their control of certain sea-lanes.[39]

The Duke's attacks against the Ottomans followed along similar lines and were attempts both to confront Ottoman hegemony in different parts of the sea and to gain protection for Spanish coastal areas. They also reflected the activities of a local authority who was attached to a state but also able to act in his own interests. Naples was the only part of the Spanish crown outside Castille that was able to finance its own operations independently; thus the Duke could undertake his own naval operations and exercise his own authority.[40] Lauren Benton states that "the administration of empire depended, meanwhile, on the exercise of delegated legal authority."[41] Authority could be delegated to local governors, ships and even pirates. Regional forces could be assembled to confront one's enemies. In December of 1616, Pedro Téllez-Girón wrote that he had been informed that Francisco Ruiz de Castro, the viceroy of Sicily had been asked to take his ships into the Adriatic to "to divert" the Venetians. The use of the term divert is relevant in that it did not imply war; it was a strategy to force the Venetians to concentrate their forces elsewhere. This plan demonstrates that while the government was responsible for

---

[36] Duro, *Duque de Osuna*, Relacion de la gran que hizo en el Duque de Osuna…, pp.274–8

[37] Duro, *Duque de Osuna*, Veradera relacion de la Victoria que tre galeras del señor Duque de Osuna, pp. 326–30.

[38] Greene, *Catholic Pirates*, pp. 78–9.

[39] Anne Pérotin-Dumon, "The Pirate and the Emperor," in *The Political Economies of Merchant Empires*, ed. James Tracy (Cambridge, UK: Cambridge University Press, 1991), p. 213.

[40] Linde, *Don Pedro Girón*, p. 125.

[41] Benton, *A Search for Sovereignty*, p. 3.

organizing the different parties involved, confrontation or diversion was at the discretion of the regional actors.[42]

With the understanding that he was to disrupt the Venetians' activities in the Adriatic, Téllez-Girón informed the government in Madrid in a letter drafted on June 2, 1617 that he had received a communication telling him not to enter the Adriatic. He had ignored the command because it was not written in code, choosing instead to assemble a force to challenge the Venetians. The fact that he had chosen to act in opposition to what he had been told in the letter indicates the degree of ambiguity that existed between the two parts of the empire. The Crown had variety of means for communicating its wishes, and recipients had different ways in which they could interpret what had been transmitted.

Appealing to the Spanish Crown to support his actions, the Duke explained what had transpired to date. Deciding to act against the Venetians, Téllez-Girón assembled a group of ships at Brindisi, one of which was captained by Admiral Ribera, a man who had been very successful in confronting the Ottomans. The Duke provided Ribera with 19 extra galleys to support the mission. Skirmishes had already taken place between Spanish and Venetian ships, and the Duke decided to prepare for a larger battle. He commented that the mission related to a direct order from the king to disrupt commerce, though he also noted that he understood the complex politics of the Adriatic and disguised the fleet's military intentions. Support came from different sources, and both the Count of Castro and Genoa contributed ships to the flotilla. Part of the success of the Duke's fleet also came from the support it received from the ports of Brindisi, Dubrovnik and Trieste, the latter of which was controlled by the Archduke of Styria. The Ottoman navy would not be a threat in this encounter, because, according to the Duke, the Ottomans knew that the squadrons of the Pope, Florence and Malta were stationed in Malta.[43]

That the Téllez-Girón, as the viceroy of Naples, was willing to gather together these forces demonstrates the importance of regional actors in carrying out imperial ambitions. Part of Téllez-Girón's argument was based on his knowledge of these types of affairs. He showed he was aware of the balance of power in the sea, and he was willing to commit the necessary ships to gain a military advantage. The presence of these ships in the Adriatic would restore the Crown's reputation and would allow the King to maintain his agreements with others. If he were to back down, the crown would lose face. This point must have been critical, because Spain's ability to project its power throughout the Mediterranean was tied to its reputation with its allies. Given these alliances, the Duke was confident that these forces would be superior to those of the Venetians. He felt that his squadron was prepared to establish a permanent presence in an area that had been dominated by Venice.

---

[42]   Duro, *Duque de Osuna*, Carta del Duque de Osuna a SM acerca de armamentos y disposiciones contra Venecia, pp. 318–21. "...hacer alguna diversion..."

[43]   Archivio General de Simancas, Estado, legajo 1880, numero 64.

The Duke's actions were also connected to a plea that had been sent to him on April 28, 1617 by the Archduke of Styria. Other regional actors were dependent on support from individuals such as the Duke of Osuna, because of their geographical vulnerability. The Habsburg Empire contained certain core areas, but it also had borderlands that were subject to attack. The Austrian Archduke noted that 1,200 Englishmen and a number of Ottomans calling themselves Dalmatians had gathered in Venice, and he believed that the assembly meant that a plan had been hatched by the Venetians to conquer Habsburg lands. The powerful Neapolitan forces could defend Habsburg interests or at least create a major deterrent for the Venetians. Even though the Venetians had signed a peace treaty with the Archduke of Styria in 1615, the threat of conflict still existed and regional power brokers were important actors in both fighting wars and in maintaining peace.[44]

That the Archduke associated the malicious intentions of the Venetians with the presence of foreigners in Venice and with threats to his own subjects indicates the degree to which maritime jurisdiction framed issues of security. The Venetians could project their political power by granting access in the Adriatic to English, Dutch and Ottoman merchants. Access was also denied to others such as the Spanish who stood in opposition to this alliance. But if the Archduke of Styria designated the Adriatic as an uncontested space dominated by the Venetian hegemons, in his letter to the crown regarding his confrontation with the Venetians, Téllez-Girón contended that the Gulf and its surrounding territories were areas in which the Spanish could increase their influence. The Spanish had allies in the region, and Téllez-Girón believed that with the assistance of these allies, Venetian subjects would be willing to turn on their overlords and assist the Spanish.

On June 20, the government sent a reply to the Duke stating that it had been informed by their ambassador in Venice, the Marquis of Bedmar, that the Venetians were planning on attacking Spanish ships that had entered the Adriatic, particularly those of the Duke of Osuna. The Duke was to prevent this attack from happening because the Venetians needed to be disabused of the notion that they were the masters of the Adriatic. In fact, the Spanish crown was older than the Venetian Republic and the Venetians had no right to be in control of the sea. In light of these developments, the Duke was to make sure that he had assembled a group of ships that were more powerful than those of the Venetians.[45]

The letter from Philip III to Téllez-Girón contains a number of clues as to how the Spanish justified their claims. First, the Spanish contention that the Venetians were determined to use force against Spanish ships demonstrates their belief that given the principle of the maritime access to all parties, the Venetians desire to attack Spanish ships interfered with Spain's right to navigate freely in waters that the Venetians could not claim as their own. The Spanish even contested Venice's historical claim. Yet the only way to handle this problem was to confront the

---

[44] Archivio General de Simancas, Estado, legajo 1880, numero 68.

[45] Duro, *Duque de Osuna*, Despacho de SM al Duque de Osuna, ordenádole defender sus dercechos en el Adriático, pp. 337–8.

Venetians militarily. Territory, whether on land or sea, was acquired through force and not through a time-honored right, and thus much of the Duke of Osuna's power was tied to how much force he could muster.

Given the authority to act, the Duke placed the fleet that besieged the Venetian ships in July of 1617 under his corsair flag. Comprised of 18 galleons, 33 galley ships and 4 brigs, his fleet sailed towards the island of Lesina and the port of Split in Venetian waters along the Dalmatian coast. Here, they confronted a squadron of Venetian ships. Because of the overwhelming Spanish naval superiority, the encounter did not produce much of a battle, and the forces of the Duke of Osuna were able to take a number of Ottoman merchants as prisoners and to abscond with a significant number of goods, which were transferred to Brindisi.[46]

The Ottomans: Defining Jurisdiction

To understand the attack, we must consider that it involved groups with very different viewpoints on what happened and on how relations should move forward. In effect, each side had a narrative that attempted to create a consistent and plausible story. The Ottoman merchants who were attacked and who had their goods taken had a particular perspective. They were looking to place blame on who they thought were responsible, were attempting to define how jurisdiction worked and were trying to assess what evidence and which testimonies would hold sway with decision makers. In this regard the attack was more complicated than just a top-level diplomatic matter, and while the event did involve the Spanish, Ottoman and Venetian states, local groups also contributed to how jurisdiction was framed and how the event narrative was shaped.

In breaking from a strict understanding of cores and peripheries, John Marino comments that the early modern state needs to be seen "as a mosaic of overlapping jurisdictions in which local lordships, bishoprics, towns and village communities continued to have a certain degree of independence ...". Marino's point emphasizes the complexity involved in sorting through how a dispute could be negotiated. Conflict could not always be resolved through direct negotiation. The Spanish and Ottomans were officially in a state of war. Although this political relationship was more flexible than two states engaged in a perpetual fighting, the Spanish did not claim responsibility for the attack. Communication channels had to be established which would allow contact to be made. While Spanish merchants did trade along the Ottoman coasts of the Adriatic, many times they did it disguised as either Ragusans or even Venetians.[47]

The best option open to the Ottomans, at least diplomatically, was to file their grievances with the Venetians. As the Porte had noted, the Venetians had given

---

[46]   Linde, *Don Pedro Girón*, p. 147.

[47]   Suraya Faroqhi, "The Venetian Presence in the Ottoman Empire, 1600–30" in *The Ottoman Empire and the World Economy*, ed. Huri İslamoğlu-İnan (Cambridge, UK: Cambridge University Press, 2004), p. 321.

guarantees to the Ottoman subjects through their representative in Sarajevo and their consul in Split. In both cases, these officials had made pledges to Islamic judges Nurullah, the chief judge of Sarajevo, and Ismail, the kadi from Klis, who came to Split.[48] The fact that Ismail could go Split and issue a hüccet indicates that a borderland jurisdiction existed in which officials could cross boundaries and participate in legal agreements. In his study of nineteenth-century Egypt, Ziad Fahmy notes that "I define a jurisdictional borderland as a significant contact zone where there are multiple and often competing legal authorities and where some level of jurisdictional ambiguity exists."[49] That Ismail was part of the legal culture of Split demonstrates that the Venetians realized that their best hope of having the merchants put their cargo on the ships sailing to Venice was by participating in this "jurisdictional ambiguity."

By working together, Ismail and Velutello, the Venetian governor, not only reached an agreement, they also represented part of the cooperative legal system that existed in many locations from Africa to Asia. Crossing borders, enlisting different types of people and filling in where a state presence was limited, the system was set up in many cases to provide an assurance and the Ottomans needed a pledge because they feared the presence of the Spanish in the Adriatic. K.N. Chaudhuri points out that "there was no question even in our period (the early modern) of history of a political kingdom or an empire that took pride in its sense of sovereignty and the power of law enforcement allowing foreign merchants to suffer at the hands of pirates and robbers, while they were in its sphere of jurisdiction."[50] This type of protection and the legal guarantees attached to it should be thought of, as Chaudhuri notes, as part of a general strategy that states used to maintain "law enforcement." Traders had reason to seek the protection of law enforcement. Threats existed both on land and at sea, and the practice of assigning galleys to protect merchant ships from attacks by hostile competitors had become quite common for Venetians by the latter half of the sixteenth century.[51]

Protection from these threats was one of the competitive factors the Venetians used to attract trade to Venice and away from Ancona and Dubrovnik, and traders came to expect it. These sorts of guarantees were extended, and the Venetians developed the port of Split to gain further control over trade and also to give Ottoman merchants greater protection and more guarantees.[52] Renzo Paci points

---

[48]   A.S.V., Senato, Deliberazioni Constantinopoli , registro 12, fogli 48V–49V, March 4, 1618.

[49]   Ziad Fahmy, "Jurisdictional Borderlands: Extraterritoriality and 'Legal Chameleons' in Pre-colonial Alexandria," *Comparative Studies in Society and History*, vol.55, issue 2 (2013), p. 309.

[50]   K.N. Chaudhuri, *Trade and Civilization in the Indian Ocean: An Economic History from the Rise of Islam to 1750* (Cambridge, UK: Cambridge University Press, 1985), p. 12.

[51]   Alberto Tenenti, *Piracy and the Decline of Venice: 1580–1615* (Berkeley: University of California Press, 1967).

[52]   On the creation of the port of Split see Paci, *La scala di Spalato*.

out that "The Venetian government, which paid close attention to the execution of the agreements, was anxious to ensure that merchants coming to Split found support and protection …".[53] Clearly, the Ottoman government was approving of the efforts to promote trade through Split; in 1610, the *provveditore alla sanità* of Split said, "To establish and maintain this port, without regard to the great expenses involved, [The Ottomans] have cleared not only woods, but also mountains to open the way to roads, built bridges, constructed mosques and *caravansarays* in order to facilitate the crossing of caravans that pass from Constantinople to Split, so that now [these merchants] can in 43 days transport their considerable goods to the port."[54] These developments point to the type of cooperation that existed between states.

The letter from Sultan Mustafa I, mentioned at the beginning of the chapter, noted that the port of Split had been constructed to guarantee the safety of Ottoman merchants. If the damages were not reimbursed, Muslim merchants would not return to this trading post. Their absence would be great loss to Venetian customs.[55] Nearly a half a year later, Sultan Osman II wrote the Doge stating that caravans coming to Split from the Balkans were not coming anymore because of the fear of a lack of protection.[56]

The correspondence of Sultan Osman II indicates that this development did not relate to an order from the top, but instead it was initiated by the actions of independent groups. The first correspondence to the Venetians came from the merchants who had been affected by the attack. Each of the 51 merchants listed his place of origin. As noted, this way of identifying oneself was chosen because an individual's first loyalty would have been to his town or city, and noting a location would have been a way to identify that person. Yet the range of places listed, including Istanbul, Sofia, Sarajevo and Mostar may also have been a means of expressing the trans-imperial nature of the contingent and showing the type of solidarity that existed between different groups.

The petition was composed days after the attack had taken place. While the petition did not have a date, an accompanying letter from the Venetian admiral Giacomo Zane from July 21 indicates that the complaint was filed soon after the attack. The merchants stated that they did not have fear traveling on the Venetian ships because they felt they received such a solid guarantee that they would be protected. This sense of security undoubtedly had to with their awareness of

---

[53]   Ibid., p. 105.

[54]   Ibid., pp. 104–5. "Per incaminamento et continuazione di detta scala, senza riguadar a spesse grandissime, (I turchi) hanno talgiato non pur boshci, ma motagne per accomodamento delle strade, fatto ponti, fabricato moschee et cavarsarie per facilitare il camino alle carovane che passano da Costantinopoli a Spalato, in maniera che in giorni quarantatre capitano I loro cavedalli di soma importanza alla predetta scala."

[55]   A.S.V., Senato, Deliberazioni Constantinopoli, registro 12, fogli 48V–49V, March 4, 1618.

[56]   A.S.V., I Documenti Turchi, busta 11, fascicolo 1231.

View of the Ruin of Spalatro from the East

Fig. 5.3   Robert Adam, *View of the port of Split from the East, Ruins of the Palace of the Emperor Diocletian at Spalatro in Dalmatia*, plate III (1764). Special Collections, University of Delaware Library.

the Spanish threat and also their confidence in the Venetians' ability to protect them. This reasoning indicates that they had a significant amount of geo-political knowledge and understood that the Venetians' reputation was closely tied to their ability to live up to their promises. In their petition, they included the name of Mümin, a çavuş from the Porte. Having a person of this status included in the petition informed the Venetians of the types of connections they had back home. They also addressed their petition to the Doge and the Cinque Savi alla Mercanzia. The fact that they included the Cinque Savi in their correspondence probably indicates that they had an understanding of how decision-making worked in Venice and had made contact with the magistracy to resolve the dispute.[57]

The narrative of the story was very similar to the one from the Porte, indicating that the account had been corroborated at number of different levels. A Bosnian official confirmed to the Venetians that the merchants came from a variety of different towns in Bosnia. He emphasized that these individuals came from a tradition of cooperation with Venice. He also restated many of the points that had been made at the Porte, noting that blame lay with the Venetian consul in Sarajevo and the count of Split. The Venetians credibility had been compromised by their inability to deliver on the guarantees that they had made to the merchants prior to the attack.[58]

Accounts of the attack moved from different contact points in the Ottoman Empire such as Istanbul and Sarajevo to Venice and to Split. The dissemination of information demonstrates the way in which different people were enlisted to tell the story. While, in theory, the hüccet should have been enough to make the Venetians act, the event was considered sufficiently important that the intervention of higher officials to find a resolution was necessary; thus, the merchants went to the Divan to have their case heard. Much of presenting the story also involved linking the different jurisdictions. Ultimately though, because the attack had taken place in the Adriatic and fell under Venetian jurisdiction, in the minds of the Ottomans, the Venetian were responsible for damages.

Maintaining jurisdictional responsibilities involved having the capacity to use violence effectively against one's competitors. The Venetians understood that if a state could eliminate competitors in violence, costs were reduced, hegemony was established and legitimacy was accepted.[59] In describing Venetian attempts to gain jurisdiction over trading routes, Frederic Lane notes that "there were advantages of scale when organizing protection, ships were directed to sail in convoys in periods of danger and Venetian merchants were then required, if they shipped at

---

[57]   A.S.V., I Documenti Turchi, busta 11, fascicolo 1210. While most references were made to Bosnian merchants, it is unclear if these individuals originally came from Bosnia and then lived in other parts of the empire.

[58]   A.S.V., Senato, Deliberazioni Constantinopoli , registro 12, foglio 51R, March 4, 1618.

[59]   Frederic Lane, " Economic Consequences of Organized Violence," *The Journal of Economic History*, Vol. 18, no. 4 (1958), p. 404.

all, to freight specified wares on these convoys only."[60] The Ottoman merchants' decision to travel from Split with the Venetian convoy was based on the scale of Venetian protection. The Ottoman merchants had two choices: they could choose the most heavily-armed ships and pay higher tariffs, or travel from less secure ports and risk attack. Their appeal to Venetian authorities indicates that they and their backers believed that the Venetians and the Venetians military entrepreneurs would make good on their claim of making reparations, because the Venetians believed in their jurisdictional sovereignty and stood behind their guarantees to deliver protection against the Spanish.

The Venetians: Assessing Power

On August 9, 1617, The Venetian Senate sent a letter to the bailo regarding the attack. In the letter, the Senate explained that they had received letters from Ottoman merchants who had been affected by the incident. Other Ottomans had come to the Collegio to voice their concerns and to ask for restitution for the goods that had been taken. The Venetians were clear that they did not want to make this payment, asserting that on the numerous occasions in the past when the Uskoks had attacked their ships, the Venetians never had to pay damages. In addition, the Spanish were enemies of the Porte, and because they had assembled such a large flotilla in the waters off of Puglia, the Venetian galley protecting the merchant ships was incapable of responding to this type of naval force. Part of the problem was also related to larger Mediterranean political dynamics. The Ragusans stood to gain from the misfortunes of the Venetians, and they had provided the Spanish with assistance. The Austrian Habsburgs also were enemies of the Porte and tried to foment trouble through their proxies, the Uskoks.

The letter continued that, given these threats, the Venetians had assigned more galleys to protect merchant ships. They understood the importance of security, and they were willing to take the necessary measures to ensure that merchants received protection. Efforts had also been taken to make amends, and after the attack, the Venetians had ordered their naval personnel in the Adriatic to search for the goods. These measures were not only attempts to restore goodwill but also to ensure that the Ottomans and the Venetians remained allies against their enemies. To convey these sentiments and to guarantee that the Venetians concerns were heard, the government asked the bailo to make sure that he enlisted the right people to state the Venetian case.[61]

As has been shown, many ties that were established between both the principals and the subjects of different states were the result of a series of personal contacts and patronage relationships rather than an attachment to an impersonal bureaucracy. This applies not only to the types of connections that Ottomans tried

---

[60] Ibid., p. 415.

[61] A.S.V., Senato, Deliberazioni Constantinopoli, registro 12, foglio 20R, August 9, 1617.

to forge with powerful Ottoman officials, but also to the types of contacts that the Venetians attempted to make.[62] Establishing an alliance at one level brought the possibility of not only establishing a relationship, but also of influencing people in higher positions of power. In this regard, the Venetians realized that the individuals standing in front of them were only as strong as the people by whom they were backed or to whom they were attached. In a letter to the bailo related to the Spanish attack in November of the same year, the Venetian government stated that "the Turkish merchants in the city, who have claims upon the merchant galleys, have presented to us a strongly argued document, and we have dismissed them in a suitable fashion, but they have let it be known that they wish to have recourse to Constantinople, to complain to the pasha and other ministers."[63] In expressing their concern to the bailo, the Venetians were interested in how the merchants could sway Ottoman officials. Influence moved from one circle of power to the next and ultimately those with access to the sultan and his inner circle were in a position to create problems that could not be dismissed easily.

The connections that were made and strategies that were used to influence powerful officials provide insight into how bridges were built between local groups and the political center. One of the ways that this worked was through gifts. In a dispatch to the Senate, the bailo suggested that they make a gift of 1,000 *cecchini* to a *mufti* who was involved in deliberating over the particulars of the Spanish case.[64] Undoubtedly, gaining the support of the mufti was important if the Venetians were to receive a favorable hearing. For similar reasons other individuals were also approached, and to earn the good graces of another important jurist who expressed support for the Venetian position, the *kadiasker* [65] of Anatolia, the Venetians also offered money.[66]

The Venetians recognized that a financial reward could be used to influence certain officials. A *çavus*, who arrived in Venice with 20 merchants with claims related to the attack, expressed an interest in working on the Venetians' behalf in a discussion with the Venetian dragoman de Nores. Thereupon it was agreed that for the sum of 200 cecchini, which the Venetian called an amount "that usually is

---

[62]   See Figure 5.4 for Europeans at the Ottoman court .

[63]   A.S.V., Senato, Deliberazioni Constantinopoli, registro 12, foglio 31V, November 14, 1617. "Li merchanti Turchi, che sono in questa città interessati nelle galee di mercantia, ne hanno presentato certa la loro scrittura con cetti assai vivi, sono stati da noi, con buona maniera licentati, ma si hanno lasciati intendere volersi conferir in costessa citta, per farne condoglienza col bassá et altri ministri."

[64]   A.S.V., Senato, Dispacci Constantinopoli, filza 84, fogli 145R–151V, November 11, 1617.

[65]   One of the head kadis. He was also considered a military official.

[66]   A.S.V., Senato, Dispacci Constantinopoli, filza 84, fogli 182R–184V, November 29, 1617.

Fig. 5.4   Antonio Guardi, *Dinner Given by Grand Vizir to European Ambassador* (1740). British Government Art Collection.

given to those that bring news of the assumption of power by a new emperor," the çavus would return to Istanbul with a letter favorable to the Venetians.[67]

Natalie Davis points out that

> though there are big shifts in systems of gift and exchange over time, there is no universal pattern of evolutionary stages, where a total gift economy dwindles to occasional presents. Rather, gift exchange persists as an essential relational mode, a repertoire of behavior, a register with its own rules, language, etiquette and gestures. The gift mode may expand or shrink somewhat in a given period, but it never loses its significance.[68]

---

[67]   A.S.V., Senato, Deliberazioni Constantinopoli, registro 12, foglio 65R, April 24, 1618.

[68]   Natalie Zemon Davis, *The Gift in Sixteenth Century France* (Madison: University of Wisconsin Press, 2000), p. 9. On gift-giving in the Spanish Empire see Diana Carrió-Invernizzi, "Gift and Diplomacy in Seventeenth Century Italy," *The Historical Journal* 51, no. 4 (2008), pp. 881–99. Carrió-Invernizzi argues that certain gift Spanish gift giving practices were different in Italy from that of the Italians, but over time after observing the Italians, the Spanish began to use many of the same practices in the mid-seventeenth century, as they began to see the gift as a part of diplomacy.

In fact, gifts were so commonplace in dealing with Ottoman officials that the bailo Marin Cavalli attempted to introduce a certain amount of control over this type of spending, contending that these gifts only served to put the Venetians in a position of weakness in relation to the Porte.[69] Gifts were not only powerful forms of persuasion, they also helped build bridges to powerful figures who could become powerful allies. Deborah Howard notes that "the choice of diplomatic gifts constituted a display of power that no amount of ritualized etiquette could disguise." Historically, gifts were given to place the recipient under a certain obligation. This message could be also understood in a Venetian/Ottoman context when the Venetians offered the Ottomans textiles, clothes or cheese, or the Ottomans presented riding equipment or different types of animals.[70] Yet gifts did not always win people over, nor were they the only ways to establish alliances. In this case neither the mufti nor the kadiasker of Anatolia was willing to accept the gifts that the Venetians had offered him. In his letter to the Senate, the bailo wrote that the kadiasker of Anatolia "in order to maintain a clear conscience had not wanted to accept a gift of money."[71] Oddly enough, the çavus also turned on the Venetians when he reached Venice in late November of 1617.[72] Here, we must move away from the assumption that political struggles such as this one were nothing more than competition where victory went to the highest bidder. Ottoman officials were conditioned and motivated by a series of different concerns. The gift, thus, was only one component in a struggle that involved many different factors. In a case such as this one, if it became known that the Venetians were paying someone to testify on their behalf, the discovery could be used to discredit the witness.[73] This type of discovery not only underscored the ability of a foreign power to interfere with the affairs of the Ottoman government, but also potentially threatened to undermine the integrity of those who administered Islamic law.

The dynamics of the case evolved in relation to a variety of strategies that the different factions had staked out, and thus Venice argued the case along different lines than the merchants and their supporters. For one, the Venetians contended that these sorts of situations were not covered in capitulations. A precedent existed to argue along these lines: in the case of the attack by the Uskoks against the Venetian ship in 1588,[74] the Venetians put forward the same argument, that they were not

---

[69]   Horatio Brown, *Studies in Venetian History*, vol. 2 (New York: John Murray, 1907), pp. 23–4.

[70]   Deborah Howard, "Cultural Transfer between Venice and the Ottomans in the Fifteenth and Sixteenth Centuries," p. 143–5. On the nature of obligations and gifts in archaic societies see Marcel Mauss, *The Gift: Forms and Functions of Exchange in Archaic Societies* (London: Cohen and West, 1966).

[71]   A.S.V., Senato, Dispacci Constantinopoli, filza 84, foglio 182R, November 29, 1617. "di questo homo il qual se ben non ha voluto per serupso di consienza accetar danari in dono."

[72]   A.S.V., Senato, Dispacci Constantinopoli, filza 85, fogli 226R–234V, July, 1618.

[73]   A.S.V., Senato, Dispacci Constantinopoli, filza 84, fogli 182R–184V, November 29, 1617.

[74]   See the closing section of Chapter 2 for a full description of this incident.

responsible for the restoration of any of the goods. Given that the merchants did not argue the case in terms of the capitulations, some validity to this claim must have existed. In this regard we must be careful to assume that Ottomans were loath to honor their international agreements. Each side struggled to classify and to define who was ultimately responsible. In a letter to Sultan Mustafa in March of 1618, the Venetians argued that the attack was the action of corsairs supported by state interests in Spain and in Ragusa. Presenting the case in this manner was done to try to define what constituted legitimate versus illegitimate activities. If the Venetians could convince the Ottomans that they were upholding a trans-cultural standard, the Ottomans would understand the Venetians were trying to protect order in the face of chaos. In seeking to explain the reigning chaos, the Venetians argued that the Venetian state and their subjects had suffered just as much as the Ottoman subjects who were affected by the attack.[75]

In looking to implicate Ragusa, an Ottoman protectorate and a rival of Venice, the Venetians were suggesting to members of the Ottoman court that the Ragusans were not interested in protecting the interests of Ottoman subjects. In this regard, Venice was trying to identify Ragusa as a rogue state. They tried to create this perception because they knew that the Ragusans had a lot of influence in Istanbul. Ragusa had been a protectorate of the Ottoman Empire since the middle of the fifteenth century. In return for tribute, the Ragusans were able to establish a trading community in the Ottoman Empire and they maintained a significant amount of influence. Lovro Kunĉević comments that

> Although the partners in this relationship were dramatically unequal in power, and one paid for the protection of the other, it was still seen as a contract between two ultimately equal states. In other words what Ragusan diplomats tried to legitimize was the idea that tribute-paying and fidelity meant not acknowledging the rule of the sultan, but entering a somewhat asymmetric relationship with the Ottoman Empire.[76]

This partnership benefited the Spanish and gave them inroads that they would not normally have had. Similar to the way that Ottomans in Venice worked through influential people such as Michele Membre, the Spanish were able to gain an audience through the favored status of certain Ragusans at the Porte.[77]

---

[75] A.S.V., Senato, Deliberazioni Constantinopoli , registro 12, foglio 53RV, March 16, 1618.

[76] Lovro Kunĉević, "Discourses on Liberty in early modern Ragusa," in *Freedom and the Construction of Europe: Religious Freedom and Civil Libery*, eds. Quentin Skinner and Martin Van Gelderen (Cambridge, UK: Cambridge University Press, 2013), p. 202.

[77] A.S.V., Senato, Deliberazioni Constantinopoli, registro 12, foglio 53 RV, March 16, 1618. The case of Ragusa is a complicated one in that while a protectorate of the Ottomans, the Ragusans enjoyed good relations with the Spanish. Suraiya Faroqhi postulates that the Ragusans acted as intermediaries between the Ottomans and the Spanish, and in one case they were forced to send back Spanish emissaries who were on a peace mission to the Ottoman Empire. See Faroqhi, "The Venetian Presence," p. 323.

While acknowledging the role of the Spanish, the different Ottoman correspondences did not believe that this absolved the Venetians of guilt. Part of the Ottomans' reasoning was that because Muslims were on the ship the Venetians who were hired to protect them were either in league with those who attacked them or so sympathetic as not to get involved in fending off the assault. The letter also argued that one of the Ottoman government's concerns was that the goods of the Christian merchants on the ship had been returned to them, while those of the Muslims were still missing.[78] The Venetians were quick to dismiss this charge as ridiculous, stating that they protected Muslim merchants in the same manner that they did their own.[79] Undoubtedly, these types of incidents must have been aroused Muslim suspicions that the Christians were in league with one another. If some chose to believe that factions formed in relationship to particular military and economic interests, as the Venetians contended in the case of the Ragusans and the Spanish, others could insinuate that clearly this was a case of Christians conspiring against Muslims.

This point, however, was only used to buttress the main thrust of the merchants' argument that the Venetian governor had given the merchants a guarantee prior to their departure. This guarantee was certainly an important claim, for a mufti who was involved in the case issued a *fetva*, a legal opinion that acknowledged the Venetian promise. This issue became a major sticking point; after the Bosnian merchants came to the Porte and filed their complaint, the Venetian dragoman in Istanbul, Borisi, stated that it was ridiculous to think that Venetians should be accountable for damages that were not covered in treaties, but instead by hüccet of a kadi who was paid a mere 30 *aspri* a day.[80] Borisi's thinking indicates that the Venetians were unhappy with the idea that a lowly official should have so much influence in a case of such importance. Clearly, they believed that people at the top of the hierarchy should work out these issues.

In adopting this position, the Venetians may have been working through what it meant to come up against people drawn together by loyalties that existed beyond mere connections to the state. In all likelihood, regional and local solidarities combined with state connections to produce a blend of local and state politics. As noted earlier, as a result of the Spanish attack, a group of 50 merchants filed a petition with the Venetian government, but these signatories were only a small part of the number of people who had been affected by the attack.[81] Indicating the scope of the people involved, the dragoman Grillo told the Collegio that the Ottoman emissary to Venice had told him the Bosnians who wanted restitution

---

[78]   A.S.V., Senato, Deliberazioni Constantinopoli, registro 12, fogli 48V–49R, March 4, 1618.

[79]   A.S.V., Senato, Deliberazioni Constantinopoli, registro 12, foglio 53V, March 16, 1618.

[80]   A.S.V., Senato, Dispacci Constantinopoli, filza 84, fogli 215R–222V, December 8, 1617.

[81]   A.S.V., Documenti Turchi, busta 11, fascicolo 1210.

from the attack "are not ten, or twenty but are in excess of three thousand."[82] Other ties probably existed with the merchants from Istanbul, for five merchants who signed the petition stated that their home was the capital. Undoubtedly, a regional block of this size with connections in Istanbul must have weighed heavily not only with provincial Ottoman officials, but with officials at the Porte as well.

The kadiasker of Rumelia or even the grand vizir may have had connections to the Bosnian merchants along ethnic lines. I.M. Kunt points out that in the early- to mid-seventeenth century the *cins* that formed created a division in Ottoman politics between Albanians and Bosnians on one side and those from the Caucasus region on the other. In fact, Veysî, the author of a political treatise in the 1620s, lamented that most of those in power were Bosnians and Albanians.[83] If these individuals were in power at the time of the Spanish attack, the Bosnians undoubtedly would have used these connections to advance their cause.

Other ties to important officials could have been based on even more personal patron/client relations between some of the merchants and powerful figures at the Porte. The mufti mentioned that his friend Monla Sherif had lost 2,000 cecchini on the ship and asked that the money be given back to him.[84] This comment certainly points to a more personal tie. This connection probably also existed with others as well, for a powerful official stepped forward, by the name of Resul Aga, whom the Venetian bailo referred to as "a rich man very esteemed by the Turks." Aga pleaded to the Venetians that if they "could not satisfy so many people, could they make sure that at least in his case things did not go badly."[85] The issue of dealing with powerful patrons was undoubtedly a commonplace occurrence when the Venetians tried to negotiate matters in Istanbul. In a case that came to their attention in 1594, the Venetians decided to arrest a certain Francesco, the servant of Cristoforo Brutti, who had paid a man to have one of their merchants roughed up at the Galata bazaar. Hearing of his arrest, Brutti went directly to his patron, the beylerbey of Rumelia, and asked that Francesco be returned. Sending a representative to the presiding governor, the beylerbey demanded that Francesco be returned to his patron. Yet the governor refused, stating that Francesco could only be released to the office of the bailo. Undaunted, the beylerbey helped Francesco escape to the safety of his custody.[86]

Relations had to be maintained between states, and while many issues were addressed in a public manner, others were more private. These areas formed a parallel world, an arena that might be addressed in public terms but in fact was

---

[82] A.S.V., Senato, Dispacci Constantinopoli, filza 85, foglio 66, April 26, 1618. "questi non sono dieci, ne vinti má che eccedeno il numero di tre mille."

[83] Kunt, "Ethnic-Regional Solidarity," p. 237.

[84] A.S.V., Deliberazioni Constantinopoli, registro 12, foglio 77V, June 5, 1618.

[85] A.S.V., Dispacci da Constantinopoli, filza 85, fogli 275–280, August, 1618. "huomo molto ricco, et stiamo assai fra Turchi se non si vuol sodisfar l'interesse de tanti almeno si procuri che il mio non vadi á male …".

[86] Brown, *Studies in Venetian History*, p. 31.

more private, based on associations and attachments. In this regard it is interesting to note that in the case of the Spanish attack, the Venetians seemed anxious to make sure that certain powerful individuals were compensated for at least part of their losses. While some individuals could be dismissed others could not. The dichotomy of the state and personal relationships constituted a complex question; the state comprised powerful individuals, who, in turn, were dependent on the state. Much of the Venetian success not only depended on the nature of the riddle's solution, but also on their ability to sort through the different power configurations forming the basis of these types of encounters. In the end even treaties could be interpreted in a variety of different ways. These sets of relations presented a complicated dynamic, for though the rhetoric of disputes was couched in terms of agreements and mutual cooperation, the parallel narrative was characterized by behind-the-scenes negotiations and payoffs. Both sides not only understood these rules, but also did everything in their power to ensure that they dictated the terms of official business, by winning the parallel game.

The Other Parallel Game

Whether the Duke of Osuna took action against the Venetians with the full consent of the Spanish government is questionable. While the Crown had given orders to disrupt Venetian activities, the type of the attack may have gone beyond the expectations of the Spanish regarding the scale of the confrontation and the ongoing nature of the conflict.[87] But if the Duke of Osuna was operating somewhat independently, what were his intentions and what type of parallel game was he involved in?

One person important to understanding the parallel game was Bedmar, the Spanish ambassador to Venice. Bedmar was the chief intelligence agent for the Spanish in Venice, and he was also someone who was strong advocate of an aggressive policy towards the Venetians, believing that Venice was a major threat to Spanish interests. In March of 1618, Bedmar wrote the Spanish government about the arrival of an Ottoman çavuş. He commented that the çavuş had come to announce the ascension to the throne of Mustafa I, to tell the Venetians not to scheme against Ragusa and to inform the Venetians to make a satisfactory payment to the Muslim and Jewish merchants who had lost their goods in the attacks against the Venetian ships. Bedmar also noted that an individual named Achmet had sent the çavuş principally to underscore the importance of the Ottoman/ Ragusan connection. The correspondence is revealing in that it demonstrates the importance that Bedmar placed on informing the Spanish government of the fissures in the Ottoman/Venetian relationship.

In Bedmar's view, Achmet's connection of the ascension of the new sultan with the issue of Ragusa had favorable connotations for the Spanish given their

---

[87]   Linde notes that some believed that the attack did not come from Madrid but instead was instigated and carried out by the Duke of Osuna. Linde, *Don Pedro Girón*, p. 148.

ties with the Dalmatian state.[88] But if Bedmar was quick to speak of Ottoman/ Venetian difficulties, he was also careful to warn the Spanish of the dangers of the Venetian/Ottoman alliance. On April 4, 1618, he sent a letter stating that he had been warned by a confidant in Venice that the Venetian bailo was trying to influence the Ottomans to work against the Spanish. In May of the same year, he repeated this warning and noted that the Venetians had given money to an Ottoman official who represented a threat to the Duke of Osuna and his forces.[89]

Part of Bedmar's commentary reflected the constant flow of diplomacy across the Mediterranean. While through their connections, the Venetians were active at the Spanish court trying to convince the Spanish to return the goods of the Ottoman merchants, other alliances formed in relationship to the prevailing politics. Practice in certain cases trumped ideology, and on October 13, 1618, the Venetian Senate reported to the bailo in Istanbul that the Duke of Osuna had sent a boat to bring an Ottoman çavuş to Naples with a contingent of Ottoman subjects all dressed in gold and silk. According to the Venetians, the Ottomans were there to establish relations with the Duke and the Spanish to the disadvantage of both the Venetians and the Ottoman Porte. The letter continued that an Ottoman named Achmet Rais was in Naples serving the interests of the Ottoman admiral and head of the Turkish fleet, Ali Pasha, who was working with the Spanish. Was this Achmet the same individual who had sent the çavuş to Venice to warn the Venetians of interfering in Ragusan affairs? The Ragusans would have been in natural position to arrange contact between the Duke and the Ottoman admiral. The Duke had sent a ship to Preveza in northern Greece where the Ottoman fleet was located.[90] There they made contact and transported the Ottoman contingent back to Naples. Earlier warnings had been issued that the Ottoman admiral was working against the Venetians with the help of corsairs from Algiers. Ali Pasha had taken a Venetian captain, Bernandino Harda, his family and a group of soldiers captive. They were held somewhere in the area of Preveza where the Venetians believed that contact was established between the Duke of Osuna's men and Ali Pasha's men.[91]

Ali Pasha had been a sanjack bey in Anatolia and the beylerbey of Tunis and also kapudan paşa on three separate occasions. In an attack that would increase his prominence, he captured a number of Venetian and French merchants and took them, their money and their goods to Istanbul where he presented them to Sultan Osman II. The Venetians sent an envoy to protest this action and received support from the Grand Vizir Öküz Mehmed Pasha. Claiming that Ali Pasha was a rogue and should be punished for actions, the Venetians' and the Grand Vizir's plea fell

---

[88] Archivio General de Simancas, Estado, legajo 1930, numero 60.

[89] Archivio General de Simancas, Estado, legajo 1930, numero 84.

[90] A.S.V., Deliberazioni Costantinopoli, registro 12, fogli 108V–109R, October 13, 1618.

[91] A.S.V., Deliberazioni Costantinopoli, registro 12, fogli 105R–107V. See also Senato, Dispacci degli ambasciatori e residenti, Napoli, filza 36.

on deaf ears and Sultan chose to keep the money. Soon thereafter Ali Pasha was rewarded with the position of grand vizir in which he remained until his death in 1621.[92]

The rise of Ali Pasha and his relationship with the Duke of Osuna indicates the importance of network connections on the periphery. While the Spanish and Ottomans were involved in an ongoing war against one another, this tie represented a particular type of relationship that seems to have formed in the contact zones of imperial borderlands. Shortly thereafter on November 3, the Venetians wrote the bailo again stating that Duke of Osuna had agreed to return the Ottomans' goods.[93] Was this decision connected to the relationship between the Duke and Ali Pasha? The shift in Ottoman court politics certainly influenced alliances and state relations. On December 1, the Venetians wrote to the bailo in Istanbul that the Spanish and the Ottomans had agreed to a 20-year treaty. The negotiations had been conducted through an intermediary named Gratiani, a representative of the sultan. The bailo was to use everything at his disposal to understand the extent of this agreement and to inform Ottoman officials of the negative intentions of the Spanish. Also the Porte needed to be informed that the Spanish were duplicitous and though they appeared to want to make a peace agreement with the Ottomans, at the same time, they were consolidating their forces in Naples and in other territories to conduct a war against the Porte and to invade territories in Algeria. The Venetians would be very content if the bailo could ensure that the treaty was never finalized. A Spanish/Ottoman alliance was contrary to the public good in Venice.[94]

The notion of public good represents one way in which the Venetians thought about their relations in Mediterranean politics. This perception reflected a world in which states built alliances and competed against one another for resources and political influence for the general good of the state. But this type of competition ran parallel with a factional politics that not only crossed imperial boundaries but also challenged existing state relations. While the attack against the Venetian ship involved Ottoman merchants and seemed to represent the so-called civilizational battle between Muslims and Christians, upon closer analysis it reflected different interests in the Adriatic and the Mediterranean. These relationships were constantly changing, and Ali Pasha's rise to power benefited the Duke of Osuna and his allies and threatened the position of the Venetians in the Adriatic. Ironically, not long afterward the Duke of Osuna's fortunes changed, and he was replaced as the viceroy of Naples.[95]

---

[92]   İsmail Hakkı Uzunçarşili, *Osmanli tarihi* (Türk Tarih Kurumu yayinlardan) cilt 3, kisim 1 (Ankara: Türk Tarih Kurumu Basimevi, 1954), pp. 373–4.

[93]   A.S.V., Deliberazioni Costantinopoli, registro 12, fogli 116V–117R, November 3, 1618.

[94]   A.S.V., Deliberazioni Costantinopoli, registro 12, fogli 178V–179R, December 1, 1618.

[95]   On the fall of the Duke of Osuna see Linde, *Don Pedro Girón*, pp. 212–58

Fig. 5.5   Türbe of Ali Pasha: Yahya Efendi Mosque Beşiktaş. Photo: Nancy
Ortega.

Epilogue

The case of the attack of the Duke of Osuna and his fleet against Venetian ships was finally resolved just a few years before the opening of the *Fondaco dei Turchi* on the Grand Canal in 1621. The irony of the opening of the Fondaco dei Turchi is that it came at a time when, according to Osman II, Ottoman traders were no longer using the port of Split and coming to Venice because of fears that the Venetians could not guarantee a sufficient level of protection. Can we assume then that the demise of the Duke of Osuna and a reduction in the Spanish threat brought Ottoman merchants back to Venice? Or given that the threat of attack on the sea always remained high is it more reasonable to assume that Osman II's pronouncement reflected the words of someone who was not aware of the type of exchange that was taking place across the Adriatic, even at the time he made his announcement?

A difficulty in addressing either of these questions is that much of our understanding of the type of exchange that was taking place can be identified only through evidence gleaned from some type of contact with a state. The individuals who do not appear in state documents are harder to find; some were noted by travelers but others who must have played a significant role in the amount of the exchange that was taking place remain out of view. Thus if Osman II was wrong, we have a difficult time refuting his claim, because if the people who conducted their business independent of state supervision did not leave documentary traces, they remain out of view.

But what does this quandary between Osman II's claim of the absence of Ottoman Muslims who were willing to trade in Venice and the sustained dialog about finding a permanent place for Ottoman Muslims in Venice tell us about what might have been taking place independent of state supervision? For one, while no reference was made about the Spanish attack in documentation discussing the plan for lodging Ottoman Muslims nor any about the fondaco in correspondence about the attack, the negotiations about the incident and the discussion about housing were both about the ability of states to track and control people who were not easily identified and who were operating outside of accepted rules established by states. As we have seen, early modern states were constantly looking for new ways to exercise control, to collect taxes more effectively, and to supervise the activities of those who were identified as being on the margins.

As has become evident in this study, the notion of a periphery and a center is one of the conceptual barriers to understanding how power worked in the early modern world. The Duke of Osuna, who in the Venetians' eyes represented a rogue and an outcast, not only was at the center of Spanish politics but also deeply involved in relations with the Ottoman Empire. Was this relationship something he wanted to keep secret from the Spanish government or was this a contact that was sanctioned by Madrid? Operating out of view had certain advantages if one wanted to challenge the existing set of power relations.

This profile certainly fits in the case of Lucia, who wanted to disappear and come to Venice so that she could live in a place inaccessible to her family. Ironically, her decision did not pan out because her family was able to pursue her and return her home. In Lucia's case, what was thought to be central to relations between the Islamic and Christian worlds—religious identity—was considered secondary to other concerns such as male power and honor.

Also central to the case of Lucia was the connection between her native Bosnia and Venice. Increasingly, studies on the Ottoman Empire have emphasized the complex relationship between Istanbul and other parts of the empire. Much less is known about the relationship between Ottoman territories and places outside the empire. Cases in this study have shown that the western Balkans was an area that was linked to both Venetian territories and Venice itself. Ottoman officials and powerful people in Bosnia and Herzegovina had a significant amount of influence with the Venetian government.

Part of this influence undoubtedly had to do with the western Balkans' dynamism; cities such as Sarajevo and Thessonalilki were not only trading centers, they were also places that accepted large numbers of Jewish and Muslim refugees from Spain and Portugal.[1] This flow of people from West to East has largely been ignored in studies of the Mediterranean. Ariel Salzman contends that this movement was directly tied to the moral economies of both the Christian and Muslim worlds, and while states such as Spain chose to expel non-Christians, the Ottomans allowed these groups to immigrate to their territories.[2] Could this development and the movement of people from Ottoman territories into the Balkans also have contributed to the growth of the presence of Muslims in Venice? While the assumption has always been that the Venetians' decision to give up their monopoly on trade contributed to the rise and to the influence of foreign merchants, including Ottomans, in the city, this assessment ignores the fact that growth, prosperity and increasing political and economic power in a region that bordered Venetian territories contributed to new patterns of movement and exchange that have largely been ignored because of a tendency to focus on the power of centers as opposed to the power of regional places of prominence.

---

[1]   Halil İnalcik and Donald Quataeret eds., *An Economic and Social History of the Ottoman Empire, 1300–1600*, vol. 1 (Cambridge, UK: Cambridge University Press, 1994). pp. 266–7.

[2]   Ariel Salzman, "The Moral Economies of the Pre-Modern Mediterranean," in *Living in the Ottoman Ecumenical Community: Essays in Honor of Suriaya Faroqhi* (The Ottoman Empire Empire and its Heritage), eds. Vera Costantini and Markus Koller (Leiden: E.J. Brill, 2008), pp. 453–78.

Bibliography

Archives

Archivio General de Simancas
Archivio di Stato, Venezia
Başbakanlik Arşivi (Istanbul)
Research also done at: State Archives in Dubrovnik and Zadar, Croatia, Biblioteca
   Nazionale Marciana, Venezia, Biblioteca Museo di Correr, Venezia, Istituionzi
   di Ricovero e di Educazione, Casa de Catacumeni, Venezia

Primary Sources

Alberi, Eugenio, ed., *Le relazioni degli ambasciatori veneti al senato,* series 3,
   vol. 1 (Firenze: Società Editrice Fiorentina, 1840).
Blount, Henry, *A Voyage in the Levant* (London: Andrew Crook,1637).
de Busbeq, Ogier Ghiselin, *The Turkish Letters of Ogier Ghiselin de Busbeq*, trans.
   Edward Seymour Forster (Oxford: The Clarendon Press, 1927).
De Lorenzi, Giovanni, *Leggi e memorie venete sulla prostituzione* (Venice: M.
   Visentini, 1872).
de Tournefort, Joseph Pitton, *A Voyage into the Levant: Performed by the
   Command of the Late French King, vol. 2* (London: n.p.,1741) http://books.
   google.com/books?id=qQt_L-BSe8sC
*Diario de viaggio da Venezia a Constantinopoli fatta da M Jacopo Soranzo al
   Sultana Murad III in compagnia di M Giovanni Correr Bailo alla Porta
   Ottomana,* Descritto da Anonimo che fu al seguito de Soranzo, (Venezia:
   n.p.,1856).
Düzdağ, M. Ertuğrul, *Şeyhülislam Ebusuûd Efendi Fetvaları* işğinda 16 asır Türk
   hayatı (Istanbul: Enderun Kitabevi, 1972).
Firpo, Luigi ed., *Le relazioni degli ambasciatori veneti al senato,* vol. 13 (Torino:
   Bottega d'Erasmo, 1984).
Gentili, Alberico, *Hispanicae Advocationis*, vol. 1 (New York: Oxford University
   Press, 1921).
Gökbilgin, Tayyib, ed, "Venedik Devlet Arşivindeki Türkçe Belgeler Kolleksiyonu
   İslerine İlgili Dilgi Belgeler," *Belgeler*, cilt 5–8, sayi 9–12 (Ankara: Turk
   Kurumu Basimevi, 1971).
Membre, Michele, *Relazione de Persia*, ed. Gianroberto Sarcia (Napoli: Istituto
   Universitario Orientale, 1969).
Sanudo, Marino, *I diarii di Marino Sanudo,* 58 vols., eds. Rinaldo Fulin et al.
   (Venezia: F. Visentini, 1879–1903).

Sarpi, Paolo, *Domino del Mar Adriatico della Serenissima Republica di Venezia* (Venezia: Roberto Mietti, 1685), http://books.google.com/ books?id=Fn45AAAAcAAJ&printsec.

Solitro, V., ed., *Documenti storici sull'Istria e La Dalmazia,* vol. 1 (Venezia: Coi tipi della ved. di G. Gattei, 1844).

Secondary Sources

Abulafia, David, *Mediterranean Encounters: Economic, Religious, Political: 1100–1550* (Aldershot, UK: Ashgate Press, 2000).

Adams, Robyn and Rosanna Cox, eds., *Diplomacy in Early Modern Culture* (New York: Palgrave Macmillan, 2011).

Ágoston, Gábor and Bruce Masters, eds., *Encyclopedia of the Ottoman Empire* (New York: Facts on File, 2009).

Alberti, Annibale and Roberto Cessi, *Rialto: l'isola, il ponte, il mercato* (Bologna: Nicola Zanichelli, 1934).

Allen, E. John B., *Post and Courier Service in the Diplomacy of Early Modern Europe* (The Hague: Martinus Nijhoff, 1973).

Allouche, Adel, *The Origins of the Ottoman-Safavid Conflict (906–962/1500– 1550)* (Berlin: Klaus Schwarz, 1983).

Amelang, James S., "People of the Ribera: Popular Politics and Neighborhood Identity in Early Modern Barcelona," in *Culture and Identity in Early Modern Europe: Essays in Honor of Natalie Davis (1500–1800)*, eds. Barbara B. Diefendorf and Carla Hesse (Ann Arbor: University of Michigan, 1993), pp. 119–37.

Anderson, Benedict, *Imagined Communities: Reflections on the Origin and Spread of Nationalism* (London: Verso, 2006).

Anderson, N.S., *The Rise of Modern Diplomacy, 1450–1919* (London: Longman, 1993).

Andrews, Walter and Mehmet Kalpaklı, *The Age of the Beloved: Love and the Beloved in the Early Modern Ottoman and European Culture and Society* (Durham: Duke University Press, 2005).

Arai, Masami, *Turkish Nationalism in the Young Turk Era: Social, Economic and Political Studies of the Middle East,* vol. 43 (Leiden: E.J. Brill, 1992).

Arbel, Benjamin, *Trading Nations: Jews and Venetians in the Early Modern Mediterranean* (Leiden: E.J. Brill, 1995).

Arı, Bülent, "Early Ottoman Diplomacy: Ad Hoc Period," in *Ottoman Diplomacy*, ed. A Nuri Yurdisev (New York: Columbia University Press, 2004), pp. 36–65.

Baer, Marc, "Islamic Conversion Narratives of Women: Social Change and Gendered Hierarchy in Early Modern Istanbul," *Gender & History*, vol. 16, no. 2 (2004), pp. 425–58.

Bağış, Ali İhsan, *Osmanlı Ticaretinde Gayri Müslimler, Kapitülasyonlar-Beratlı Tüccarlar, Avrupa, ve Hayriye Tüccarları (1750–1839)* (Ankara: Turhan Kitabevi, 1983).

Bakhit, Muhammad Adnan, "The Christian Population of the Province of Damascus in the Sixteenth Century," in *Christians and Jews in the Ottoman Empire*, vol. 2, eds. Benjamin Braude and Bernard Lewis (New York: Holmes & Meier, 1982), pp. 19–66.

Balagija, Abdusalem, *Les Musulmans yougoslaves* (Algiers: La Maison de livres, 1940).

Ball, James, "The Greek Community in Venice: 1470–1620," (Ph.D. thesis, University of London, 1984).

Baram, Uzi and Linda Carroll, "The Future of the Ottoman Past," in *A Historical Archaeology of the Ottoman Empire: Breaking New Ground*, eds. Uzi Baram and Linda Carroll (New York: Kluwer Academic/Plenum Publishers, 2000), pp. 3–36.

Barkey, Karen, *Bandits and Bureaucrats: The Ottoman Route to State Centralization* (Ithaca: Cornell University Press, 1994).

———, *Empire of Difference: The Ottomans in Comparative Perspective* (Cambridge, UK: Cambridge University Press, 2008).

Belin, Par M. "Relations diplomatiques de la République de Venise avec la Turquie," *Journal Asiatique*, Novembre–Décembre 1876, pp. 381–424.

Bennassar, Bartolomé and Lucile Bennassar, *Les chrétiens d'Allah: L'histoire extraordinaire des renégats* (Paris: Berin, 1989).

Benton, Lauren, *Law and Colonial Cultures: Legal Regimes in World History 1400–1900* (Cambridge, UK: Cambridge University Press, 2002).

———, *A Search for Sovereignty: Law and Geography in European Empires, 1490–1900* (Cambridge, UK: Cambridge University Press, 2009).

Bethencourt, Francisco, *The Inquisition: A Global History, 1478–1834* (Cambridge, UK: Cambridge University Press, 2009).

Bianchi, Francesco and Deborah Howard "Life and Death in Damascus: The Material Culture of the Venetians in the Fifteenth century," *Studi Veneziani*, N.S., 46 (2003), pp. 233–300.

Birdal, Mehmet Sinan, *The Holy Roman Empire and the Ottomans: From Global Imperial Power to Absolutist State* (New York: I.B. Tauris, 2011).

Blok, Anton, "Rams and Billy Goats: A Key to the Mediterranean Code of Honour," *Man*, New Series, vol. 16, no. 3 (1981), pp. 427–40.

Boğac, Ergene, *Local Court, Provincial Society and Justice in the Ottoman Empire* (Leiden: E.J. Brill, 2003).

Bombaci, A. "Una lettera turca in caraterri latini del dragomanno ottomano Ibrahim al veneziano Michele Membre (1567)," *Rocznik Orjentalistyczny* 15 (1948), pp.129–44.

Borgherini-Scarabellin, Maria, "Il magistrato dei Cinque Savi alla Mercanzia dalla istituzione alla caduta della republica," *Miscellanea di storia Veneto-Tridentina*, vol. 2 (Venezia: Deputazione *di storia* patria per le Venezie, 1926).

Bosworth, C.E., et al., eds., *The Encyclopedia of Islam*, New Edition, vol. 8 (Leiden: E.J. Brill,1994).

Bracewell, Wendy Catherine, *The Uskoks of Senj: Piracy, Banditry and the Holy War in the Sixteenth Century Adriatic* (Ithaca: Cornell University Press, 1992).

Braudel, Fernand, *Civilization and Capitalism: The Perspective of the World* (Berkeley: University of California Press, 1992).

————, *The Mediterranean and the Mediterranean World in the Age of Philip II*, trans. Siân Reynolds (New York: Harper & Row, 1972).

Brooks, James, *Captains and Cousins: Slavery, Kinship and Community in the Southwest Borderlands* (Chapel Hill: University of North Carolina Press, 2002).

Brown, Horatio, *Studies in Venetian History*, vol. 2 (New York: John Murray, 1907).

Brummett, Palmira, "Imagining the Early Modern Ottoman Space," in *The Early Modern Ottomans*, eds. Virginia Aksan and Daniel Goffman (Cambridge, UK: Cambridge University Press, 2007), pp. 15–58.

————, *Ottoman Seapower and Levantine Diplomacy in the Age of Discovery* (Albany: SUNY Press, 1994).

————, "The Ottoman Empire, Venice and the Question of Enduring Rivalries," in *Great Power Rivalries*, ed. William R. Thompson (Columbia: University of South Carolina Press, 1999), pp. 225–53.

Burckhardt, Jacob, *The Civilization of the Renaissance in Italy* (London: The Phaidon Press, 1944).

Burke, Peter, *Popular Culture in Early Modern Europe* (New York: New York University Press, 1978).

Calabi, Donatella, "Gli stranieri nella capitale della repubblica Veneta nella prima età moderna," *Mélanges de l'Ecole francaise de Rome, Italie et Méditerranée*, vol. 111, no. 2 (1999), pp. 171–91.

————, "Foreigners and the City: An Historiographical Exploration for the Early Modern Period," *Fondazione Eni Enrico Mattei Working Papers*, Paper 15 (September, 2006) http://www.researchgate.net/publication/5023555_Foreigners_and_the_City_An_Historiographical_Exploration_for_the_Early_Modern_Period

Carrió-Invernizzi, Diana, "Gift and Diplomacy in Seventeenth Century Italy," *The Historical Journal* 51, no. 4 (2008), pp. 881–99.

Casale, Giancarlo, *The Ottoman Age of Exploration* (Oxford: Oxford University Press, 2010).

Cavallo, Sandra and Simona Cerutti, " Female Honor and the Social Control of Reproduction in Piedmont between 1600 and 1800," in *Sex and Gender in Historical Perspective: Selections from Quaderni Storici*, eds. Edward Muir and Guido Ruggiero (Baltimore: John Hopkins University Press, 1990), pp. 73–109.

Chambers, David and Brian Pullan, *Venice: A Documentary History* (Oxford: Blackwell, 1992).

Chaudhuri, K.N., *Trade and Civilization in the Indian Ocean: An Economic History from the Rise of Islam to 1750* (Cambridge, UK: Cambridge University Press, 1985).

Cipolla, Carlo, *Guns, Sails and Empires: Technological Innovation and the Early Phases of European Expansion 1400–1700* (New York: Pantheon Books, 1965).

Colley, Linda, *The Ordeal of Elizabeth Marsh: A Woman in World History* (New York: First Anchor Books, 2007).

Cohen, Amnon, "On the Realities of the Millet System: Jerusalem in the Sixteenth Century," in *Christians and Jews in the Ottoman Empire: The Functioning of a Plural Society*, vol. 2, eds. Benjamin Braude and Bernard Lewis (New York: Holmes & Meier, 1982), pp. 7–18.

———, *The Guilds of Ottoman Jerusalem* (Leiden: E.J. Brill, 2004).

Cohen, Sherrill, *The Evolution of Women's Asylums since 1500: From Refuges for Ex-Prostitutes to Shelters for Battered Women* (New York: Oxford University Press, 1992).

Cohen, Thomas, "Three Forms of Jeopardy: Honor, Pain and Truth-Telling in a Sixteenth-Century Italian Courtroom," *The Sixteenth Century Journal*, vol. 29, no. 4 (1998), pp. 975–98.

Concina, Ennio, *Fondaci: Architettura, arte, e mercatura, tra Levante, Venezia, Alemagne* (Venezia: Marsilio, 1997).

Constable, Olivia, *Housing the Stranger in the Mediterranean World: Lodging Trade and Travel in Late Antiquity and the Middle Ages* (Cambridge, UK: Cambridge University Press, 2003).

Cozzi, Gaetano, "Authority and Law in Renaissance Venice," in *Renaissance Venice*, ed. J.R. Hale (Totowa, NJ: Rowman & Littlefield, 1973).

———, *Paolo Sarpi tra Venezia e l'Europa* (Torino: G. Einaudi, 1978).

———, *Repubblica di Venezia e Stati italiani: politica e giustizia dal secolo XVI al secolo XVIII*, (Torino: G.Einaudi, 1982).

———, *Stato, Società e Giustizia* (Roma: Jouvence, 1980).

Dankoff, Robert and Robert Elsie, *Evliya Çelebi in Albania and Adjacent Regions* (Leiden: E.J. Brill, 2000).

Darling, Linda, "Mediterranean Borderlands: Early English Merchants in the Levant," in *The Ottoman Empire: Myths, Realities and 'Black Holes'*, eds. Eugenia Kermeli and Oktay Özel (Istanbul: Isis Press, 2006).

Davis, Natalie Zemon, "Boundaries and the Sense of Self in Sixteenth Century France," in *Reconstructing Individualism: Autonomy, Individuality, and the Self in Western Thought*, eds. Thomas C. Heller et al. (Stanford: Stanford University Press, 1986).

———, *Fiction in the Archives: Pardon Tales and Their Tellers in Sixteenth Century France* (Stanford: Stanford University Press, 1987).

———, *The Gift in Sixteenth Century France* (Madison: University of Wisconsin Press, 2000).

———, *Trickster Travels: A Sixteenth Century Muslim between Worlds* (New York: Hill & Wang, 2006).

Davis, Robert, "Slave Redemption in Venice," in *Venice Reconsidered: The History and Civilization of an Italian City-State, 1297–179,* eds. John Martin and Dennis Romano (Baltimore: Johns Hopkins University Press, 2000).

De Filippis, Mary, et al., *Dutch New York between East and West: The World of Margrieta van Varick* (Bard Graduate Studies for Studies in the Decorative Arts) (New Haven: Yale University Press, 2009).

De Vivo, Filippo, *Information and Communication in Venice: Rethinking Early Modern Politics* (Oxford: Oxford University Press, 2007).

Duro, Cesáreo Fernandez, *Duque de Osuna e su marina: Jornadas contra Turcos e Venecianos* (Madrid: Sucesores de Rivadenyera, 1885), Google books, pdf.

Dursteler, Eric, *Renegade Women: Gender, Boundaries and Identity in the Early Modern Mediterranean* (Baltimore: Johns Hopkins University Press, 2011).

———, "The Bailo in Constantinople: Crisis and Career in Venice's Early Modern Diplomatic Corps," *Mediterranean Historical Review* 16 (2001), pp. 1–25.

———, *Venetians in Constantinople: Nation, Identity and Coexistence in the Early Modern Mediterranean* (Baltimore: John Hopkins University Press, 2006).

———, "Veneto-Ottoman Trade in the Early Modern Era," *Turcica*, vol. 34 (2002), pp. 105–33.

Earle, Peter, "The Commercial Development of Ancona," *The Economic History Review*, New Series, vol. 22, no. 1 (1969), pp. 28–44.

Eldhem, Edhem, "Foreigners at the Threshold of Felicity: The Reception of Foreigners in Ottoman Istanbul," in *Cites and Cultural Exchange in Europe, 1400–1700* (Cultural Exchange in Early Modern Europe), vol. 2, eds. Donatella Calabi and Stephen Turk Christensen (Cambridge, UK: Cambridge University Press, 2007), pp. 114–31.

Elliot, John, *The Count Duke of Olivares: The Statesmen in the Age of Decline* (New Haven: Yale University Press, 1986).

Fahmy, Ziad, "Jurisdictional Borderlands: Extraterritoriality and 'Legal Chameleons' in Pre-colonial Alexandria," *Comparative Studies in Society and History*, vol.55, issue 2 (2013), pp. 305–29.

Faroqhi, Suraiya, "The Venetian Presence in the Ottoman Empire, 1600–30," in *The Ottoman Empire and the World Economy*, ed. Huri İslamoğlu-İnan (Cambridge, UK: Cambridge University Press, 2004), pp. 311–44.

———, "Women and Wealth in the Eighteenth Century Anatolian Countryside," in *Women in the Ottoman Empire: Middle Eastern Women in the Early Modern Era*, ed. Madeline C. Zilfi (Leiden: E.J. Brill,1997), pp. 6–27.

Fenlon, Ian, *The Ceremonial City: History, Memory and Myth in Renaissance Venice* (Yale University Press: New Haven, 2007).

Finlay, Robert, *Politics in Renaissance Venice* (New Brunswick: Rutgers University Press, 1980).

Fleet, Kate, *European and Islamic Trade in the Early Ottoman State: The Merchants of Genoa and Turkey* (Cambridge, UK: Cambridge University Press, 1999).

Foucault, Michel, "The Subject and Power," *Critical Inquiry*, vol. 8, no. 4 (1982), pp. 777–95.

Fubini, Ricardo, "Diplomacy and Government in the Italian City States of the Fifteenth Century, (Florence and Venice)," in *Politics and Practice in Early*

Modern Italy: The Structure of Diplomatic Practice, ed. Daniela Frigo (Cambridge, UK: Cambridge University Press, 2000), pp. 25–48.

Garcia Arenal, Mercedes, *Conversions islamiques: Identities religieuses en Islam méditerranéen* (Paris: Maisonneuve et Larose, 2001).

Gilmore, David, ed., *Honor and Shame and the Unity of the Mediterranean* 22, special publication (Washington, DC: American Anthropological Association, 1987).

Ginzburg, Carlo, *The Cheese and the Worms*, trans. Ann and John Tedeschi (Baltimore: Johns Hopkins University Press, 1992).

Goffman, Daniel, "Negotiating with the Renaissance State: the Ottoman Empire and the new diplomacy," in *The Early Modern Ottomans: Remapping the Empire*, eds. Virginia Aksan and Daniel Goffman (Cambridge, UK: Cambridge University Press, 2007), pp. 61–74.

———, *The Ottoman Empire and Early Modern Europe* (Cambridge, UK: Cambridge University Press, 2002).

Gökbilgin, Tayyib, "Le relazioni veneto-turchi nell'eta di Soliman il Magnifico," *Il Veltro*, Marzo-Agosto 1979, pp. 277–90.

Greene, Molly, *A Shared World: Christians and Muslims in the Early Modern Mediterranean* (Princeton: Princeton University Press, 2000).

———, *Catholic Pirates and Greek Merchants: A Maritime History of the Mediterranean* (Princeton: Princeton University Press, 2010).

———, "The Ottomans in the Mediterranean," in *The Early Modern Ottomans: Remapping the Empire*, eds. Virginia Aksan and Daniel Goffman (Cambridge, UK: Cambridge University Press, 2007), pp. 104–16.

Gully, Adrian, *The Culture of Letter Writing in Pre-Modern Islamic Society* (Edinburgh: Edinburgh University Press, 2008).

Hale, John, *The Civilization of Europe in the Renaissance* (New York: Atheneum, 1993).

Handžić, Adem, *Population of Bosnia in the Ottoman Period: A Historical Overview* (Istanbul: Research Centre for Islamic History, Art and Culture, 1994).

Harris, Jonathan, et al., eds., *Byzantines, Latins and Turks in the eastern Mediterranean World after 1150* (Oxford: Oxford University Press, 2012).

Harvey, Leonard Patrick, *Muslims in Spain 1500–1614* (Chicago: The University of Chicago Press, 2005).

Heyd, Uriel, *Ottoman Documents on Palestine, 1552–1615: A Study of the Firman according to the Mühimme Defteri* (Oxford: Clarendon Press, 1960).

Heywood, Colin, "Bosnia Under Ottoman Rule," in *The Muslims of Bosnia-Herzegovina: Their Historic Development from the Middle Ages to the Dissolution of Yugoslavia*, ed. Mark Pinson (Cambridge, MA: Distributed for the Center for Middle Eastern Studies of Harvard University by Harvard University Press, 1996), pp. 22–53.

Howard, Deborah, "Cultural Transfer between Venice and the Ottomans in the Fifteenth and Sixteenth Centuries," in *Forging European Identities, 1400–1700* (Cultural Exchange in Early Modern Europe) vol. 4, ed. Herman Roodenburg (Cambridge, UK: Cambridge University Press, 2007), pp. 138–77.

————, *Venice and the East: The Impact of the Islamic World on Venetian Architecture* (New Haven: Yale University Press, 2000).

————, *Venice Disputed: Marc'Antonio Barbaro and Venetian Architecture, 1550–1600* (New Haven: Yale University Press, 2011).

Imber, Colin, *The Ottoman Empire 1300–1650: The Structure of Power* (New York: Palgrave MacMillan, 2002).

————, "Women, Marriage and Property: Mahr in the Behcetü'l-Fetava of Yenişehirli. Abdullah," in *Women in the Ottoman Empire: Middle Eastern Women in the Early Modern Era*, ed. Madeline Zilfi (Leiden: E.J. Brill, 1997), pp. 81–104.

Imhaus, Brunehilde, *Le minoranze orientali a Venezia 1300–1510* (Roma: Il Veltro, 1997).

İnalcik, Halil, "Ottoman-Venetian Relations," in *Venezia centro di mediazione tra Oriente e Occidente, secoli XV–XVI: aspetti e problem*, a cura di Hans- Georg Beck et. al, vol. 1 (Firenze: Olschki, 1977), pp. 83–90.

————, *The Ottoman Empire: The Classical Age* (London: Weidenfeld & Nicholson, 1973).

İnalcik, Halil and Donald Quataeret, eds., *An Economic and Social History of the Ottoman Empire, 1300–1600*, vol. 1 (Cambridge, UK: Cambridge University Press, 1994).

Isom-Verhaaren, Christine, "Shifting Identities: Foreign State Servants in France and the Ottoman Empire," *Journal of Early Modern History, vol. 8, issue 1/2* (2004), pp. 109–34.

Ivanova, Svetlana, "The Divorce Between Zubaida Hatun and Esseid Osman Ağa: Women in the Eighteenth Century Shari'a Court of Rumelia," in *Women, the Family and Divorce Laws in Islamic History*, ed. Amira El Azhary Sonbol (Syracuse: Syracuse University Press, 1996), pp. 112–25.

Jennings, Ronald C., "Women in Early Seventeenth Century Ottoman Judicial Records: The Sharia Court of Anatolian Kayseri," *Journal of the Social and Economic History of the Orient*, vol. 18, part I (January 1975), pp. 53–114.

Jütte, Robert, *Poverty and Deviance in Early Modern Europe* (Cambridge, UK: Cambridge University Press, 1994).

Kafadar, Cemal "A Death in Venice (1575): Anatolian Merchants Trading in the Serenissima," *Journal of Turkish Studies* 10 (1986), pp. 191–218.

Kedar, Benjamen ed., *East-West Trade in the Medieval Mediterranean* (London, Variorum Reprints, 1986)

Kolodziejczyk, Dariusz, *Ottoman-Polish Diplomatic Relations (15th–18th Century): An Annotated Edition of 'Ahdnames and Other Documents* (Leiden: E.J. Brill, 2000).

Kunĉević, Lovro, "Discourses on Liberty in early modern Ragusa," in *Freedom and the Construction of Europe: Religious Freedom and Civil Libery*, eds. Quentin Skinner and Martin Van Gelderen (Cambridge, UK: Cambridge University Press, 2013), pp. 195–214.

Kunt, I.M., *The Sultan's Servants: The Transformation of Ottoman Provincial Government, 1550–1650* (New York: Columbia University Press, 1983).

Lane, Frederic, "Economic Consequences of Organized Violence," *The Journal of Economic History*, vol. 18, no. 4 (1958), pp. 401–17.

———, *Venice: A Maritime Republic* (Baltimore: Johns Hopkins University Press, 1973).

Lee, Wayne, "Projecting Power in the Early Modern World," in *Empires and Indigenes: Intercultural Alliance, Imperial Expansion, and Warfare in the Early Modern World*, ed. Wayne Lee (New York: New York University Press, 2011), pp. 1–16.

Lesure, Michel "Michel Cernovic 'explorator secretus' a Constantinople (1556–1563)," *Turcica: revue d'etudes turques,* Tome 15 (1983), pp. 127–54.

Lewis, Bernard, *The Muslim Discovery of Europe* (New York: W.W. Norton, 1982).

Liang, Gen, *Family and Empire: The Férnandez de Córdoba and the Spanish Realm* (Philadelphia: University of Pennsylvania Press, 2011).

Linde, Luis, *Don Pedro Girón, duque de Osuna: La hegemonia espnaola en Europa a comienzos del siglo XVII* (Madrid: Ediciones Encuentro, 2005).

Lopasic, Alexander, "Islamization of the Balkans," *Journal of Islamic Studies*, vol. 5, no. 2 (1994), pp. 163–86.

Mack, Rosamond, *Bazaar to Piazza: Islamic Trade and Italian Art* (Berkeley: University of California Press, 2002).

Mackenney, Richard, "Myth, Legend and the 'Spanish' Conspiracy against Venice in 1618," in *Venice Reconsidered: The History and Civilization of the Italian City State*, eds. John Jeffries Martin and Dennis Romano (Baltimore: John Hopkins University Press, 2000), pp. 185–216.

———, *Tradesmen and Traders: The World of the Guilds in Venice and Europe* (London: Croon Helm, 1987).

Malcolm, Noel, *Bosnia: A Short History* (London: Macmillan London Limited, 1994).

Malkiel, David Joshua, *A Separate Republic: The Mechanics of Venetian Self-Government, 1607–1624* (Jerusalem: Magnes Press, 1991).

Mantran, Robert, "Foreign Merchants and Minorities in Istanbul during the Sixteenth and Seventeenth Centuries," in *Christians and Jews in the Ottoman Empire*, vol. 1, eds. Benjamin Braude and Bernard Lewis (New York: Holmes & Meier, 1982), pp. 127–37.

Marcus, Abraham, *The Middle East on the Eve of Modernity: Aleppo in the Eighteenth Century* (New York: Columbia University Press, 1989).

Mardin, Şerif, "Civil Society and Culture in the Ottoman Empire," *Comparative Studies in Society and History* 2 (1969), pp. 258–81.

Marghetitch, S.G., *Étude sur les fonctions des dragomans des missions diplomatique ou consulaires en Turquie,* Constantinople n.p. 1898, reprint (Istanbul: Isis Press, 1993).

Marino, John, "The Venetian Territorial State: Constructing Boundaries in the Shadow of Spain," in *Spain in Italy: Politics, Society and Religion, 1500–1700*, eds. Thomas James Dandelet and John Marino (Leiden: E.J. Brill, 2007), pp. 227–50.

Mattingly, Garrett, *Renaissance Diplomacy* (New York: Dover Publications, 1988).

Mauss, Marcel, *The Gift: Forms and Functions of Exchange in Archaic Societies* (London: Cohen and West, 1966).

McGowan, Bruce, "Ottoman Political Communication," in *Propaganda and Communication in World History: The Symbolic Instrument in Early Times*, vol. 1, eds. Harold D. Lasswell et al. (Honolulu: University of Hawaii Press, 1979–80), pp. 444–93.

Minkov, Anton, *Conversion to Islam in the Balkans: Kisve Bahasi Petitions and Ottoman Social Life, 1670–1730* (Leiden: E.J. Brill, 2004).

Monahan, Patrick, "Sanudo and the Venetian Villa Surbana,"*Annali di architettura* 21 (2009), pp.45–64.

Mueller, Reinhold, "The Procuratori di San Marco and the Venetian Credit Market: A Study of the Development of Credit and Banking in the Trecento" (Ph.D. thesis, Johns Hopkins University, 1969).

———, *The Venetian Money Market: Banks, Panics and the Public Debt: Money and Banking in Renaissance Venice*, vol. 2 (Baltimore: Johns Hopkins University Press, 1997).

Muir, Edward, *Civic Ritual in Renaissance Venice* (Princeton: Princeton University Press, 1981).

Muldrew, Craig, *The Economy of Obligation: The Culture of Credit and Social Relations in Early Modern England* (New York: St. Martin's Press, 1998).

Mullett, Michael, *Popular Culture and Popular Protest in Late Medieval and Early Modern Europe* (London: Croom Helm, 1987).

Murphey, Rhoads, "Patterns of Trade along the Via Egnatia in the Seventeenth Century," in *The Via Egnatia Under Ottoman Rule: Halycon Days in Crete II: A Symposium held in Rethymnon 9–11 January 1994*, ed. Elizabeth Zachariadou (Rethymnon: Crete University Press, 1996), pp. 171–91.

Musi, Aurelio, "The Kingdom of Naples in the Spanish Imperial System," in *Spain in Italy: Politics, Society and Religion 1500–1700*, eds. Thomas James Dandelet and John Marino (Leiden: E.J. Brill, 2007).

Nirenberg, David, *Communities of Violence: Persecution of Minorities in the Middle Ages* (Princeton: Princeton University Press, 1996).

Nubola, Cecelia, "Supplications between Politics and Social Conflicts in Early Modern Europe," in *International Review of Social History*, ed. Lex Heerma Van Voss, vol. 46, supplement 9 (Cambridge, UK: Cambridge University Press, 2001), pp. 35–56.

O'Connell, Monique, *Men of Empire: Power and Negotiation in Venice's Maritime State* (Baltimore: The Johns Hopkins University Press, 2009) Ortega, Stephen, "Across Religious and Ethnic Boundaries: Ottoman Networks and

Spaces in Early Modern Venice," *Mediterranean Studies: The Journal of the Mediterranean Studies Association*, vol. 18 (2009), pp. 66–89.

———, "Pleading for Help: Gender relations and Cross-Cultural logic in the Early Modern Mediterranean," *Gender & History*, vol. 20, no. 2 (2008), pp. 332–48.

———, "Shaping Legal Decisions: Power across borders in the early modern Mediterranean," *Interpreting the Past: Essays from the 4ᵗʰ International Conference on European History*, eds. Kenneth E. Hendrickson and Nicolas C.J. Pappas (Athens: Atiner, 2007), pp. 205–14.

Özkaya, Belgin, "Theaters of Fear and Delight: Ottomans in the Serenissima," in *Thamyris/Intersecting Place, Sex and Race: After Orientalism: Critical Entanglements, Productive Looks*, vol. 10, ed. Inge Boer (New York: Rodopi, 2003), pp. 45–61.

Paci, Renzi, *La scala di Spalato e il commercio veneziano nei Balcani fra cinque e seicento* (Venezia: Deputazione di storia patria per le Venezie, 1971).

Pamuk, Şevket, *A Monetary History of the Ottoman Empire* (Cambridge, UK: Cambridge University Press, 2000).

———, "Institutional Change and the Longevity of the Ottoman Empire," *Journey of Institutional History*, vol. 35, no. 2 (2004), pp. 225–47.

Panaite, Viorel, *The Ottoman Law of War and Peace*, Eastern European Monographs, no. 571 (New York: Columbia University Press, 2000).

Parveva, Stefka, *Village, Town and People in the Ottoman Balkans: Sixteenth–mid Nineteenth century* (Istanbul: Isis Press, 2009).

Pedani, Maria Pia, *I documenti turchi dell'Archivio di Stato di Venezia* (Roma: Minestero per i beni culturali e ambientali, Ufficio centrale per i beni archivistici, 1994).

———, *In nome del Gran Signore: inviati ottomani a Venezia dalla caduta di Costantinopoli alla guerra di Candia* (Venezia: Deputazione Editrice, 1994).Pérotin-Dumon, Anne, "The Pirate and the Emperor," in *The Political Economies of Merchant Empires*, ed. James Tracey (Cambridge, UK: Cambridge University Press, 1991), pp. 196–227.

Perruso, Richard, "The Development of the Doctrine of *Res Communes* in Medieval and Early Modern Europe," *Tijdschrift voor Rechtsgeschiedenis* 70 (2002), pp. 69–94.

Persitany, Jean, *Honour and Shame: The Values of Mediterranean Society* (London: Weidenfield & Nicolson, 1965).

Philpott, Dan, "Sovereignty," in *The Stanford Encyclopedia of Philosophy*, ed. Edward N. Zalta, Summer 2010, http://plato.stanford.edu/archives/sum2010/entries/sovereignty.

Pierce, Leslie, *Morality Tales: Law and Gender in the Ottoman Court of Aintab* (Berkeley: University of California Press, 2003).

Poni, Carlo, "Local market rules and practices: Three guilds in the same line of production in early modern Bologna," in *Domestic strategies: Work and Family in France and Italy 1600–1800*, ed. Stuart Woolf (Cambridge, UK: Cambridge

University Press and Editions de la Maison des Sciences de l'Homme, 1991), pp. 69–101.

Poulon, Hugh, *Top Hat, Grey Wolf and Crescent: Turkish Nationalism and the Turkish Republic* (New York: New York University Press, 1997).

Preto, Paolo, *I servizi segreti di Venezia* (Milano: Il Saggiatore, 1994).

———, *Venezia e i turchi* (Firenze: G.C. Sansoni, 1975).

Pullan, Brian, *Rich and Poor in Renaissance Venice: The Social Institutions of a Catholic State to 1620* (Cambridge, MA: Harvard University Press, 1971).

———, *The Jews of Europe and the Inquisition in Venice* (London: I.B. Tauris, 1997).

———, "The Occupations and the Investments of the Venetian Nobility in the Middle and Late Sixteenth Century," in *Renaissance Venice*, ed. John Hale (London: Faber & Faber, 1973), pp. 379–408.

Ravid, Benjamin, "The Legal Status of the Jewish Merchants in Venice (1541–1638)" (Ph.D. thesis, Harvard University, 1973).

———, "The Religious Economic and Social Background nd Context of the Establishment of the Ghetti in Venice," in *Gli Ebrei e Venezia: secoli XIV–XVII: Atti del convegno internazionale organizzato dall istituto di storia della società e dello stato veneziano della Fondazione Giorgio Cini*, ed. Gaetano Cozzi (Milano: Edizioni Comunità, 1987), pp. 211–60.

Raymond, Andre, *Artisans et commergants au Caire au XVIIIeme siecle* (Damascus: Institut Francais de Damas, 1973).

Reychman, Jan, and Ananiasz Zajaczowski, *Handbook of Ottoman Diplomatics* (The Hague: Mouton, 1968).

Riedlmayer, András, "From the Ashes: Bosnia's Cultural Heritage," in *Islam and Bosnia: Conflict Resolution and Foreign Policy in Multi-Ethnic States*, ed. Maya Shatzmilller (Montreal: McGill's-Queens University Press, 2002), pp. 98–135.

Roitman, Jessica, *The Same but Different?: Intercultural Trade and the Sephardim, 1595–1640* (Leiden: E.J. Brill, 2011).

Romano, Dennis, "Gender and Urban Geography of Renaissance Venice," *Journal of Social History*, vol. 23, no. 2 (1989), pp. 339–53.

Rostagno, Lucia, *Mi faccio Turco: Esperienze ed immagini dell'Islam nell'Italia moderna* (Roma: Istituto per l'Oriente C.A. Nalino, 1983).

Rothman, E. Natalie, *Brokering Empire: Trans-Imperial Subjects between Venice and Istanbul* (Ithaca: Cornell University Press, 2012).

Rubini, Edoardo, *Giustizia veneta: lo spirito nelle leggi criminali della Repubblica* (Venezia: Filippi, 2003).

Rublack, Ulinka, *Dressing Up: Cultural Identity in Renaissance Europe* (Oxford: Oxford University Press, 2012).

Ruggiero, Guido, *Binding Passions: Tales of Magic, Marriage and Power at the End of the Renaissance* (New York: Oxford University Press, 1993).

———, *The Boundaries of Eros: Sex Crime and Sexuality in Renaissance Venice* (New York: Oxford University Press, 1985).

———— *Violence in Early Modern Venice* (New Brunswick: Rutgers University Press, 1980).

Sahillioğlu, H., "Bursa kadı Sicillerinde İç ve Dış Ödemeler Aracı Olarak 'Kitabü'l-kadı' ve 'Süftecele'ler," in *Türkiye İktisat Tarihi Semineri: Metinler/Tartışmalar* (8–10 Haziran 1973) ed. O. Okyar (Ankara: Hacettepe Üniversitesi,1973), pp.103–41.

Şahin, Kaya, *Empire and Power in the Reign of Süleyman: Narrating the Sixteenth Century* (Cambridge, UK: Cambridge University Press, 2013).

Sahlins, Peter, *Boundaries: The Making of France and Spain in the Pyrenees* (Berkeley: University of California Press, 1989).

St. Claire, Alexandrine, *The Image of the Turk in Europe* (New York: Metropolitan Museum of Art, 1973).

Salzman, Ariel, "The Moral Economies of the Pre-Modern Mediterranean," in *Living in the Ottoman Ecumenical Community: Essays in Honor of Suriaya Faroqhi* (The Ottoman Empire Empire and its Heritage), eds. Vera Costantini and Markus Koller, (Leiden, E.J. Brill, 2008), pp. 453–78.

Samarčić, Radavan, *Sokollu Mehmed Paşa* (Istanbul: Sabah Kitapları, 1996).

Sapori, Armando, *The Italian Merchant in the Middle Ages* (New York: Norton, 1970).

Scaraffia, Lucetta, *Rinnegati: Per una storia dell'identità occidentale* (Roma: Laterza, 1993).

Schneider, Jane, "Of Vigilance and Virgins: Honor, Shame and Access to Resources in Mediterranean Societies," *Ethnology*, no. 3 (July 1971), pp. 1–23.

Schulz, Jürgen, *The New Palaces of Medieval Venice* (University Park: Pennsylvania State University Press, 2004).

Schwoebel, Robert, *The Shadow of the Crescent: The Renaissance Image of the Turk in Europe* (New York: St. Martin's Press, 1967).

Scott, Joan Wallach, *Gender and the Politics of History* (New York: Columbia University Press, 1999).Seneca, Frederico, *Il Doge Leonardo Donà* (Padova: Antenore, 1959).

Setton, Kenneth, *Venice, Austria and the Turks in the Seventeenth Century* (Philadelphia: The American Philosophical Society, 1991).Shaw, Christine, *The Politics of Exile in Renaissance Italy* (Cambridge, UK: Cambridge University Press, 2000).

Shoemaker, Karl, *Sanctuary and Crime in the Middle Ages, 400–1500* (New York: Fordham University Press, 2010).

Shulvass, Moses Avigdor, *The Jews in the World of the Renaissance* (Leiden: E.J. Brill, 1973).

Simonsfeld, Henry, *Der Fondaco dei Tedeschi in Venedig*, 2 vols. (Stuttgart: Cotta, 1887).

Simonsohn, Shlomo, *The Apostolic See and the Jews,* vol. 7–8 (Toronto: University of Toronto Press, 1991).

Smail, Daniel, *Imaginary Cartographies: Possession and Identity in Late Medieval Marseille* (Ithaca: Cornell University Press, 1999).Somel, Selçuk Akşin,

Historical Dictionary of the Ottoman Empire (Lanham, MD: Scarecrow Press, 2003).

Soykut, Mustafa, *Image of the 'Turk' in Europe: A History of the 'Other' in Early Modern Europe 1453–1682* (Berlin: K. Schwarz, 2001).

Sperling, Jutta Gisela, *Convents and the Body Politic in Late Renaissance Venice* (Chicago: University of Chicago Press, 1999).

Stillman, Norman "Charity and Social Service in Medieval Islam," *Societas: A Review of Social History*, Spring, 1975, pp. 105–10.

Stoianovich, Traian, *Between East and West: The Balkan and Mediterranean Worlds*, vol. 2 (New Rochelle: Caratzas, 1992).

Subrahmanyam, Sanjay, "Connected Histories: Notes towards a Reconfiguration of Early Modern Eurasia," in *Beyond Binary Histories: Re-imagining Eurasia to c.1830*, ed. Victor Lieberman (Ann Arbor: University of Michigan Press, 1999), pp. 289–316.

Sugar, Peter, *Southeastern Europe under Ottoman Rule, 1354–1804* (Seattle: University of Washington Press, 1996).

Tamburini, Filippo, *Santi e peccatori*: *Confessioni e suppliche dai Registri della Penitenzeria dell'Archivio Segreto Vaticano (1451–1586)* (Milano: Istituto di Propoganda Libraria, 1995).

Tenenti, Alberto, *Piracy and the Decline of Venice*: *1580–1615* (Berkeley: University of California Press, 1967).

Tezcan, Baki, *The Second Ottoman Empire: Political and Social Transformation in the Early Modern World* (Cambridge, UK: Cambridge University Press, 2010).

Theunissen, Hans, "Ottoman-Venetian Diplomatics: The *'Ahd-Names*. The Historical Background and the Development of a Category of Political-Commercial Instruments together with an Annotated Edition of a Corpus of Relevant Documents" (Phd thesis: Utrecht University, 1960).

Thomas, George Martin, *Diplomatarium, veneto-levantinum sive acta et diplomata res Venetas Graecas atque Levantis (1351–1454)* vol. 2 (New York: B. Franklin, 1966).

Tilly, Charles, *Trust and Rule* (Cambridge, UK: Cambridge University Press, 2005).

Todorova, Maria, *Imagining the Balkans* (New York: Oxford University Press, 1997).

Trexler, Richard, *Public Life in Renaissance Florence* (Ithaca: Cornell University Press, 1980).

Trivellato, Francesca, *The Familiarity of Strangers: The Sephardic Diaspora, Livorno, and Trade in the Early Modern Period* (New Haven: Yale University Press, 2009).

Tucci, Ugo, "The Psychology of the Venetian Merchant in the Sixteenth Century," in *Renaissance Venice*, ed. John Hale (London: Faber & Faber, 1973), pp. 346–78.

Tucker, Ernest, "From the Rhetoric of War to the Realities of Peace: The Evolution of Ottoman-Iranian Diplomacy through the Safavid Era," in *Iran and the*

World in the Safavid Age, eds. Willem Fleur and Edmund Herzig (New York: I.B. Tauris, 2012), pp. 81–90.

Urban, Lina, *Locande a Venezia* (Venezia: Centro Internazionale della Grafica, 1989).

Uzunçarşili, İsmail Hakkı, *Osmanli tarihi* (Türk Tarih Kurumu yayinlardan) cilt 3, kisim 1 (Ankara: Türk Tarih Kurumu Basimevi, 1954).

Van Den Boogert, Maurits H., *The Capitulations and the Ottoman Legal System* (Leiden: E.J. Brill, 2005).

Van Voss, Lex Heerma, "Petitions in Social History," in *International Review of Social History*, ed. Lex Heerma Van Voss, vol. 46, supplement 9 (Cambridge, UK: Cambridge University Press, 2001), pp.1–10.

Vanzan, Anna, "In Search of Another Identity: Female Muslim-Christian Conversions in the Mediterranean World," *Islam and Christian-Muslim Relations*, vol. 7, no.3 (1996), pp. 327–33.

———, "La pia casa dei Catecumeni in Venezia, Un tentativo di devshirme Christiana?" in *Donne microcosmi culturali*, a cura di Adriana Destro (Bologna: Pàtron, 1997), pp. 221–55.

Vaughn,Virginia Mason, *Emissaries in Early Modern Literature and Culture: Mediation, Transmission, Traffic, 1550–1700*, eds. Brinda Charry and Gitanjali Shahani (Farnham, UK: Ashgate Press, 2009).

Vercellin, Giorgio, "Mercanti turchi e sensali a Venezia," *Studi Veneziani* 4 (1980), pp. 45–78.

Viallon, Marie, *Venise et la Porte Ottomane (1453–1563): un siècle de relations vénéto-ottomanes de la prise de Constantinople à al mort de Soliman* (Paris: Economica, 1995).

Vianello, Andrea, *L'arte dei calegheri e zavateri di Venezia tra XVII e XVIII secolo* (Venezia: Istituto veneto di scienze, lettere ed arti, 1993).

Villian-Gandossi, Christiane, "Les attributions du Baile de Constantinople dans le fonctionement des Èchelles du Levant au XVI siècle," *Recueils de la Societè Jean Bodin* 33, part 2 (1972), pp. 227–42.

Wallerstein, Immanuel, *The Modern World-System: Capitalist Agriculture and the Origins of the European World-Economy in the Sixteenth Century* (New York: Academic Press, 1976).

Waugh, Daniel Clarke, *The Great Turkes Defiance* (Columbus: Slavica Press, 1978).

Weber, Max, *Charisma and Institution Building: Selected Papers* (Chicago: The University of Chicago Press, 1968).

Weissman, Ronald F.E., "Reconstructing Renaissance Sociology: The 'Chicago School' and the Study of Renaissance Society," in *Persons in Groups: Social Behavior as Identity Formation in Medieval and Renaissance Europe*, ed. Richard C. Trexler (Binghamton: Center for Medieval and Early Renaissance Studies, 1985), pp. 39–46.

Wilkins, Charles L., *Forging Urban Solidarities: Ottoman Aleppo 1640–1700* (Leiden: E.J. Brill, 2010).

Wilson, Bronwen, *The World In Venice: Print, the City and Early Modern Identity* (Toronto: University of Toronto Press, 2005).

Wright, Diana Galliand and Pierre MacKay, "When the Serenissima and the Grand Turco Made Love: The Peace Treaty of 1478," *Studi Veneziani* 53 (2007), pp. 261–77.

Würgler, Andreas, "Voices from Among the 'Silent Masses': Humble Petitions and Social Conflicts in Early Modern Central Europe," in *International Review of Social History*, ed. Lex Heerma Van Voss, vol. 46, supplement 9 (Cambridge, UK: Cambridge University Press, 2001), pp. 11–34.

Yi, Eujong, *Guild Dynamics in Seventeenth Century Istanbul: Fluidity and Leverage* (Leiden: E.J. Brill, 2004).

Yurdusev, A. Nuri, "The Ottoman Attitude toward Diplomacy," in *Ottoman Diplomacy: Conventional or Unconventional* (New York: Palgrave MacMillan, 2004), pp. 5–35.

Ze'evi, Dror, *An Ottoman Century: The District of Jerusalem in the 1600s* (Albany: SUNY Press, 1996).

Zele, Walter, "Aspetti delle legazioni ottomane nei *Diarii* di Marin Sanudo," *Studi veneziani* 18 (1989), pp. 241–84.

Zilfi, Madeline, "'We Don't Get Along': Women and Hul Divorce in the Eighteenth Century," in *Women in the Ottoman Empire: Middle Eastern Women in the Early Modern Era*, ed. Madeline Zilfi (Leiden: E.J. Brill, 1997), pp. 264–96.

Index

Bolded page numbers indicate illustrations.